DATE DUE

MY 16			
JE 2 03			
AG 12			
SE 18			

DEMCO 38-296

OLD AGE
IN GLOBAL
PERSPECTIVE

*Cross-Cultural and
Cross-National Views*

SOCIAL ISSUES IN GLOBAL PERSPECTIVE

David Levinson
Melvin Ember

General Editors

The Social Issues in Global Perspective series is prepared under the auspices and with the support of the Human Relations Area Files at Yale University. HRAF, the foremost international research organization in the field of cultural anthropology, is a not-for-profit consortium of twenty-two sponsoring members and 300 participating member institutions in twenty-five countries. The HRAF archive, established in 1949, contains nearly one million pages of information on the cultures of the world.

Old Age in Global Perspective

Cross-Cultural and Cross-National views

Steven M. Albert
Maria G. Cattell

G. K. HALL & CO.
An Imprint of Macmillan Publishing Company
NEW YORK

Maxwell Macmillan Canada
TORONTO

Maxwell Macmillan International
NEW YORK   OXFORD   SINGAPORE   SYDNEY

roduced or
: or
by any
ermission in

New York, NY 10022

Maxwell Macmillan Canada, Inc.
1200 Eglinton Avenue East Suite 200
Don Mills, Ontario M3C 3N1

Macmillan Publishing Company is part of the Maxwell Communication
Group of Companies

Library of Congress Catalog Card Number: 93–18773

Printed in the United States of America

Printing number
1 2 3 4 5 6 7 8 9 10

Library of Congress Cataloging-in-Publication Data

Albert, Steven M.
    Old age in global perspective : cross-cultural and cross-national
views / Steven M. Albert, Maria G. Cattell.
      p.   cm. — (Social issues in global perspective)
    Includes bibliographical references and index.
    ISBN 0–8161–7393–1. — ISBN 0–8161–1604–0 (pbk.)
    1. Aging—Social aspects—Cross-cultural studies. 23. Old age—
Cross-cultural studies.   3. Aged—Family relationships—Cross-
cultural studies.   I. Cattell, Maria G.   II. Title.   III. Series.
HQ1061.A488   1993
305.26—dc20   93–18773
CIP

The paper used in this publication meets the minimum requirements
of American National Standard for Information Sciences-Permanence
of Paper for Printed Library Materials. ANSI Z39.48–1984.∞™

Contents

Preface

The purpose of this book is to integrate cross-cultural, or ethnographic, research on old age with survey-based cross-national research to give what we hope is a better picture of aging across the globe. Cross-cultural and cross-national research represent two alternate streams of information on the aging experience, and the reasons for bringing them together are outlined in chapter 1. Following this methodological introduction, we turn in section I to three alternative approaches to the temporal component of aging. These correspond to three versions of "time": the biologic, chronologic, and social dimensions of age. For each, we invoke a different discipline: biodemography, comparative demography, and anthropology.

In section II, we narrow our discussion and examine four dimensions of old age in detail, using a variety of sources. These include living arrangements, intergenerational transactions, intragenerational relationships, and conflict over succession to seniority. Section III continues the investigation with a special focus on health decline and death, the ultimate endpoint for old age. The goal throughout is a conscious attempt to combine ethnographic and survey data in order to generate hypotheses for future research. Twenty-three such hypotheses are presented in the final chapter of the book.

Every book has its biases. In cross-cultural research, such bias is usually most visible in an author's predilection for singularity or universality. Does one stress variability and the unique quality of each culture's organization of experience? Or does one instead seek pancultural regularities and hence run the risk of slighting unique variations on a theme? We have tried to steer a middle ground. We are not happy with crude applications of the "ethnographic veto." The common biologic basis of aging, the presence of clearly invariant biodemographic features of aging in human populations, and regularities in the psychology of aging across cultures all suggest that cultures face a set of common constraints in what they can make of old age. However, as we have tried to show, within this set of common constraints, cultures still show great variation in a wide variety of domains. "Disability" is a good example. It is variably linked with age and physical impairment across societies and thus presents a great challenge for the construction of valid transcultural measures.

While we do not feel we have identified every constraint on the experience of aging, and hence have not specified the full range of cultural possibility in the case of "old age," we are reasonably confident that what passes for universal features of aging in research is mostly culture-bound. Throughout this book, readers will find that many conclusions drawn from research with American elderly are not applicable to other societies. The range of variation in the experience of aging is much wider than the American experience would suggest.

This, we feel, is a richer book for combining cross-cultural and cross-national perspectives. It differs from strictly ethnographic surveys, such as Foner's research on inequality between young and old (Foner 1984) or holocultural analyses based on the Human Relations Area Files, in that it tries to apply concepts taken from social gerontology across the globe. The book differs from standard cross-national surveys in that it is critical of measures that are developed in one cultural context and applied to another without due regard for cultural variation. We feel that readers of this book will get the best of both worlds. But they will need to invest a certain amount of effort: anthropologists will have to learn a little demography, and gerontologists a little anthropology.

Finally, because it is a sensitive subject, it is worth saying a word on how we speak of societies that differ in technological capacity. We have followed the United Nations designation of "more developed" and "less developed" nations. However, we often use a shorthand: "developed" versus "developing" nations. We have tried to avoid "pre-literate" or "non-literate" as opposed to "literate"; "simple" as opposed to "complex"; "non-industrial" as opposed to "post-industrial"; and related formulations. There is truly no satisfying way to speak about such global differences between societies, especially when the terms of the contrast carry such loaded connotations.

Any errors are the responsibility of the authors. Given that, it may be valuable to assign blame. The bulk of the book (all chapters except chapter 4 and 11) was written by Steven M. Albert; however, many chapters were written twice, and the final versions represent a collective effort, especially chapters 1, 4, 5, and 11, and all three section introductions. The authors also collaborated on the initial design of the book and on bibliographical resources.

We thank the many journals that allowed us to reprint figures and tables. Special gratitude is due also to Michael Billig (Franklin and Marshall College), who reviewed parts of chapters 2 and 3; to Miriam Moss (Philadelphia Geriatric Center), who provided unpublished data and also reviewed chapter 6; to Mary Chamie (United Nations), who offered information on the U.N. disability statistics database; and to Kevin Kinsella (Center for International Research, U.S. Bureau of the Census), who provided unpublished materials, including the data for Figure 3–2. Our colleagues at the Polisher Research Institute of the Philadelphia Geriatric Center must once again be thanked for their collegiality and support, especially Joyce Post, MLS. We thank Ruthe Karlin for preparing a number of the figures.

1

Introduction: Integrating Ethnographic and Cross-National Perspectives on Old Age

In comparative research on the experience of old age, "ethnographic" or "cross-cultural" studies may be contrasted with "cross-national" research. The former rely on a predominantly qualitative, or anthropological, orientation, the latter on a sociological or survey-based paradigm. The contrast can be characterized in a number of ways. Most cross-cultural research consists of detailed case histories, intensive studies of the social context of aging as it is perceived, and often manipulated, by those involved. The goal, to borrow a phrase from a different discipline, is to capture such social experience in "real time," that is, as it happens, and in its multiple meanings, for a limited number of discrete settings. Standardized elicitation of data, in which every respondent answers the same question, is less important in such research than sensitive probing tailored to the particular respondent.

The cross-national or survey-based program of research, by contrast, abandons the search for this level of detail, leaving that effort for the "thick description" (Geertz 1973) characteristic of ethnography. Instead, it seeks population-level regularities about facets of old age. Sampling considerations become critical because the goal is to generalize

1

characteristics of the sample (whether prevalence estimates or statistical associations) to the population at large. It follows that a carefully chosen set of standardized questions, with identical response formats, is critical in such research. The intensive detail of the case history is lost, but the loss is counterbalanced by a corresponding gain in the relevance of the conclusions drawn from such research.

Ethnographic or Cross-National Research?

We cannot review all the literature that has appeared regarding the comparative virtues of the two approaches in research on aging. Rubinstein (1992) provides a convenient summary and identifies two large differences between cross-cultural and cross-national approaches in comparative research on aging. The first involves differences in methodology (and ultimately epistemology); the second involves different assumptions about sampling units in the assessment of cultural variation.

Beginning with differences in methodology, ethnographic methods are best for detecting variation in individual experience and personal meaning. As Rubinstein points out, "anthropological methods are good ways to learn about elders as individuals and members of communities: about experience, about what things mean." Cross-national research, relying as it does on the standardized survey, is not likely to tap this level of social experience. Because questions are fixed and probing is rigidly controlled, the influence of contextual variation on responses (or in the interpretation of questions) is not normally recognized (or is only recognized after the fact in broad psychometric patterns). The anthropological approach, in contrast, suggests that such context-centered meaning is what matters most in social experience.

Some of this context-centered meaning may in fact be tapped by survey questionnaire items. There is a large body of research that indicates that interviewer effects and response styles necessarily work against the survey ideal of a common stimulus for all respondents. Here too the different responses of the anthropologist and survey researcher are revealing. For the survey researcher, such context sensitivity is a source of bias. The survey researcher responds by trying to minimize such bias by attending more carefully to the wording of questions and through statistical control. The anthropologist, in contrast, makes such dissonance between the elicitation of information and the respondent's construction of the question the center of his or her research.

The second difference between cross-cultural and cross-national research strategies involves sampling units. Cross-national investigation by and large assumes that national boundaries represent cultural boundaries, yet it is clear that national aggregates "lump a variety of cultural entities together" (Rubinstein 1992). The best cross-national surveys are sensitive to such within-country cultural variation and accordingly choose samples that adequately vary by race, ethnicity, and religion, the most obvious proxies for cultural difference. Yet it is clear that these broad markers of culture are in some ways no better than nationality as indicators of cultural difference. For one thing, every attempt at defining *race* or *ethnic group* coherently for survey purposes appears to have failed. Most recently, Hahn (1992) examined definitions of *race* used by the National Center for Health Statistics in survey enumeration and found that the criteria used to establish racial affiliation are arbitrary and inconsistently applied. For example, children of mixed-race marriages are classified in a great variety of ways depending on the weight attached to the race of the mother or father, which is different in different surveys. Simply asking people their race is no help, because people may change racial designations from one survey to the next (as when people move from one neighborhood to another). Also, great differences in the racial composition of the same sample are possible depending on what racial designations are available on a survey form. Thus, some "Hispanics" will classify themselves as "black" or "white," if these are the only options available for a "race" question. The "obviousness" of racial identity is evidently much less obvious than people think, for in a study of infant mortality, Hahn also found that infants classified as "nonwhite" at birth were likely to be reclassified as "white" at death (Hahn et al. 1992).

If race is not coherent as a social category for survey purposes, *ethnicity* and *religion* fare even worse. The heterogeneity of social characteristics among those who call themselves Jews or Italians, for example, is well known. Even among Americans who claim an ethnic identity, great variation is evident in the degree to which people consider themselves "hyphenated Americans," in the language spoken in the home, in the degree of contact with extended family in the native land, in the length of time since immigration, in the preparation of traditional cuisine, and in participation in cultural organizations. On the other hand, for some outcomes relevant to aging research (such as co-residence with an elder), ethnic or religious differences appear to be less significant than differences in income or social class. Religion shows similar variability. Among those professing a certain religion, adherence to beliefs, knowledge of the liturgy, attendance at religious services, and charitable contributions to religious organizations all vary. Clearly, using ethnic or religious identity as an independent variable for comparing facets of old age among cultural groups does not make much sense if variability within any of these groups approaches the degree of variability between groups.

Once again, survey researcher and anthropologist are likely to respond to such variability in different ways. The anthropologist will focus on increasingly finer components of social experience in the hope of characterizing cultural differences between groups. The survey researcher is likely to deny the relevance of culture for some outcome of interest if mean differences between the groups are not statistically significant.

Are the two approaches, then, irreconcilable? Reading the strong words written by proponents of one view against the other makes one wonder. Take Sudman's (1983) criticism of qualitative methods, a wonder of damning with faint praise: "The lowest quality samples generally consist of 20–50 respondents usually chosen at the convenience of the researcher. . . [but] any sort of sample may be useful when very little is known." Since convenience samples of 20–50 respondents are the bread and butter of most ethnographic studies of old age, the pointedness of Sudman's challenge is hard to ignore. Campbell and Stanley (1963) are even less restrained: ethnographic case studies have "such a total absence of control as to be of almost no scientific value. . . . Such studies often involve tedious collection of specific detail, careful observation, testing and the like, and in such cases involve the error of misplaced precision" (their emphasis). So much for "thick description."

These harsh words come from researchers whose contributions to social science research have been substantial and quite influential. But the replies of the qualitative researcher are no less strident. One statement will speak for many. Research on family caregiving to impaired elders is well established, with perhaps hundreds of survey-based reports published each year on the prevalence of such caregiving, the dimensions of caregiver commitment to such care, and the burdens and satisfactions of the home care experience. Gubrium and Sankar (1990), however, consider this research shallow for all the reasons mentioned above:

> Concepts have been defined, variables selected, hypotheses formulated, measures and scales constructed, samples selected, inquiries conducted, data analyzed—all as if the basic meanings and concepts of the home care experience were known. . . . Rarely, if ever, has anyone ever raised the question of whether there might be different versions of the home's going-on as a sickroom, which would imply that measurement would necessarily produce multiple, perhaps contradictory, "figures." (p. 8)

Fortunately, these strident claims are belied by the actual practice of social science research. Survey researchers use qualitative inquiry to design and test questionnaire items, and qualitative researchers, for the most part, do administer closed-end surveys to establish the similarity of their samples to the large samples used in survey research. Most recently, qualitative researchers have gone on to code the narratives they elicit from informants to take advantage of new data processing techniques for the analytic reduction of text material. In this way, the "themes" established in ethnographic research are now being derived in more explicit and replicable ways. Likewise, event recording software allows the anthropologist to assess a much wider and more complex set of behaviors in real time. We can expect a convergence of quantitative and qualitative approaches, perhaps over the protests of the more vocal practitioners of each approach. One result, we predict, will be "thicker" closed-ended questions for surveys that sensitively incorporate relevant features of the context of inquiry (Albert 1992a).

Why Bring Cross-Cultural and Cross-National Perspectives Together?

In this book we bring together ethnographic case studies and cross-national surveys to assess variation in the experience of old age. We could have used a single approach to the exclusion of the other, which would have made the book much easier to write because combining the two approaches is not always easy. In addition, combining cross-national and ethnographic studies requires mastery of two very different literatures. Cross-cultural studies appear for the most part as self-contained monographs, in which comparative interests are not foremost. Cross-national studies appear for the most part in journals and span a number of disciplines. Thus, in writing this book, we have had to survey explicitly anthropological monographs along with literature drawn from gerontology, sociology, psychology, human biology, medicine, demography, and economics.

Why combine the two? The short answer is that we were driven to it. We felt we could not do justice to the problem of cross-cultural variation in aging without taking advantage of every type of data available. Simply put, little is known about the different facets of old age outside the more developed countries. Data are at a premium. Ethnographic studies provide a wealth of detail about the aged, but such studies do not typically cover the same ground with the same depth. One study may stress intergenerational relationships, another death-hastening behavior, and another kin fosterage by childless elder women. Ethnographers have different interests and, given the nature of fieldwork, are drawn into particular circuits of social life, which accordingly become most prominent in published reports. There is still, unfortunately, no common set of variables or measures routinely collected in ethnographic field research. Attempts to code disparate ethnographies to form a true cross-cultural data set, as, for example, in the Human Relations Area Files, are extremely valuable but are restricted to a limited set of behaviors and institutions that can be inferred from an often spotty ethnographic literature.

As a result of this limitation in the ethnographic record, we decided to search for cross-national surveys of the aged in the developing countries to supplement available case studies. Fortunately, we were rewarded with important data on variations in living arrangements, the disablement process, intergenerational exchange, and many other facets of late life. The key was to look for data on the aged in surveys that do not explicitly focus on the elderly. For example, fertility surveys often gather data on household composition and hence elder living arrangements; likewise, surveys designed to establish the general prevalence of disability often provide information on the disease morbidities of late life, which are also recorded in such research. In this book, we have used these survey results to broaden the ethnographic picture.

Combining cross-cultural and cross-national approaches had a price, of course. We were forced to be selective in summarizing the ethnographic literature; but the cross-national survey material helps, we think, in contextualizing the more detailed ethnographic reports. For more encyclopedic accounts of the ethnographic data on old age, we refer readers to such studies as that of Simmons (1945) or, more recently, Foner (1984) and Cowgill (1986).

Thus, the quick answer to the question of why one might want to combine such disparate approaches is simply stated: we needed data. If we wanted to examine variation in elderly intragenerational relationships, different constructions of intergenerational solidarity, or differences in the last year of life of the decrepit elder, we needed to supplement ethnographic accounts with other types of data; the ethnographic record in these areas was simply too spare. Likewise, cross-national research is explicitly comparative, but the range of societies surveyed is quite limited. As mentioned earlier, very few cross-national studies include societies outside Europe and North America. Thus, the ethnographic record allows us to expand the range of societies investigated. As it is, the book still has gaps because of the insufficiency of data. We have indicated these gaps throughout the text and have also tried to summarize in a concluding chapter which areas are of highest priority for future research.

The longer answer to the question involves a theoretical issue. The shortcomings of each approach, we felt, could be partly overcome by combining studies that had used the different methodologies. Here we have followed Whiting (1968) and his important exposition on the value of cross-cultural research for social psychology. Extending this line of inquiry, it is clear that *the ethnographic material increases the range of variation of many of the traditional variables assessed in social gerontology.* Restricting one's sights to a single society (or single type of society, as in the case of the developed nations) may result in a truncated range of variation for behaviors of interest, and thus makes it difficult to develop theories that might be applicable to all societies. Whiting uses the case of child weaning to make this point. Weaning ages in American society range from 0 to 7 months (in a 1950 study), but the range across thirty-seven other societies is much wider, from 12 months to 6 years. Examining weaning age as a predictor of childhood emotional disturbance yields very different results according to whether one restricts the range to the American case or goes further to use the range evident across a wider sample of thirty-seven societies. The American data revealed an association between later weaning age and increased emotional disturbance, but the cross-cultural survey showed a curvilinear rather than a linear relationship: early and late weaning were not associated with increased emotional disturbance, but weaning around the 1-year mark was. Thus, having a broader range of values for a variable allows one to develop theories of increased generality. Such theories will be applicable to all societies and are thus likely to be better approximations of universal behavioral regularities.

A similar example in aging research is presented in chapter 5 for the case of elder living arrangements. In the United States, greater age and widowhood are strong predictors of co- residence with adult children. These predictors seem obvious enough. After all, greater age implies more health limitations and increased frailty; likewise, widowhood often brings with it dissolution of a household and increased dependency on adult children. The obviousness of these associations, however, actually depends on a host of culture-specific factors that do not become evident until we look at other societies and broaden the range of values that the "living arrangement" variable can take on. Thus, in the Dominican Republic *married* men are more likely to co-reside with adult children than unmarried men, the reverse of the U.S. pattern; the living arrangements of elderly women, on the other hand, follow the U.S. pattern (De Vos 1990). In this case we must understand that sharing a residence with a married elderly couple is normal outside the developed nations, and that rates of divorce and separation in late life are, on the whole, also much higher outside the developed nations. Combining these two factors with the matrifocal household organization characteristic of Caribbean societies, it becomes clear that separated or divorced elder women are less likely to move out of such a joint living arrangement than are their husbands. Thus, marital status functions in more varied ways as a predictor of living arrangement than the American data would have led us to imagine.

We can multiply these cases, and we have purposely tried to do so in this book to show the value of a cross-cultural perspective in aging research. In this way, we are able to broaden therange of values typical of the variables assessed in gerontological research. This is an important first step in developing theories that will be applicable across the globe. Such theories are likely to be better candidates for assessing what is universal in the aging experience than theories based on single-culture research.

Part I

THE NATURE OF AGE: BIOLOGY, CHRONOLOGY, AND CULTURE

In 1981 the sons of Koroi, a weak old man, began celebrating his death. The mortuary ceremonies were completed by 1982 and from then on Koroi was socially dead. He did not die, physically, until 1984.

All humans age. Aging is a biologic process leading first to maturity and ultimately to functional decline and death. Aging is also a biosocial (Rossi 1985) or biopsychosocial process (Gove 1985) in which such biologic change carries with it more general alterations in human experience. Finally, aging is linked to social distinction, as societies use age to categorize individuals. The distinction between the relatively *junior* and *senior* is central for allocating resources, knowing to whom to defer, and indexing cultural expertise. These are all universals, yet the experience of aging and old age also differs greatly across societies, with variation in sociocultural environments and biodemographic processes playing key roles in these differences.

Biologic aging is not uniform for every human but varies among individuals and among groups. Physical and sociocultural environments have different effects on individuals, so that some persons grow "old" before others of the same chronological age (individual genetics also play a role). These different environments also have different effects on whole populations and their patterns of nutrition, fertility, morbidity, and mortality. Hence the proportion of elderly, as one example, varies widely in different societies and nations.

Sociocultural differences also play major roles in the different experiences of aging and old age. For example, the passage of time is not everywhere nor always marked by years, even where chronological age is commonly known; and the meaning of social distinctions such as *young* and *old* may vary considerably from culture to culture. An *infant* or *old person* may be defined by differing criteria, and behavioral expectations for age-related roles are not the same everywhere. Nor is the lifecourse divided into the same stages in all cultures, nor even by all persons within one culture (Fry 1976). Thus social aging varies from society to society.

Sociocultural and biodemographic variation represent two central cross-cultural influences on experiences of aging and old age. These two sources of variation are not independent and are perhaps best conceived as overlapping or interactive spheres of influence. For example, the number of elderly there are in a society (a biodemographic fact) influences younger persons' supportive or nonsupportive behavior toward the elderly (a sociocultural fact). In turn, how the elderly are treated, with gerontocide as the extreme case, affects the proportion of elderly in a society, although pressures or opportunities to limit or increase fertility (a sociocultural fact) may more significantly affect the proportions of youth and elderly in a society.

In addition, the proportion of elderly in the environment affects individuals' experiences of old age. As research in age-segregated communities has shown, when an older person's *supra-personal environment* (i.e., immediate zone of contact with objects and people) is populated by a greater number of elderly, an old person's perceptions of health, patterns of friendship, sense of personal autonomy and vulnerability, and much else are all altered (Fry 1985; Keith 1990; Lawton 1990a). Thus, sociocultural and biodemographic processes are intimately connected, with causality a two-way street. Cultural norms and institutions and their associated behaviors have biodemographic consequences, and vice versa. Anthropological demographers, who examine linkages between sociocultural and biologic influences on population processes, offer a promising reconciliation of the microlevel perspective typical of sociocultural research and the macrolevel perspective of biodemographic research (Greenhalgh 1990; Hammel 1990; Hammel and Howell 1987; Howell 1986; see Weiss 1989b for a recent review of human biodemography).

The three chapters that make up this section of the book all examine the temporal component of aging. Together they show that one must combine a biologic, chronological, and social perspective on time if we wish to understand aging in a cross-cultural framework.

A first task for the comparative study of aging is to recognize that chronology, the measurement of age in some standard unit of time (e.g., years), is only one approach to age. The defining characteristics of old age vary from culture to culture. Definitions of old age may include markers of the passage of time, physical criteria, social criteria, or other factors. Chronological age may be important and closely linked with social differences, or chronological age may be unknown or just not especially relevant.

In the United States, people tend to link old age with chronology, with number of years lived. Gerontological researchers almost always rely on chronological age to define *elderly* persons; ages of 60 or 65 years are commonly used to designate *elderly* persons. The state plays a powerful role in defining old age and other life stages by chronological age. For example, *retirement* from active employment is often defined in terms of the years one has lived. The age basis of this status transition has become increasingly fixed (although only recently: see Cowgill 1986) through an array of formal institutions such as Social Security, Medicare and other health insurance, and lobbying groups such as the American Association of Retired Persons.

Such uses of chronology may seem simple, easy, or even necessary (as in survey research or in managing a bureaucratic behemoth such as the U.S. Social Security system). But they are not necessarily accurate when it comes to people's attitudes, nor are they uniformly applied in individual behavior, as in the case of the 80-year-old who has not yet retired from employment. From another vantage point, we will see that chronological age is in fact only a moderately good predictor of older persons' performance (Shock, Greulich, and Andres 1984). On an even more basic level, it is also worth noting that a person's chronological age is often not obvious. Knowing one's chronological age depends on a system of time-reckoning that may be absent in some societies (Fry 1990). Nor can we overlook cultural norms that lead people to inflate or deflate reported age, even when it is accurately known.

The passage of time may be marked in a variety of ways other than by the solar year. For example, alternation of seasons and moons, or various concepts suggesting a long time, have all been used to index seniority. One definition of old people among the Samia of Kenya—where many older people do not know their chronological age—is those "who have cleared many granaries," that is, those who have eaten the harvests of many seasons (Cattell 1989a). Social criteria, such as having a married child or being a grandparent, may influence ideas about being old, as can physical characteristics such as menopause, physical frailty, grey hair, wrinkles, or walking with the aid of a walking stick.

Finally, it is important to recognize that the biologic, chronological, and social components of age need not correspond within a society, even in one that reckons time strictly according to chronology. American examples of such disjunction would include the middle-aged American man who has not yet "grown up" because he is unmarried, still "finding himself," or has not yet "settled down"; or perhaps the "dirty old man" whose sexual conversation or behavior is, by implication, inappropriate for his years. An example from Melanesia is the case of Koroi (ment[...] at the beginning of [...] this section), whose ritual or social death pr[...]ed[...] his physical death.[...]

Koroi, wh[...] lived on the [...] of New Britain (Papua New Guinea), was a leader [...] he had lived many years, but that was not important [...] old age, who [...] did not count years. In 1981 Koroi had become [...] no longer had the mental ability to participate i[...] [...] material exchanges that define a person as a member o[...] [...] Koroi took shell money to his daughter's i[...] forgot to [...] ontribute it because all he could think and ta[...] was how his children were neglecting him. After that, his so[...] decided to acknowledge their father's retirement from active life by [...] series of mortuary rituals, which, they said, would show the old man how his sons honored him.

The mortuary rituals began in 1981 and continued into 1982. During these rituals all of Koroi's lifetime credits and debts were discharged, all his obligations were met, and hence all his ties to the community were severed. Since he longer participated in exchanges, he was no longer an active or living person so far as the community was concerned. This situation was unusual, but it released Koroi's sons from their father's leadership and enabled them to become leaders in their own right before their father's death.

As for Koroi, while he was socially dead, he was not dead to his family. They continued to care for him, as they had been doing, in spite of his complaints to the contrary. When he died in 1984, it was only a family matter. There was no public mourning (that had already been done), only minimal rites by his family to express their private grief. Koroi's experience is described by Counts and Counts (1985).

If definitions of *death* have such a social component, how much more variable will definitions of *old age* be? In some cases salient age may be age relative to other persons, such as birth order or generational difference (Hammel 1984, Legesse 1973, Rosenmayr 1988). Classic instances of the salience of relative age include the age-group systems of East African pastoral societies (Stewart 1977). In many of these societies, dramatic initiation rites mark entrance to the age-group system, and individuals (usually males) are distributed among groups (or age sets) that are permanently *senior* or *junior* to one another. These distinctions of *social age,* while only partly linked to chronological age, nevertheless are significant factors in access to resources, including marriageable females, material goods, and ritual or other knowledge.

These comments on aging highlight the need for different levels of analysis. Thus we take up, in chapter 2, biologic aging and biodemographic variability. In chapter 3, we turn to the comparative demography of aging, focusing on population aging and the demographic transition. Chapter 4 examines social age, in particular, cross-cultural variation in the conceptualization of the human lifecourse.

2

Cultural Variation and the Biodemography of Aging

This chapter sets out the biodemographic component of cross-cultural variation in the experience of aging and old age. In it we examine the ways in which biologic aging constrains sociocultural variation. We begin with biologic perspectives on aging and longevity and the characteristic features of human aging, in particular, senescence. We then survey cross-cultural variation in the biodemography of human populations.

The Biology of Aging

While this book surveys variation in the experience of being old, it is valuable to begin by specifying what is common in the aging experience. The "culture-free" component of aging is evident in biologic processes variably linked to the passage of time. Crews (1990) includes in biologic aging "all time-dependent structural and functional changes, both maturational and senescent, that normally occur in the postpubertal period among males and females of a species." This definition is valuable for drawing a distinction between the process of *senescence* in normal aging and disease. Senescence includes the progressive and

17

cumulative functional deterioration associated with longer lifespan, while disease involves pathological processes that are distinct from aging, even if such pathologies are more prevalent among the old. If such pathologies occur more frequently with age, as in the case of certain kinds of cancer, for example, this may have more to do with longer environmental exposure times (Rowe and Minaker 1985) than with age-related changes in physiology.

The senescent changes in function typical of normal aging follow from physiological and organ system decline, as, for example, in the loss of "organ reserve" capacity. In the young, organ systems such as the heart, lungs, and kidneys have four to ten times as much reserve function as needed in a resting state; thus, during exercise the heart can increase output sixfold, and kidneys still function adequately even when five-sixths of the nephrons are destroyed (Fries and Crapo 1981). With aging, this reserve capacity declines, making the organism more susceptible to general health perturbations. Thus, it is possible to die of old age; the trauma or disease responsible for the death is secondary to more general biologic changes that make the body less capable of responding to such challenges. As Turke (1990) puts it, "senescence is why influenza regularly kills octogenarians but rarely kills teenagers." Aging, then, is closely bound up with senescence, which can be defined as increased vulnerability to environmental insults (Alexander 1987).

What is responsible for senescence? Hayflick (1985) has reviewed a range of biologic theories of aging, which include changes in organ function, alterations in physiologic processes, and more general genetic mechanisms, but concludes that no single effect in aging is primary. No biologic mechanism that could plausibly account for the range of structural and functional changes typical of aging has been identified (Kirkwood 1985). In fact, the search for such a biologic mechanism may itself be misplaced. Aging is a product of natural selection in human populations, and the great variety of senescent changes typical of old age can be explained in terms of the declining force of natural selection in the postreproductive period. Evolutionary theories further suggest an important role for selection of pleiotropic genes, genes that produce early positive effects and late negative effects on fitness. These genes would be selected because they contribute to reproductive fitness even as they adversely affect individuals in the postreproductive period. Rose and Graves (1989) conclude that "there is no physiological necessity about senescence; it arises only when natural selection fades out with increasing age (28)." We return to these points when we examine the evolution of human longevity.

More pertinent for research on variation in the experience of old age is the biologic variability typical of late life. A sample of 80-year-olds is likely to represent a range of health statuses, extending from the hale, active individual with no cognitive impairment to the demented, bedbound patient. We might say that the two individuals differ in *biologic age* (i.e., in their position relative to the maximum human lifespan) despite their common chronological age. This is another way of saying that chronological age is not the same as biologic age. In fact, the two are only moderately correlated. This can be demonstrated through an analysis of the standard biomarkers used to assess biologic age. Such biomarkers include sensory acuity (fingertip sensitivity, the highest audible pitch one can detect, focal range of the eye), respiratory capacity (forced vital capacity, or the total volume of air exhaled after a deep breath), memory, and a series of psychomotor indices (for example, auditory and visual reaction times). Correlations between scores on biomarker performance and chronological age vary widely, ranging from over .50 for highest audible pitch and forced vital capacity to as low as .23 for measures of reaction time (Hochschild 1989b). Thus, chronological age is not a reliable indicator of biologic age, except perhaps in extreme old age (i.e., 80 and above).

Another important source of variability in biologic aging emerges from the moderate, rather than strong, correlation between disease and functional limitation in late life. Examining diseases prevalent in old age (e.g., arthritis, congestive heart disease, diabetes, dementia, chronic obstructive pulmonary disease) and the degree to which individuals are unable to perform the activities of daily living (tasks ranging from the ability to perform household chores to personal care self-maintenance) shows a surprisingly low rate of overlap; one study reports no correlation greater than .57 (Ford, Folmar, Salmon, et al. 1988). Clearly, disease leads to functional limitation, which ultimately leads to mortality; but a series of careful studies has also shown that functional disability has a strong association with mortality that is independent of physical health status (Ferrucci, Guralnik, Baroni, et al. 1991). Thus, two individuals with the same stage of disease may still have very different prognoses, with the more highly functional patient at lower risk of early death. In fact, *level of disability* is a more powerful predictor of mortality than the *number of disabling diseases* an individual has. In the case of the chronic diseases typical of old age in the developed countries, there is evidently a variable range of functional disability within each type and stage of disease. For this group especially, functional limitation (a behavioral outcome) may be more informative than disease state and other standard biomedical criterion measures (Kaplan 1990).

Senescence, then, is a feature of aging and can be roughly expressed in terms of biologic age, but the connection between biologic and chronological age is imperfect, and the biologic basis of senescence is unclear. Variability in the expression of senescence is marked and clearly significant for cross-cultural variation in treatment of the elderly. That is, if senescence is only moderately associated with age, then there will be many highly functional older individuals, as well as impaired elderly. Cultures are likely to differ according to which side of aging they emphasize.

The Biologic Expression of Senescence

How does the body change with age? Since our focus is the elderly, we ignore very early signs of senescence such as the loss of athletic prowess. Indeed, for a number of the biomarkers described earlier, humans are already in decline by their late 20s.

Crews (1990) separates the biological characteristics of senescence in late life according to (1) changes in body composition; (2) alterations of skeletal mass, (3) biochemical alterations; and (4) neurobiological change. The medical and public health consequences of such biologic change are set out in systematic fashion in the Institute of Medicine's survey of health and "the second fifty years" (Berg and Cassells 1990). Our knowledge of the biologic features of aging is drawn primarily from Western societies and even in Western societies we have only recently begun to trace changes among the healthy, as opposed to diseased, elderly. In this section, we draw heavily on Crews's extensive review.

With age, body composition changes in a number of ways. These trends appear to hold across a wide variety of cultural and ecological conditions. Perhaps the most marked change is redistribution of fat. Western samples show increasing fat infiltration in body tissue, especially in the central and upper body (Mueller, Deutsch, Malina, et al. 1986). This process is described as the "masculinization" of body shape because, with age, fat distribution in females begins to resemble that in men. Such masculinization has been reported for Papua New Guinea as well, although fat infiltration did not increase in this sample (Norgan 1987). Elderly samples show a corresponding decline in muscle mass, leading to lower metabolic rates and reduced energy requirements (Wurtman et al. 1988).

Progressive bone loss seems to be a universal characteristic of human aging; women ultimately lose two to three times as much bone as do men (Plato 1987). Accordingly, osteoporosis, a pathological loss in bone mineral density, affects women to a much greater degree than men (Berg and Cassells 1990). However, within this pattern of overall bone density decline, population variation has been documented, which may be linked to cultural differences. African blacks showed greater rates of bone loss after age 40 than African whites (Solomon 1979), and bone density among Amerindians in the United States declined more rapidly than in matched white samples (Evers, Orchard, and Haddad 1985). The cause of such differences may be genetic or cultural (as in practices that encourage nutritional insufficiency in the elderly), or some combination of the two.

Crews (1990) suggests that age-related increases in blood glucose may be another universal characteristic of human aging (see also Reaven and Reaven 1985). The relationship between age and blood glucose is evidently independent of obesity or diet, for Crews and Bindon (1989) found in a Samoan sample that the relationship between age and blood glucose remains if body mass index, skinfold size, and percent of trunk fat are taken into account. There is also evidence of reduction of immune function with age that is independent of diet (Goodwin and Garry 1988).

Primary neurological degenerative diseases also become more prevalent with age, perhaps most striking is the case of Alzheimer's disease. Alzheimer's disease is also more common among relatives of those affected with the disease, suggesting a genetic component in its etiology (Duijn, Clayton, Chandra, et al. 1991).

Not all age-related biologic changes are negative. The elderly report lower rates of depression than the young (Lawton 1990b); and a growing body of research shows that older adults report fewer swings of mood and more control over affective expression (Lawton and Albert 1990). Confirming a popular stereotype, the elderly may in fact be wiser, as suggested by more confidence in decisions, greater reflection on issues, and increased tolerance for different views (Baltes and Baltes 1990). While certain measures of mental ability decline in old age, such as speeded (i.e., timed) performance tasks, others evidently improve, such as command of vocabulary (Labouvie-Vief 1985).

Also, a number of diseases run less virulent courses when they afflict individuals in the later stages of life (Rowe and Minaker 1985), and altered pharmacodynamics with senescence make the use of some drugs less problematic among the elderly than among younger people (Patterson, Schnell, Martin, et al. 1990).

Finally, elderly consistently report "excellent" or "good" health at higher rates than the young, at least in American samples (Ferraro 1980), although such self-reports may reflect cohort differences; having grown up under different historical circumstances, these elderly may be less willing to be seen as "complaining" about their health than are people at younger ages. It should be noted that in the postindustrialized nations, more elderly are living longer, with less disability, than ever before (Brody 1985). Dying of "old age" is still beyond the reach of most the world's population.

Aging and Survivorship

We have seen that chronological age is a rough but not exact indicator of senescence. Chronological age thus provides only a partly satisfactory "culture-free" definition of aging. An alternative approach is to examine how aging affects populations, rather than how it affects individuals. In this way, we see a stronger association between aging and senescence.

Examining populations as a whole, we can view mortality risk as a proxy for the expression of senescence, because senescence ultimately leads to death and age is the single most informative risk factor for mortality (Weiss 1989b). The complement of mortality risk is survivorship. From the perspective of the population, then, aging can be viewed as a factor that decreases the rate by which people within one age category (e.g., age 60 to 64) survive to enter the next (e.g., age 65 to 69). Here we do not specify exactly what decreases survivorship. Rather, we note that aging has this effect at the population level and use this invariant relation for a second attempt to create a culture-free definition of aging.

Viewing aging in these terms shows an interesting universal feature of population processes. In any society (indeed, in all mammalian species), survivorship plotted against age yields the same more or less rectangular shape, shown in the upper panel of Figure 2–1. The rectangularization of the survival curve becomes more pronounced as societies begin to control infectious disease and limit infant mortality. Plotting mortality rates against age, shown in the lower panel of Figure 2–1, yields a j-shaped or flattened u-shaped curve.

As the plot shows, survivorship declines slightly in infancy, remains constant for a period (with the death rate at a minimum between 10 and 15 years of age), and then declines rapidly (Weiss 1989b; Kirkwood 1985). Interestingly, wild mammalian populations (and many other species) subjected to domestication show a similar rectangularization in their survival curves (Hayflick and Finch 1977). Nondomesticated animal populations do not show the characteristic rectangular shape in their survival curves because they are subject to greater variability of mortality at every age. Rectangularization of the survival curve, then, indicates a reduction of "accidental" deaths linked to environment and greater expression of the biologically determined lifespan limit (Fries and Crapo 1981).

Figure 2–1 shows that the survival curve flattens out in late life. However, comparing the upper and lower panels of the figure also shows that the death rate for those surviving to old age continues to accelerate. Thus, the flattening is partly artifactual; rates of death are higher, although survivorship seems more stable because there are fewer people in the population at risk of death. The Gompertz-Makeham equation specifies the shape of mortality-survivorship curves and shows that the "force" of mortality (i.e., the rate at which people are removed from the population) increases exponentially with age (Sacher 1978, Kirkwood 1985). However, Manton and Soldo (1985) have also shown that more old-old elders (age 80+) are alive in the United States than would be predicted by the Gompertz-Makeham equation.

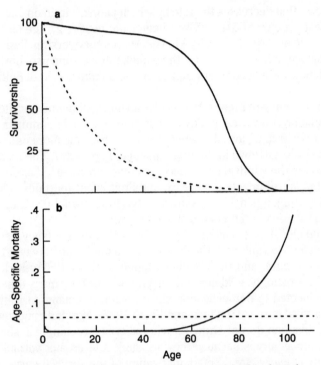

Figure 2–1 (a) Relationship between survivorship, l_x, and age, x, for a typical industrialized population in the late twentieth century (continuous curve) and for a hypothetical population of organisms which do not age (broken curve). (b) Relationship between age-specific mortality rate, μx, and age, x, for the same populations as in (a).

Reprinted, by permission, from T. B. L. Kirkwood, "Comparative and Evolutionary Aspects of Longevity," *The Handbook of the Biology of Aging* (New York: Van Nostrand Reinhold, 1985), p. 28.

The rectangular shape for survivorship is evident in preindustrial, industrializing, and postindustrial societies, as shown in Figure 2–2, although the Yanomama curve appears less rectangular than it might because of small sample size. The preindustrial Yanomama of Venezuela and Brazil are horticulturalists who have only recently begun to adopt a sedentary lifestyle (Early and Peters 1990). Figure 2–2 shows that

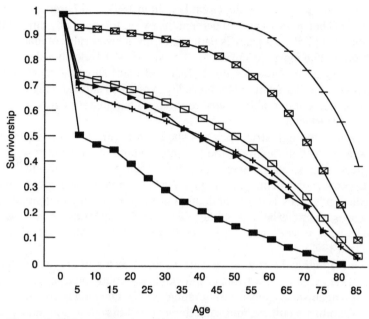

Figure 2–2 Female survivorship curves from representative human populations: Yanomama Indians (■), Sweden 1780 (+), Great Britain 1861 (▶), Laredo, Texas 1900 (□), United States 1930 (⊠), United States 1980 (—).

Reprinted, by permission of Kluwer Academic Publishers, from K. M. Weiss, "A Survey of Human Biodemography," *Journal of Quantitative Anthropology,* Vol. 1 (1–2), p. 85.

only 50 percent of Yanomama females survive to age 5, that age-specific mortality is fairly constant until age 15, and that survivorship rapidly declines beyond that age. The high infant mortality is primarily due to infectious disease and nutritional insufficiency, while the steep decline in survivorship following age 15 is due to maternal mortality, interpersonal violence, and warfare. The mortality curves for the industrializing societies show the same overall pattern (i.e., same curve shapes), although all show the "shift to the right" in the curve characteristic of societies that have begun to improve sanitation and thus control infectious disease (Mausner and Kramer 1980). Female infant survivorship to age 5 for Sweden in 1780, Great Britain in 1861, and Laredo, Texas, in 1900 is between 70 and 75 percent; likewise, the mortality curve for women of childbearing age is flatter, indicating lower rates of maternal mortality. The mortality curves for the two industrial societies depicted in the figure (the United States in 1930 and 1980) show the more obviously rectangular form. Infant mortality is reduced substantially (more than 90 percent of children survive to age 5) and maternal mortality is similarly reduced.

Even in the industrial societies shown in Figure 2–2, survivorship begins to decline rapidly in the fourth decade of life. Recent research suggests that survival curves in the industrialized nations are unlikely to become more rectangular, implying a fixed limit on longevity even if medical advances lead to elimination of the the chronic degenerative diseases characteristic of old age (Fries and Crapo 1981; Fries 1988; Olshansky, Carnes and Cassel 1990; yet see Manton, Corder, and Stallard 1993).

One additional virtue of viewing aging in terms of survivorship is that it very clearly shows that an individual's chronological age must be viewed against a society's demographic profile. *Old* means one thing in the Yanomama culture, and something very different in postindustrial nations, even by the criterion of chronological age. That is, a year of life for a Yanomama and a year of life for a postindustrial American are simply not the same, despite the common time unit. It is not simply that average life expectancy differs (although that too is true and significant: see chapter 3), but rather that a year of life in each society carries with it vastly different biologic and cultural significance. The compressed Yanomama lifespan means a very different trajectory for such events as marriage, childbearing, leadership, and the transition to seniority.

Aging and the Evolution of Human Longevity

The *average life expectancy* of humans has increased dramatically with development; that is, the age at which a person is likely to die has increased in industrial societies and continues to do so. It is currently highest in Japan, where a woman born today is likely to live until age 76. The *maximum lifespan* of humans, on the other hand, has remained constant at about 100–110 years for the past 100,000 years. As part of hominid evolution, maximum lifespan doubled between roughly 3,000,000 and 100,000 years ago (Cutler 1975; Turke 1990). Estimates of maximum lifespan in mammalian species rely on the strong correlation between lifespan and relative brain size (Sacher 1959), as well as on correlations with other lifespan indicators, such as eruption of first molars, as these are applied to fossil evidence (Turke 1990).

Comparing average life expectancy with maximum lifespan is instructive. Early hominids had a maximum lifespan of about 50 years (Cutler 1975), yet Weiss (1981, 1984, 1989a), using life table data, has calculated average life expectancies of 15 years for Australopithecines and 18 years for Neanderthals, both an indication of the saliency of infant and maternal mortality in depressing average life expectancy. Life expectancy for neolithic agriculturalists and medieval Europeans was little better and has been estimated at 25 years (Weiss 1981, 1984; Crews 1990). The low average life expectancy should be contrasted with an already much longer capacity for longevity, as the maximum lifespan had already evolved to its current maximum.

Longevity so far beyond the reproductive period raises a number of questions from an evolutionary standpoint. The long postreproductive survival of humans evidently dates back to the Paleolithic period; and ethnographic research with modern hunter-gatherers confirms that the majority of women who survive to age 15 live to age 45, long enough to experience menopause (Lancaster and King 1985). Jones (1976) reports that 29 percent of all medieval women were likely to have reached menopausal age. Menopause is a straightforward marker of postreproductive survival, although menopausal age itself varies, with median ages ranging from 43 to 51 years (Beall and Weitz 1989), depending on a range of genetic and environmental factors. For example, Tibetan women experience menopause at a mean age of 47 (Beall 1983), and !Kung women of the Kalahari Desert region experience menopause at a mean age of 40 (Howell 1979). The current mean age for menopause among American women is 51 (Crews 1990). In any case, menopause appears to be unique, or nearly unique, to the human female (Kirkwood 1985). This emphasizes the evolutionary puzzle that surrounds human longevity. Why should humans live so long beyond the reproductive period?

Theories designed to explain the evolution of aging can be roughly divided into two camps: those viewing extended longevity as adaptive, and those taking a nonadaptive view of longevity (Kirkwood 1985). Adaptive theories stress that while the postreproductive individual can make no further direct genetic contribution to evolution, such individuals can still affect the fitness of their progeny, particularly in their role as grandparents, and in this way contribute to the "inclusive fitness" of the species (Hamilton 1964, 1966; Turke 1990). Nonadaptive theories stress that senescence and hence longevity may be nothing more than random accumulations of mutations, which persist in the species because the force of natural selection diminishes in the postreproductive period (Medawar 1952). Thus, senescence and extended longevity are seen in natural populations only when domestication or improved health care reduces mortality risk at early ages. Yet nonadaptive theories fail to account for the timing of senescence (Kirkwood 1985); moreover, recent research shows strong evidence of selection pressures relating to senescence (Nesse 1988).

Adaptive theories have trouble explaining why selection that benefits the group or species has been more effective than selection among individuals, for the latter mechanism is almost always a more powerful force for selection (Maynard Smith 1976, Kirkwood 1981). However, Turke (1990) has made a plausible case for group selection in the evolution of longevity. Escalating social competition during hominid evolution may have promoted conditions "under which the elderly increasingly would have become social assets to their children, grandchildren, other close relatives, and perhaps to their group as a whole." Turke has identified four factors that would increase the reproductive value of the elderly: longer lengths of time in which children were dependent on parents, and hence the need for stable, powerful kinship networks; greater advantages for stable mating relationships; an increased value for learning and the accumulated knowledge conveyed by the elderly; and the value of the elderly in tying kin groups together, which would increase kin-group size and solidarity, and thus give such social groups competitive advantage. Turke (1990) goes on to conclude that "the resulting increase in the reproductive value of the elderly selected for delayed senescence, eventually extending the maximum lifespan."

Kirkwood (1985) suggests an alternative adaptive theory in which the evolution of longevity is understood in terms of a trade-off between level of somatic repair and other sorts of investment, such as growth or reproductive efforts. Individual fitness, in this view, is maximized at a level of repair that puts a limit on longevity. Thus, the evolution of human longevity can be explained in terms of changing levels of "accidental" mortality (i.e., high infant mortality, deaths due to war or trauma, etc.). When such mortality is high, natural selection favors somatic changes associated with rapid reproduction and high fertility, leading to a shorter maximum lifespan. When accidental mortality is low, natural selection favors somatic mutations that result in greater longevity, such as we see in Western societies that have already undergone the demographic transition. This theory is supported by a well-known demographic fact, namely, the inverse correlation between longevity and fertility, which we examine in chapter 3.

Before leaving the topic of longevity, it is worth pointing out that reports of especially long-lived populations or cultures have not withstood the test of scientific scrutiny. Claims of a disproportionately large number of centenarians have been made for the Abkhasians of the Caucasus region of the former USSR (Benet 1974), the Hunza of Pakistan (Leaf 1973), and Aegean island dwellers (Beaubier 1976). But such reports usually are based on poor documentary evidence, such as inadequate vital registration, and small samples (Cowgill 1986). In fact, careful research in one culture known for such extended longevity, an Ecuadorian mountain-dwelling group, discovered quite striking patterns of age exaggeration. Mazess and Forman (1979) report that villagers claiming to be centenarians were actually in their 80s and 90s, and that age exaggeration was typical of those over age 70. Medvedev (1974) has claimed that a similar process explains Abkhasian extended longevity. Despite such claims of extended longevity, current research suggests that average life expectancy will not exceed 85 years, even with elimination of most of the chronic diseases affecting the elderly (Olshansky, Carnes, and Cassel 1990).

Comparative Analysis of Life Tables

One way to capture variation in aging across different populations is to compare life trajectories relative to the probability of dying at any particular age. That is, the probability of dying at each particular age gives a rough indication of the *pace* of the lifecourse relative to chronological time. Death probabilities are also useful in establishing the effects of disease or other mortality determinants across different populations, or across the same population at different times (Handwerker 1990). These probabilities of dying are contained in life tables, which apply a specific set of age-specific mortality probabilities to a fictitious, *stationary* birth cohort. While the rates do not represent the actual mortality experience of a real population, life tables are still useful for modeling the lifecourse in different populations.

Life tables combine the mortality rates of a population at different ages into a single statistical model (Shryock and Siegel 1971). The great advantage of life tables for comparative study of age structure is that they allow comparison of mortality across populations that differ in age and sex distribution. While life tables for most of the developed countries are available and have been compiled through a United Nations effort, life tables for developing countries remain incomplete. Life tables for hunter-gatherer bands or groups of swidden horticulturalists remain limited. Howell (1979) has shown how the model life tables of Coale and Demeny (1966) can be applied to the small populations studied by anthropologists (see also Handwerker 1990). Typical life table functions include the probability of dying, the number (or proportion) of cohort members surviving, the number of person-years lived by the cohort, and average life expectancy broken out for a set of age strata.

Given this background on life table functions, it is instructive now to compare life tables for two populations. Table 2.1 presents life tables for Yanomama and American females. Comparison of the life tables shows the huge difference between the two groups. Taking the probability of dying first, note the striking difference in infant mortality in the first year of life: 43 of every 100 Yanomama female infants, as opposed to less than 1 in 100 American female infants, are likely to die. The Yanomama show greater likelihood of dying at every age interval. The magnitude of these differences becomes especially clear when we compare the two populations in terms of the age interval in which the rates reach a rough parity. For example, the life tables show that American women reaching age 55 have a lower probability of death than a Yanomama 10-year-old (.035 and .042, respectively). This comparison is important because the 10–14-year age span is the interval in which the conditional probability of dying is typically the lowest for human populations. Indeed, it is in this interval that Yanomama mortality risk reaches its lowest point. Thus, the age interval in which Yanomama

Table 2.1 Life Tables for Yanomama and American Females

Age Interval	Probability of Dying	Proportion Surviving	Life Expectancy at Birth
Yanomama			
0–1	.430	1.00	19.8
1–4	.118	.57	33.7
5–9	.066	.50	34.0
10–14	.042	.47	31.2
15–19	.130	.45	27.5
20–24	.134	.39	26.3
25–29	.137	.34	24.9
30–34	.140	.29	23.5
35–39	.143	.25	21.9
40–44	.147	.22	20.2
45–49	.150	.18	18.2
50–54	.154	.16	16.0
55–59	.188	.13	13.4
60–64	.251	.11	11.0
65–69	.327	.08	8.8
70–74	.432	.05	6.9
75–79	.570	.03	5.2
80+	1.000	.01	3.8
American			
0–1	.009	1.00	78.3
1–4	.002	.99	78.0
5–9	.001	.99	74.2
10–14	.001	.99	69.2
15–19	.002	.99	64.3
20–24	.003	.99	59.4
25–29	.003	.98	54.6
30–34	.004	.98	49.8
35–39	.006	.98	45.0
40–44	.008	.97	40.2
45–49	.014	.96	35.5
50–54	.022	.95	31.0
55–59	.035	.93	26.6
60–64	.054	.90	22.5
65–69	.079	.85	18.6
70–74	.121	.78	15.0
75–79	.184	.69	11.7
80–84	.298	.56	8.7
85+	1.000	.39	6.3

Sources: Yanomama (Weiss 1989b); American (*Vital Statistics of the United States 1988,* National Center for Health Statistics, 1991; DHS Pub. No. 91–1104). American life table modified to make it comparable to Yanomama table.

mortality is lowest still compares poorly to the mortality risk of the 55-year-old American woman.

In rates of survivorship (proportion surviving), we find that the likelihood of surviving to different ages does not drop below .90 for American women until age 60; in fact, more than half the American women can expect to be alive at age 80. Among the Yanomama, survivorship does not reach .90 in any age interval. Fewer than half the Yanomama entering the 5–9-year age interval survive to enter the next interval.

Despite the great differences in the *level* of mortality at different ages, we do not find obvious differences in the *pattern* of mortality for American and Yanomama female populations. In other words, the curves relating mortality and survivorship to age have the same general shape in both populations; only the age parameters (i.e., mean numbers surviving at a given age) differ. Put another way, great differences in rates of mortality are not accompanied by obvious differences in the *pivoting* of mortality around age. For example, mortality is at a minimum for both populations at roughly the same ages (ages 5–15), despite striking differences in the level of mortality. This common pattern of death across societies that are so obviously different in susceptibility to mortality is noteworthy and has been reported for other societies as well. Howell's research on the demography of the Dobe !Kung (Howell 1979), for example, shows that mortality among Kalahari hunter-gatherer bands follows the same pattern. As Howell suggests, the life table functions would appear to capture "general features of human biological processes that are sensitive to environmental fluctuations in level but not in age patterns of mortality" (Howell 1979, 79–80).

It should also be mentioned that the Yanomama estimates shown in the Table 2.1 have been challenged by more recent research. Early and Peters (1990) have criticized the Yanomama life tables of Neel and Weiss (1975; see also Weiss 1989b), whose data appear in Table 2.1, on the grounds that there are insufficient data for infant and childhood deaths. Recognizing this deficiency, Neel and Weiss relied on estimates of deaths in the early ages (primarily to compensate for female infanticide), which in turn were derived from the model life tables of Coale and Demeny (1966). But the model life tables are themselves derived from populations very different in scale, namely 326 national populations with quite different patterns of life expectancy. Based on their research among the Mucajai Yanomama, Early and Peters (1990) suggest that infant and childhood deaths are exaggerated in the Neel and Weiss table. Early and Peters also argue that the stationary population assumption of life table modeling may be inappropriate in the case of the Yanomama because of the volatility of the population at the village level. This volatility is evident in constant village fissioning, mortality from warfare, and movement of women in marriage, all of which make the life table modeling far removed from village processes (Early and Peters 1990, 132).

Still, it is notable that, even with potential exaggeration of Yanomama mortality in the 0–5 age span, Yanomama and American female patterns of mortality differ only in level and not in pattern. The Early and Peters (1990) research strengthens this conclusion by suggesting that the differences in level may in fact be less striking than those indicated in Table 2.1.

This conclusion should be kept in mind when we turn to the remaining life table functions, where the differences between Yanomama and American age structure become more glaring still. We note that average life expectancy at birth for Yanomama females is less than 20 years; for American females it is more than 78 years. Yanomama females who survive the first year have an improved life expectancy of 33.7 years, which rises to 34 for those who survive to age 5. American female life expectancy does not show this peaking pattern in childhood, but rather declines gradually from birth. This difference in age patterning is quite evident, but it can be completely attributed to the great difference in infant mortality between the two populations. In fact, the Yanomama peak of life expectancy in the 1–10-year interval is a typical feature in societies that have high infant mortality rates; the same pattern appears, for example, among the !Kung (Howell 1979) and in rural India (Shryock and Siegel 1971). Here then is an important demographic characteristic that underlies the contrast between "developed" and "developing" countries (see chapter 3).

In this discussion, we have only touched upon a few of the life table functions, and we have limited discussion of the functions to a single contrast between populations close to the extremes of demographic variability. Our goal has not been an exhaustive treatment of the life table, which would take us too far afield, but rather simply to indicate the relevance of the technique in the comparative biodemography of aging. Presentation of life tables is still the exception rather than the rule in comparative studies of aging (e.g., Cowgill's [1986] fairly extensive treatment of the demography of aging ignores the life table method), and their applicability to small populations has been challenged, as in the Yanomama research of Early and Peters (1990). Still, the life table functions show at a glance how different susceptibilities to death, or age-specific mortality, reverberate across the entire age structure of a population. They show in the strongest terms that aging is a *population process*, as well as the experience of every individual, a point that is absolutely central if one is to understand aging in a global framework. This will become clearer when we turn to population aging in the next chapter. More research on the effect of village-level volatility on demographic variables would help clarify any potential limitations of life table methods for research on small-scale populations.

3

Population Aging and Comparative Demography

We have seen that chronological age is an imperfect measure of aging: it is only moderately accurate in conveying biologic age and, as we shall see in chapter 4, it is often only obliquely related to social age. However, in the case of cross-national descriptive measures of aging, we must rely on chronological age because it is the only measure we have. Since these measures use a standard set of cutpoints to denote the elderly (ages 50, 55, 60, 65, and sometimes 75), we are forced to use them as well in reporting measures of age distribution. However, throughout the following discussion, it is important to keep in mind the limitations of chronological age as an indicator of aging.

Using age 65 and over as a rough and initial marker for "old age," how many older adults are there in the world, and how is this population of elderly distributed across the globe? Due to inadequate vital registration systems, estimates of the size of the elderly population vary. Still, with these qualifications, it is significant to note that recent estimates put the population of elderly worldwide at about 320 million, 6 percent of the world's total population (Population Reference Bureau 1991). Roughly 40 percent reside in the "developed" nations, the remainder in the "developing" world (Kinsella 1988). By the year 2000, the number of elderly worldwide will increase to 410 million (Torrey,

Kinsella, and Taueber 1987). Looking at this trend from another direction, it is significant to note that twenty-three countries had elderly populations of two million or more in 1985, and that fifty will have such populations by 2025 (Torrey, Kinsella, and Taueber 1987). As of 1990, thirty-three of 154 countries (21 percent) for which data are available have populations in which the elderly (age 65 or over) make up 10 percent or more of the total population (Population Reference Bureau 1991).

More significant than such absolute figures is a trend that is found in both developed and developing nations, and which seems to go hand in hand with development, or at least the Western model of development, that has been sucessfully imported to the developing world (Caldwell 1982). This trend is *population aging*, and the fertility decline intimately associated with such aging.

Population aging is defined as an increase in the proportion of those 60 (or 65) years and older in a population. Contrary to popular opinion, population aging is not restricted to countries designated "developed" or "more developed" in the standard United Nations classification (i.e., all countries in Europe and North America, the former Soviet Union, Japan, Australia, and New Zealand), but actually reflects a worldwide trend. Thus, a number of countries in the "less developed" category (i.e., the remaining nations of the world) are also showing clear signs of population aging. This is most apparent in Uruguay, which has crossed the 10-percent line for population aged 65 or greater; but it is also evident in a host of countries, such as Taiwan and Hong Kong (6 and 8 percent, respectively), in which the rate of increase in the proportion of the population over 65 is clearly accelerating. Population aging is also evident in a wide range of countries that have recently crossed the 5-percent mark: Israel, Cuba, Jamaica, Singapore, Albania, Yugoslavia, Chile, Argentina, Trinidad-Tobago, Sri Lanka, China, and Lebanon. In fact, the growth rate for the world's elderly population is now 2.4 percent per year, which is much higher than the growth rate for the global population as a whole (Torrey, Kinsella, and Taeuber 1987). Also, population aging is evident *within* the population of those 65 years and older. For example, the fastest growing segment of the U.S. population includes those over age 85 (Siegel and Davidson 1984), a trend that is typical of developed countries (Torrey, Kinsella, and Taeuber 1987).

These figures, striking as they are, still do not do justice to the extent of population aging in the less developed countries. Broadening the age criterion for "elderly" to age 55, which is more in line with the lower life expectancy in many developing countries, shows that population aging is quite advanced. The growth rate for persons aged 55 and over in the developing countries is 3.1 percent per year, three times the rate of the more developed countries (Kinsella 1988). Thus, the "graying" of populations is actually a global phenomenon, and its implications are only slowly being recognized; but already discussions have become public in less developed countries about whether the young still uphold their obligations to the elderly (see Cattell n.d. on Kenya) or whether nursing homes are an acceptable form of long-term care (see Rhoads and Holmes 1981 on Samoa).

Population aging has less to do with prolongation of human life (for example, through medical advances) than with fertility decline. To see why this is so, think of successive birth cohorts that decrease in size because of reduced fertility. Such declines in fertility lead to birth cohorts that are small relative to earlier, higher-fertility cohorts. As the two cohorts age, the younger, low-fertility birth cohort makes up a smaller proportion of the total population than the earlier, high-fertility cohort. The result is a shift toward a greater number of elderly in the population. Thus, even a gradual reduction in the mean number of children per family results in a major shift toward an older population. At this point, medical advances may indeed contribute to population aging, because population aging usually occurs in societies that have already reduced infant mortality, and any further reductions in mortality are likely to extend the lives of the elderly (Bannister 1988). The relationship between fertility, mortality, and population aging will become clearer when we take up the demographic (or epidemiologic) transition below.

Given this global graying of human populations, how do different societies compare in age structure? While a great many measures have been developed for comparing age structure, we will discuss three of the standard measures: proportion of the elderly relative to total population (along with the derived "dependency ratio"), life expectancy, and age–sex pyramids (including a population's median age).

Variation in the Proportion of Elderly

Table 3.1 shows the proportion of the population over age 64 in the 180 countries for which data were available in 1990. Following Cowgill's

(1986) typology, we group countries according to their status as "young" (less than 4 percent elderly), "youthful" (4–6 percent elderly), "maturing" (7–9 percent elderly), or "aged" (greater than 10 percent elderly) populations. Comparing this table to the distribution of agedness in 1980 (Cowgill 1986: 25) is instructive and shows a clear trend toward more aged populations even within so short a timespan as a decade.

None of the populations in this sample has aged to the point that 20 percent of its members are over age 65, at least as of 1990, the year for which these figures apply. Sweden, at 18 percent, represents the "oldest" population in the world. Table 3.1 also makes clear the strong association between stage of "development" and proportion of elderly in the total population. The developed countries all show proportions of elderly in excess of 10 percent. The developing countries, on the contrary, typically have proportions of elderly below 10 percent, although population trends suggest that a number of countries in this group are now in the process of joining the developed countries as "aged" societies.

Not shown in the table, but relevant here, is information on when each of the countries reached certain thresholds for population aging. For example, while Mexico, Indonesia, the Philippines, Bangladesh, and Guatemala all have current proportions of elderly below 7 percent, France reached the 7 percent threshold in 1865, and Sweden in 1890 (Torrey, Kinsella, and Taeuber 1987). Thus, fertility decline in the developed countries is a longstanding trend (Caldwell 1982). Indeed, in countries such as France or Sweden it may be that the age structure of the population has become more or less stable, in which the proportion of elderly will remain constant in the absence of a major demographic event such as war or an epidemic.

The information in Table 3.1 is often used to calculate a *dependency ratio*, that is, the ratio of young (under 15) and old (65 and over) to those between ages 15 and 64, the working years. The measure gives a rough sense of the *dependency load* of a society, since old and young would appear to be consumers of wealth relative to working-age producers of wealth. The measure, however, has a number of faults. It makes the highly inaccurate assumption that people over age 65 do not work. Of course many do, either in wage labor, as in the developed world, or in household activities that enable others to work, as in

Table 3.1 Proportion of Population Age 65 and Over

	Aged Populations (≥10%)
18	Sweden
16	Norway
15	Austria, Denmark, Germany-Fed. Rep., Switzerland, United Kingdom
14	Belgium, France, Italy
13	Finland, Germany-Dem. Rep., Greece, Hungary, Luxembourg, Netherlands, Portugal, Spain
12	United States, Uruguay, Bulgaria
11	Barbados, Canada, Japan, Czechoslovakia, Ireland, Australia, New Zealand
10	Cyprus, Iceland, Malta, Poland

	Maturing populations (7% ≤N≤9%)
9	Puerto Rico, St. Christopher-Nevis, Argentina, Israel, USSR, Romania, Yugoslavia
8	Cuba, Hong Kong, Macau
7	Dominica, Grenada, Guadeloupe, Martinique

	Youthful Populations (4% ≤N≤6%)
6	Antigua-Barbuda, Jamaica, St. Lucia, St. Vincent-Grenadines, Trinidad-Tobago, Chile, China, Seychelles, Singapore, Taiwan, Gabon
5	Costa Rica, São Tomé Principe, Haiti, Panama, Republic of Korea, Lebanon, Reunion, Albania, Cape Verde, Mauritius, Bahamas
4	South Africa, Mexico, Nicaragua, Tunisia, Bolivia, Brazil, Columbia, Ecuador, Guyana, Paraguay, Peru, Suriname, Venezuela, Afghanistan, Bhutan, Burma, Lesotho, Korea-PDR, Malaysia, Mogolia, Pakistan, Sri Lanka, Syria, Thailand, Turkey, Vietnam, Belize, Guinea-Bissau, Burkina Faso, Egypt, Chad, Equatorial Guinea, El Salvador, Ethiopia, Morocco, Algeria, French Polynesia, New Caledonia, Samoa

	Young Populations (<4%)
3	Mali, East Timor, Senegal, India, Indonesia, Iran, Iraq, Ghana, Kampuchea, Laos, Niger, Honduras, Nepal, Oman, Philippines, Saudi Arabia, Zimbabwe, Sudan, Somalia, Yemen Arab Republic, Yemen-PDR, Guatemala, Sierra Leone, Benin, Dominican Republic, Liberia, Botswana, Comoros, Central African Republic, Congo, Mozambique, Djibouti, Namibia, Mauritania, Libya, Guinea, Angola, Bangladesh, Gambia, Burundi, Cameroon, Madagascar, Fiji, Brunei, Malawi, Zaire, Solomon Islands, Vanuatu
2	Maldive Islands, United Arab Emirates, Togo, Bahrain, Tanzania, Rwanda, Jordan, Kenya, Ivory Coast, Zambia, Uganda, Papua New Guinea, Nigeria, Swaziland
1	Qatar, Kuwait

Source: Population Reference Bureau 1991; World Data Disk (World Game Institute).
Data missing for 21 countries or territories.

village-based societies. Also, the dependency ratio ignores the fact that the elderly may possess more wealth than the younger generation, even in some developing countries. This enables them to live independently for some years past age 65, and often makes the younger generation dependent on *them* (Crystal and Shea 1990; see also chapter 6).

Finally, Cowgill (1986) points out that *dependency* is misleading in this measure, for populations with a greater proportion of elderly actually have *lower* dependency ratios than younger populations. To see how this can be so, one must remember that the number of people under age 18 far outweighs the number of people over age 65 in virtually every society, barring the most aged societies such as Sweden. As a result, the child population contributes far more to the numerator of the dependency ratio than the elderly population. Given that older populations emerge when fertility declines, and hence themselves produce relatively small child populations, the numerator used in calculating dependency in aged societies will be smaller than that evident in developing countries. The result is a lower dependency ratio for the mature and aged populations.

Population aging by itself, then, does not increase dependency loads. Too rapid a decline in fertility (e.g., as a result of antinatalist policies by the state), however, can lead to increased dependency loads in combination with population aging. The case of China, discussed below, is striking on this score.

An alternative measure of demographic constraints on intergenerational support is the "familial support ratio." This ratio compares the proportion of the population in the family caregiver age range (ages 45–49) with the proportion aged 65–79, elders who presumably had these children twenty to thirty years earlier (Siegel and Hoover 1984). An alternative support ratio, particularly relevant in aging populations, compares the number of people aged 65–69 with the number of those aged 80 and over (Myers 1992). Myers reports that the general trend in such support ratios is downward, that is, toward fewer caregivers for an increasing pool of elders. Because the family support ratio is less commonly used than the dependency ratio, we restrict our discussion to the latter.

For all its faults, the dependency ratio is still valuable for deriving a rough measure of the support a society must marshal for its dependents. The extent of such support becomes clearer with the data presented in Figure 3–1, which displays the proportion of young and old contributing to the dependency ratio in nineteen countries (selected to illustrate extremes in the dependency ratio). The ratio is expressed as the proportion of the sum of people younger than 15 and older than 65 per 100 people aged 15 to 65. The figure shows how rates of fertility decline and the timing of such declines lead to very different pictures of dependency in the developing and the developed countries.

In Figure 3–1, it is clear that global variation in the dependency ratio in 1990 is what one would expect from the previous discussion. Syria, South Yemen, Burkina Faso, and Kenya have the highest dependency ratios in the world, with fifty-two or fifty-three "dependent" persons for every 100 people in the "working years." These countries all fall in the "young population" category; indeed, in these countries nearly half the

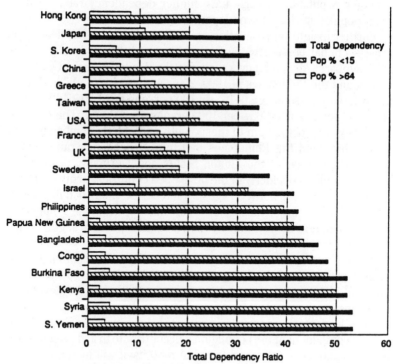

Figure 3–1 Age Components in Dependency Ratio

population is under age 15. Contrast these cases with the developed countries shown in the figure. Japan, Greece, the United States, France, the United Kingdom, and Sweden all have dependency ratios in the 31–36 range, which puts them among the lowest in the world. These countries are all "aged populations"; that is, all have populations aged 65 and over in excess of 10 percent. But these countries also have extremely small proportions of people under age 15, ranging from 18 to 22 percent. The result is a lower overall dependency ratio for developed countries.

In fact, the association between age structure and dependency ratio is quite strong. The correlation between population over age 64 and the dependency ratio for the 171 countries for which we have complete data is –.71, and the correlation between population under age 15 and the dependency ratio is .96 (Population Reference Bureau 1991).[1] Younger populations clearly have higher dependency ratios, just as older populations have lower dependency ratios.

Further insight on population aging is evident when we leave this cross-sectional perspective and examine longitudinal trends. Figure 3–2 compares dependency ratios for the United States, Germany, China, and the Philippines in 1990, 2005, and 2025. "Youth" in the figure refers to persons age 0–19 per 100 persons aged 20–64; "elderly" refers to persons aged 65+ per 100 persons aged 20–64. The total dependency ratio is the sum of these youth and elderly components. In 1990, China and the Philippines had total dependency ratios much higher than those of the United States and Germany, despite the greater numbers of elderly in the developed countries. In other words, for every 100 people between ages 20 and 64, Germany had fifty-seven people either younger than 19 or older than 65, while the Philippines had 117 people in the combined young and old population segments for every 100 people in their working years.

Note what happens, however, as cohorts age. The combination of fertility patterns and the aging of current cohorts will result in a very different picture of support relationships by 2025. For the developed countries, total dependency ratios will *increase* because low fertility will more or less remain constant and current cohorts will age. By 2025, the elderly component of the population will contribute to a greater portion of the dependency ratio, and the total ratio itself will increase. In the

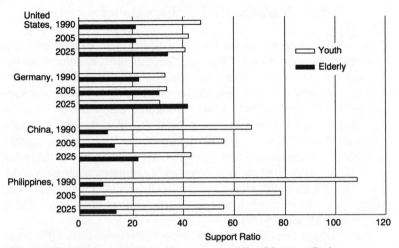

Figure 3–2 Youth and Elderly Components of Total Support Ratio
Figure provided by K. Kinsella, Center for International Research, Bureau of the Census, U.S. Department of Commerce.

developing countries, however, the picture is expected to be quite different. Declines in fertility will lead to a reduction in the size of the population younger than 19; the result will be a greater proportion of elderly contributing to the dependency ratio but a *decrease* in the total ratio. In fact, by 2025 *total* dependency ratios in the developed world will *surpass* those of the developing countries (United States, 77; Germany, 74; China, 65; Philippines, 68).

Changes in the dependency ratio, then, may mask changes in the relative contribution of young and old people as dependents. This distinction has important policy implications. That is, while the dependency ratio will certainly decline in the developing countries, the elderly will also represent a greater proportion of dependents. The fertility decline that has already begun in China, Taiwan, Korea, Hong Kong, and a number of other developing countries will lead to rapid population aging, and will reduce the time available to put appropriate programs in place for support of the elderly (Torrey, Kinsella, and Taueber 1987).

Variation in Life Expectancy

A second measure useful for the comparative demography of aging is average life expectancy. Life expectancy at birth is defined as the average number of years that a newborn is expected to live if the age-specific mortality rates (i.e., the likelihood of dying at a particular age) effective in the year of birth apply throughout his or her lifetime. To return to a distinction developed earlier, it should be noted that life expectancy at birth does not specify the maximum lifespan for a population. The life expectancy of the !Kung of Botswana is 35, yet there are many !Kung older than 35. Life expectancy estimates are heavily influenced by infant deaths (Handwerker 1990), so that anyone surviving infancy in societies like those of the !Kung foragers is likely to exceed the average life expectancy.

Table 3.2 presents life expectancies at birth in the 1985–1990 interval for the 154 countries for which we have complete 1990 data, again using Cowgill's (1986, 20) typology of fewer than 50 years, 50–59 years, 60–69 years, and 70 years and over.

Inspection of the table reveals a strong relationship between life expectancy and stage of development. Life expectancy in the developed countries exceeds 70 years, while all those falling in the 50 years or below group are developing nations, primarily African. These nations have life expectancies equivalent to those of the developing nations in the mid-nineteenth century (Cowgill 1986).

The association between population age structure and life expectancy is strong. The correlation between life expectancy and proportion of the population under age 15 for the 145 nations with complete data is −.80, and the correlation between life expectancy and proportion aged 64 and over is .69. Clearly, life expectancy is lower in high-fertility populations and higher in countries that have already experienced a decline in fertility.

By now it should be clear that the distinction between "developed" and "developing" countries can be drawn almost exclusively in demographic terms, without reference to gross domestic product, utilization of fossil fuels, urbanization, literacy, or any of the other standard markers of development. The three demographic indicators we have discussed so far—proportion of the population under age 15, proportion

Table 3.2 Average Life Expectancy, by Nation

75 Years and Over
Japan, Iceland, Sweden, Netherlands, Switzerland, Norway, Canada, Australia, France, Italy, Israel, Denmark, United States, Spain

70 Years and Over
Greece, Cyprus, Finland, Germany-Fed. Rep., United Kingdom, New Zealand, Belgium, Cuba, Austria, Jamaica, Ireland, Costa Rica, Barbados, Germany-Dem. Rep., Portugal, Singapore, Kuwait, Malta, Bulgaria, Poland, Panama, USSR, Albania, Czechoslovakia, Luxembourg, Yugoslavia, Hungary, Romania, Uruguay, Chile, Argentina, Bahrain, Fiji, Trinidad-Tobago, Sri Lanka

65 Years and Over
Guyana, Venezuela, Suriname, China, Korea-DPR, Korea-Rep., Qatar, United Arab Emirates, Malaysia, Mauritius, Mexico, Lebanon, El Salvador, Paraguay, Jordan, Ecuador, Syria

60 Years and Over
Brazil, Colombia, Dominican Republic, Mongolia, Thailand, Turkey, Iraq, Saudi Arabia, Philippines, Nicaragua, Tunisia, Honduras, Algeria, Guatemala, Cape Verde, Peru, Libya, Vietnam, Morocco, Egypt, Burma

50 Years and Over
Iran, India, Zimbabwe, Botswana, Indonesia, South Africa, Oman, Kenya, Haiti, Ghana, Papua New Guinea, Zambia, Bolivia, Tanzania, Cameroon, Ivory Coast, Togo, Pakistan, Zaire, Comoros, Laos, Madagascar, Lesotho, Uganda, Gabon, Liberia, Yemen Arab Republic, Yemen-PDR, Nigeria, Swaziland, Sudan

Under 50 Years
Bangladesh, Rwanda, Congo, Burundi, Kampuchea, Nepal, Bhutan, Mozambique, Burkina Faso, Malawi, Djibouti, Mauritania, Equatorial Guinea, Benin, Senegal, Guinea-Bissau, Central African Republic, Chad, Niger, Angola, Mali, Guinea, Somalia, Ethiopia, Afg   ne

Source: United Nations, *World Population Pros*[   ] Nations 1989), accessed through World Resources Disk [   ] missing for 55 countries.

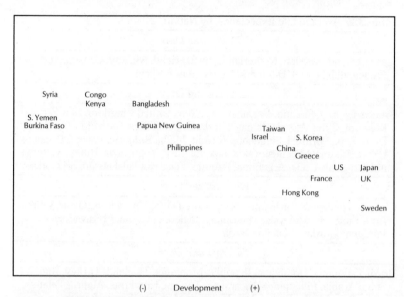

Figure 3–3 Multidimensional Scaling Plot
World Resources Data, 1990; Multidimensional Scaling Plot (MINISSA, implemented in ANTHROPAC [Borgatti 1989]).

over age 64, and life expectancy—by themselves accurately reproduce the division between developed and developing countries. This is shown in the multidimensional scaling plot presented in Figure 3–3, in which the nineteen countries examined earlier are arrayed according to their "distance" from each other based on the three indicators.[2] The figure shows tight clustering of developed and developing countries, organized along a horizontal gradient of "development."

Age–Sex Pyramids

Age–sex pyramids are a third way to assess the agedness of populations and show at a glance differences in the age and sex structure of different populations. These pyramids are histograms that show the proportion of men and women in different age strata. They are placed back to back, with age serving as the vertical axis. The width of the pyramid base gives a rough measure of current fertility, and the slope of the pyramid indicates the effect of mortality and migration at each age (Handwerker 1990).

Age–sex pyramids conveniently summarize the distinction made earlier between relatively young populations and populations that have aged. Young populations, as we have seen, are those that have high fertility and also high mortality rates. Displaying such populations in the form of an age–sex pyramid shows a marked pyramid shape: narrow at the top, wide at the base, and with a steep slope. The top panel of Figure 3–4 illustrates one such hypothetical population pyramid. Aged populations, on the other hand, have low fertility and low mortality, causing the age–sex pyramid to be more rectangular in shape. This is illustrated in the lower panel of Figure 3–4, which displays a hypothetical aged population. The age–sex pyramid has a narrow base relative to older ages and also greater width in the upper ages. As mentioned earlier, low fertility alone leads to population aging, which we now see can be shown graphically in age–sex pyramids, which appear increasingly more rectangular.

Age–sex pyramids can also be used to display the effects of temporary shifts in fertility. When fertility declines, early cohorts will be larger than more recently born cohorts. The result will be a marked bulge in the age–sex pyramid. This trend is apparent in the United States' age–sex pyramid for 1980. A bulge in the age 15–35 groups reflects the baby boom of the late 1940s through the mid–1960s. Fertility declined after the early 1960s, making subsequent cohorts appear small relative to the earlier baby boom issue. As the baby boom population moves through the age pyramid in coming years, the pyramid will take on a more or less diamond shape, although an increase in fertility will widen the base and population at lower ages.

One final feature of age–sex pyramids worth noting is the sex ratio at later ages. The sex ratio is typically expressed as the number of men per 100 women. For example, in the United States and other developed nations, women outnumber men at later ages; the sex ratio is less than 1. Yet in Liberia and Kenya, this is not the case; men outnumber women in the later age strata, resulting in a sex ratio greater than 1. This difference between the more developed and less developed countries, however, has not been consistently reported. For those age 65

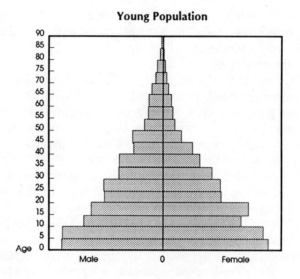

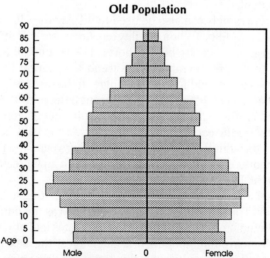

Figure 3–4 Age-Sex Pyramids for Young and Old Populations

and over, for example, United Nations data show a sex ratio of 80 males per 100 females in China, but 96 per 100 in Nepal and 123 per 100 in Bangladesh (Martin 1990). When elderly women outnumber elderly men, the reasons for the skewed ratio are not hard to uncover. There are a variety of biologic and demographic causes, such as greater male mortality from disease in late life and greater rates of early-adult male mortality in violence, trauma, and warfare. When elderly males outnumber elderly females, as in Bangladesh or Liberia, explanations are less obvious and point to cultural processes that favor men over women in late life. Of course, reporting biases are also a possibility: men have reasons for overestimating their age; women have reasons for underestimating their age.

One explanation for this disparity at late ages in the developing countries is female infanticide, or selective investment in males over females at early ages, for example in seeking aggressive medical treatment or ensuring adequate nutrition. Some evidence for the latter appears in recent research suggesting that infant diarrhea in males and females elicits different responses from families in India (Bentley 1988). Female infanticide and selective favoring of boys over girls in the early childhood years would increase female mortality rates, which in turn might result in overrepresentation of males in late life. However, such increased mortality among females should also appear in early age strata, and hence lead to narrower widths in these strata as well.

Of course, other explanations are possible. Little is known about mortality risk in late life outside the developing countries. The lower late-life sex ratio (fewer men per 100 women) in developed countries appears to have most to do with the increased *lethality* of the major killers among men in late life (Mausner and Kramer 1985). Men are more likely to die of heart failure; women are more likely to survive. The higher late-life sex ratio (more men per 100 women) in developing countries may reflect access to food in late life. For example, White (1985) reports that the body mass index (BMI = weight in kilograms/height in meters squared, a standard anthropometric measure) values of Australian aboriginal men remain relatively stable in the later decades of life, while BMI values among aboriginal women decline. This gender-linked variation may be attributed to discrimination against older women in the allocation of food, which is consistent with the relative status of the sexes in aboriginal Australian societies. Similarly, Evans (1990) has shown that men's control over income in later life, as opposed to jointly shared household income, is associated with greater BMI, and hence more adequate nutrition, among elder Javanese men. Older Javanese women do not exercise control over distinct personal income; BMI among women is related to the amount of household income they manage. Nearly half the women in Evans's community sample of Javanese families did not manage any household income. Hence Evans concludes that older Javanese women are at far greater risk for malnutrition and earlier mortality than older men. This research shows that economic status is critical for the welfare of the elderly even in societies that explicitly venerate the elderly.

Aging and the Demographic Transition

Returning to a line of inquiry begun earlier, it is clear that the developed nations are similar in that they all have lower levels of *both* fertility and mortality than do the developing nations. Development, we have argued, can easily be characterized in *demographic* terms (see Figure 3–3). The developed countries, beginning about 1790, all began to experience declines in mortality at younger ages, largely due to improved public health measures and more adequate nutrition. The result was an increase in total population. Within 100 years of this first decline in mortality, however, fertility also began to decline. Thus, in Massachusetts (the only state with reliable vital statistics collected before 1900), crude fertility and mortality rates in 1800 were both quite high (about 55 and 30 per 1,000, respectively, although mortality had started to drop earlier). By 1900, the crude birth rate had dropped to about 30 per thousand, and the crude death rate to about 18 per thousand (Mausner and Kramer 1985). Families with an average of 6–8 children became rare, replaced by families with only 3–4 children, with the average number of children declining even further later in the century (to less than 2.1, the replacement level). This relatively long-term and permanent reduction has been typical of the developed countries and has led demographers to speak of a general three-step "demographic" or "epidemiologic transition," in which crude mortality and fertility decline from 40–50 per thousand to 10–15 per thousand (Cowgill 1986). The stages of this transition are shown schematically in Figure 3–5.

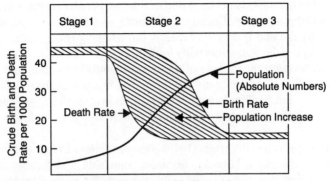

Figure 3–5 Stages of Demographic Transition
Reprinted by permission, from J. S. Mausner and S. Kramer, *Epidemiology—An Introductory Text* (Philadelphia: W. B. Saunders Company, 1985), p. 250.

Figure 3–5 presents an idealized, or prototypical, picture of the demographic transition, because cultural context may alter the rate of demographic change (Hammel 1990). In pretransition stage I, mortality and fertility are both high, and total population is relatively low. Infectious disease is the primary killer, with the preponderance of deaths due to respiratory disease, tuberculosis, parasitemia, and related *acute* illness. Measles, diarrheal diseases (such as cholera), and malaria are the primary killers. Stage II involves a decline in crude mortality and a later decline in fertility, the net result being a fairly large increase in total population. Stage III is characterized by low rates of both fertility and mortality, a more slowly increasing or stable population, and a shift to *chronic* disease as the primary cause of mortality. In this stage, cardiovascular disease, cancer, and cerebrovascular disease are the major causes of death (Brock, Guralnik, and Brody 1990; Kinsella 1988). The demographic transition thus implies population aging, for the decline in fertility means a greater proportion of older adults in the population. Also, as mentioned earlier, declines in infant mortality appear to be the driving force behind the demographic transition, brought about largely through public health measures (i.e., better sanitation, vaccination programs, improved nutrition, and access to primary health care).

Why does fertility decline follow the initial reduction in crude mortality? This question is perhaps one of the most controversial issues in historical demography. Common wisdom had sought an explanation for fertility decline in terms of a slow but growing recognition of the significance of declining mortality for family economic well-being. A decline in mortality meant less of a threat of family extinction and thus there was less need for many children. The implication in this line of thinking is that fertility is *artificially* high in pretransition societies. If economic security were a sure thing, people would have fewer children.

Beginning with Notestein (1945), demographers began to stress a stronger association between declining mortality and fertility rates. Notestein linked fertility decline to "the growth of huge and mobile city populations," which essentially dissolved the corporate-based, extended family and gave rise to a society in which individualism had free reign (Caldwell 1982). Individuals could now indulge personal preferences in ways they could never have done in the past, and along with these preferences came a new interest in the accumulation of goods and a desire to pursue a host of personal aspirations. Having more children thus became an economic issue in a new way, in which the individual had now to consider how much an additional child would mean sacrifice of other goods or aspirations.

This explanation of fertility decline seems reasonable enough until one notes that city populations in the developing world do not always reduce fertility in the expected way, and more generally, that developing nations well into stage II, as evidenced in declining crude mortality rates, do not experience the expected reductions in fertility. As Caldwell (1982) points out, maintaining the Notestein theory in the face of these data implies that fertility decisions in the developing nations are simply economically irrational. This is an unwelcome conclusion, since it points more to longstanding prejudice than to adequate explanation; and, in any case, careful surveys of fertility decisions in developing countries reveal no such irrationality. In fact, the Notestein theory faces greater difficulties. For example, Caldwell (1982) points out that following World War II fertility did not decline in urban Egypt (where it should have), but did decline in agrarian Bulgaria (where it should not have).

Caldwell (1982) has proposed an influential alternative theory, which will be discussed below when we turn to global variation in the relationship between generations. In his view, fertility decisions are always rational, in the sense that "fertility is high or low as a result of economic benefit to individuals, couples, or families in its being so" (Caldwell 1982, 152). Whether high or low fertility is economically rational is not a matter of economic modernization or development, as Notestein (1945) and mainstream economist views would have it, but rather a consequence of the flow of wealth between generations. Traditional, pretransition societies are characterized by a flow of wealth from younger to older generations; it is thus economic to have more children, and careful parents invest limited resources in the children they think are most likely to succeed. In fact, in such modernizing societies, families always gain economic benefit from having more children, because aside from long-term expectations of wealth sent by children who have gained new educational credentials and skills for wage employment, children retain their function as domestic helpers and even wage earners in the village context as well. The junior to senior direction for this intergenerational wealth flow is linked to the presence of extended families. In these societies, families are not nucleated, and parents and children do not share the affective ties typical of nuclear families. As a result, children do not occupy the pivotal position for patterns of expenditure and emotional investment so typical of developed nations.

In the developed nations, in contrast, fertility functions differently because the nuclear family implies a completely different constellation of economic and emotional investment. It is economically rational to have fewer children in the developed nations because the flow of wealth in these societies is primarily from parent to child; with the nuclear family comes a new and pivotal position for children as outlets for expenditure and affective attention. Caldwell stresses the intimate association between economic and emotional *nucleation*. With the decoupling of the nuclear family from extended kinship units, parents become masters of a *family* economy, and are free to spend on their children in ways inconceivable in extended kinship orders. With this opportunity come new expectations about parent and child roles, for example, that parents and children should have the *same* level of expenditure, or even that parents should spend more on their children than themselves.

A central implication of the Caldwell theory, then, is the lack of any necessary connection between economic development and declines in fertility. It is not economic development but rather the rise of the nuclear family and its strong conjugal tie that reverses the intergenerational flow of wealth typical of the developing nations; and it is this flow of wealth that affects fertility decisions. In fact, Caldwell reports that some areas of Europe adopted the nuclear family form and began the process of fertility reduction as early as the seventeenth century, long before economic modernization, which again shows the lack of connection between fertility decline and economic modernization. Likewise, when fertility declines in the developing countries, it occurs among urban elites that have adopted Western models of the family. Caldwell concludes that "if another culture had brought economic development, a culture with a much less nucleated family system, industrialization might well have proceeded far beyond its present levels in the Third World without reversing the intergenerational flow of wealth" (Caldwell 1982, 153).

Thus, while the evidence for the demographic transition is striking and incontrovertible, the reasons why it has taken a particular form in a particular place remain controversial. Our concern in raising the topic is limited only to pointing out its relevance to aging as a population process. First, with fertility decline comes population aging, as we have shown from a number of vantage points; second, and equally significant for comparative study of the position of the elderly, fertility decisions are embedded in a larger constellation of issues that affect relationships between the generations, such as the intergenerational flow of wealth, the relative separation of families from larger kinship units, and the nature of affective ties between parents and children. These topics will all be examined in the chapters that follow.

Fertility, Population Aging, and Government Policy

The population aging that is characteristic of the demographic transition is a gradual, long- term trend. As indicated earlier, however, government antinatalist policies can hasten population aging. The case of China is instructive. While other East Asian countries (e.g., Japan, Malaysia, and Singapore) have adopted pronatalist policies to slow population aging (Martin 1991), China remains committed to a one-child policy until the turn of the century (Bannister 1988). Chinese policymakers have only slowly accepted the inescapable connection between low fertility and a greater number of elderly relative to other population segments. In fact, publication of research showing this obvious relationship was suppressed in China until quite recently. The rapid population aging in China will mean an extraordinarily high number of urban elderly in a society that to date is still quite ill-equipped to provide for them.

Chinese fertility had been dropping even before the government instituted its one-child policy in rural areas in 1978. The total fertility rate had dropped from 5.8 births per woman in 1970, for example, to 2.7 in 1978. This decline in fertility alone already presages massive population aging. For example, Bannister (1988) reports that the number of people age 60 and over will increase from 77 million in 1982 to nearly 300 million in 2005 and, again, to 430 million in 2025. Short of a major catastrophic change in adult mortality, this population is already set in place and will appear in due course, for these cohorts have already been born. The fertility trend that produced these cohorts *precedes* the government's severe efforts to dampen fertility as a way to reduce total population. However, continuing the one-child policy will mean fewer people in the younger age intervals at these later dates, and hence a greater proportion of elderly in the population. Even with replacement of the one-child policy with a more liberal two-child policy, which seems likely after the turn of the century, the proportion of elderly in China in 2025 will still be 22 percent, almost a fourfold increase from 1990 levels.

This rapid population aging will occur in a society with little in the way of a social security system, an underdeveloped government pension system, and little development of a health-care service sector stressing chronic disease and functional health (Bannister 1988). Besides further liberalization of the antinatalist policy, we can expect China to follow Japan and other East Asian countries in promoting policies that delay the age of retirement (Martin 1991), thus keeping as many people in the work force as possible at any given time.

We raise the Chinese case to indicate that government policy may affect population aging in indirect ways, with massive consequences. Many other African, Asian, and East Asian governments have expressed interest in restricting population growth as a way to encourage economic development, but little thought is usually given to the effects of such policy on the age structure of the population. With a proportion of elderly at a low 5 percent in 1985, Chinese leaders did not realize that they *already* had an aging problem of major dimensions.

Notes

1. Pearson correlations were calculated using the Global Data Manager and World Data Disk (World Game Institute).
2. The multidimensional scaling solution uses a nonmetric algorithm (MINISSA) and is implemented in ANTHROPAC (Borgatti 1990).

4

Culture and the Lifecourse

Human lives are "researchable units," but not easily researchable units (Fry 1990); and learning about human lives as a unit (the *lifecourse*) has presented a challenging stimulus to social scientists. For gerontologists, a convergence of disciplinary perspectives into the lifecourse approach or paradigm has set a gerontological research agenda for the 1980s and 1990s with an "overflowing cornucopia" of research choices (Fry 1990).

The research choices range from examination of the entirety of individuals' lives, "the lifecourse as a cultural unit" (Fry and Keith 1982), to specific stages of the lifecourse, such as old age, and a variety of phenomena including different social and cultural contexts, historical processes, and social and economic change. Case studies point to both intracultural and cross-cultural variation in definitions of the lifecourse, with variation in its overall *shape*, the statuses and roles characteristic of its divisions (life stages), and the effects of demographic factors and historical processes. At this point in the development of lifecourse research, the concepts in the model need refinement through cross-cultural comparisons (Fry 1990).

This chapter is designed to contribute to such refinement. Here we define the *lifecourse* as a unit of analysis. We then turn to temporality, or the time-linked dimension of the lifecourse. As we will see, research has encountered difficulties in delimiting the lifecourse because of the difficulty of disentangling individual development (aging effects), a cohort's progression through time (cohort effects), and historical processes (period effects). We also examine the ways in which age and generational status may conflict and the different ways societies respond to such contradiction. We next consider variation in the overall structure, or shape, of the lifecourse, including both analytic concepts of social scientists and indigenous views of the lifecourse as "metaphors to age by." We then examine the "stages of old age" and some generic categories applied to the elderly, such as "ancients" and "ancestors."

We continue with a discussion of life stages, lifecourse transitions, and intergenerational relations as exemplified in the explicit, formal models of the lifecourse found in age-set systems and the informal lifecourse models of societies with implicit systems of age stratification. This involves a discussion of the state and its effect on definitions of the lifecourse.

We conclude with a brief discussion of historical change and the lifecourse, including commentary on old age as a new stage of life and changing lifecourse patterns.

Conceptualizing the Lifecourse

The literature on the lifecourse is vast. For reviews and some landmark studies in the burgeoning social science literature on the subject, the following studies are notable: Cain (1964); Elder (1975, 1982a, 1985); Fry (1990); Hagestad and Neugarten (1985); Hareven (1978, 1982); Neugarten (1968); Riley (1979, 1988); Riley, Huber, and Hess (1988); Riley, Johnson, and Foner (1972); Rossi (1985); Rossi and Rossi (1990); Sorensen, Weinert, and Sherrod (1986); and Spencer (1990).

Embedded in this large and growing literature is a profusion of terms suggesting that a human life represents a passage through time or follows some plan or pattern, which is at least partly external to the individual. Many terms include the word *life*, which attests to fascination with human lives and the difficulties of conceptualizing a human life so it can be the subject of research. Thus, the literature includes *lifecourse, life cycle, life line,* and *life stages.* There are *life chances* or opportunities across the lifecourse, *life crises,* and *life events.* The *life world* suggests that lives are lived in contexts, and *lifeterm* and *lifetime* are used as descriptors for an entire life, as in *life-term social arena* (Moore 1978) and *net lifetime intergenerational exchange* (Caldwell 1982). Various metaphors have been employed, some suggesting a passage or journey (*career, pathway, trajectory*), others hint at normative patterns or ideals (*pattern, plan, script*), yet others conceive of time as a linear progression (*social clock, life schedule, timetable*). *Life histories* or *life texts* are biographical narratives that have also been used as a source of data on the aging experience (Luborsky 1987).

We take the *lifecourse* as a developmental process patterned on cultural standards or norms for behavior, which summarizes the stages of life between birth and death. We use the term *lifecourse* because of its current acceptance in gerontology.

As Fry (1990) points out, there is "remarkable agreement on basic premises" among researchers adopting the life span or lifecourse perspective. Following Fry's summary, these basic premises are:

- The lifecourse is an entirety or unit: "aging occurs from birth to death" (Riley 1979). The lifecourse is multidimensional, "encompassing interdependent biological, psychological, and social processes."
- The lifecourse is linked to a secular context, that is, "linked to a specific social, environmental, and historical context."
- With increasing age, there is increasing variation among individuals in lifecourse processes. Plasticity is a lifelong characteristic, that is, "behavior and personality are malleable throughout the lifecourse" (Fry 1990).

Critical to cross-cultural research on the lifecourse is the great variability in the periodization of the lifecourse, that is, in the demarcation of the different stages that are seen to make up a life. The evidence to date suggests that such periodization of the lifecourse is institutionalized in all societies, but with varying degrees of formality and explicit articulation (Fry 1990). Moreover, the category of "old" or "aged" exists everywhere. Yet variation in the content of this last stage of life is also evident. Some societies distinguish between "intact" and "decrepit" elders (Glascock and Feinman 1981); others distinguish between the "young-old" and "old-old."

Researchers have begun to pay greater attention to the relevance of cultural norms and the lifecourse to the experience of old age, and different experiences of the lifecourse in different sociocultural and historical settings—for example, in the research of social historians who reach back into the American past (Hareven 1982; Elder 1985), in ethnic studies (Nydegger 1992), and in anthropological fieldwork in different cultures, including both single-setting ethnographies (Cattell 1989a; Thomas 1992) and large-scale comparative research such as Project AGE (Fry 1988; Ikels, Keith, and Fry 1988; Keith, Fry, and Ikels 1989). However, so far the majority of data has come from research in contemporary industrialized nations (Fry 1990).

Time and the Lifecourse

Notions of the movement, or shape, of time and the location, fuzziness, or absence of time boundaries vary across cultures and have a variety of effects on concepts of the lifecourse.

Time is culturally defined, and concepts of time are embedded in language, verb tenses, and images and metaphors. The Euro-American concept of linear time as expressed in solar calendars, chronological age, and the notion of "aging from birth to death" is not the only way in which time is conceived, although it is the prevailing view in gerontology. In linear thinking, time moves from past to present to future, and it is irreversible—"it's over and done," to use the American vernacular. In contrast, time among Hindus is circular and humans are endlessly recycled in various life forms, with accompanying beliefs in reincarnation. Concepts of time may take other shapes, and may follow various rhythms such as those of the seasons, the movements of the sun and moon, and the human biology of birth and aging (Fry 1990).

In addition to varying cultural concepts of time, time presents some serious problems when it comes to research on the lifecourse. These problems have to do with the time-related variables of age, cohort, and historical period. It is hard to know when a feature of old age should be attributed to aging, to the particular common experience of a birth cohort, or to some historical factor unrelated to either. Take, for example, the common observation that older American adults born in the 1920s differ with regard to their children when it comes to leaving food on a plate at dinner. A visit to a restaurant will usually show that older adults finish everything on the plate, while their children feel far less compunction about wasting food. Is this a function of age, such that adults become more frugal or socially conscious with age and less likely to waste food? Or is it a cohort effect, such that older adults who have lived through the Depression have acquired a particular frugality with respect to food? Or, finally, is such frugality the result of a historical period, say, a recession that cuts across the historical experience of the cohort?

The first of these variables, age or life time, has to do with individual aging—from birth to death and, in some societies, to ancestral status. These changes are linked to individual aging, the biologic, psychologic, and social changes that occur simply by getting older.

The second involves the common experience of people born at the same time. These "born togethers" constitute a birth cohort or age stratum: a number of people aging through the same time framework and sharing many similar experiences—Americans who came to maturity during the Depression era, for example (Elder 1974, 1982b). But the notion of common historical experience can be misleading, because not all members of a cohort share the same experiences in a given historical period. For example, not all youths in the Great Depression of the 1930s suffered the deprivation described by Elder (1974). In addition, any given historical experience is shared by many different cohorts.

The third time effect is history, which involves processes of change within a wider society. These historical processes are often referred to as *social change* or *modernization,* poorly defined concepts that, in spite (or perhaps because) of their vagueness and the difficulty of operational definition, have stimulated research on aging in developing countries (see chapter 8). The variables are necessarily confounded but can be disentangled to some extent by emphasizing one of the three, for example, by longitudinal research, which follows individuals over time and maximizes individual variation (age effects), or by historical research, which maximizes either cohort or period effects (Fry 1990). In addition, research in different cultural settings maximizes the effects of contextual variables.

An additional complication in the study of lifecourse processes involves ideas about age and generation. An individual's age and generational status may conflict, and societies differ in the degree to which they have established mechanisms to reconcile such disparities. In American society, the wish to see age and generation correspond is perhaps most visible in the case of a man marrying a woman "young enough to be his daughter." The phrase itself is a rebuke, as it likens the marriage to an incestuous union. Or imagine the 38-year-old woman whose daughter has just given birth at age 18, and who, not atypically, rejects the idea of being a grandmother because she feels she is "too young" for grandparenthood. In these cases, the age and generation criteria that define seniority conflict. Non-Western societies are also not immune to such unwelcome combinations of age and generation.

Kertzer (1982) reminds us that the definition of *generation* is by no means obvious. When we speak of generation, do we mean *birth cohort*, a group of people born at the same time; or rather a more or less homogeneous age group that has undergone common historical experience (e.g., *the older generation, youth*); or, finally, is the term more appropriately limited to a descent relationship, that is, the parent–child relationship, rather than to any society-wide designation? Kertzer convincingly shows that only the last usage is warranted. The two other definitions confuse generation and age, when, in fact, the two need not correspond. Consider the case of societies that use kin terms for classification. In Eastern Indonesian societies, for example, *uncles* may be younger in age than *nephews*; generational seniority is defined in terms of kinship categories rather than age. Needham (1974) reports of the Kodi of Eastern Indonesia that youths in senior categories may be deferred to by far older men in junior categories. Similarly, in societies characterized by clanship based on unilineal descent, such as the Tallensi of Ghana, strict attention is paid to the birth order of males in generations close to that of the apical clan founder. The lineage emerging from the firstborn son is the senior lineage of the clan; and the elder of this lineage, whatever his relative age, is clan leader (Fortes 1940).

Thus, age and generation represent different criteria for determining seniority. They may correspond, but they need not. In fact, even in the United States age and generation do not always correspond. For example, with remarriage late in life to a younger woman, a man may have a second wife the same age as his children from a prior marriage.

Given the lack of correspondence between age and generation, we follow Kertzer (1982) and consider them distinct social elements that can be combined in different ways.

Why so many human groups, existing in such varied conditions, insist on using a genealogical principle, generation, to think about social relations outside the family is hard to explain. The explanations range from the broadly cognitive to the psychological, even Freudian. Does it reflect a universal tendency to "tame time" (Baxter and Almagor 1978) by imposing a social relationship (generation) on a biological process (age)? Or is it rather a way to establish a more orderly succession to positions of power within societies? Assigning people of varying ages to a junior and senior group, for example, restricts competition. An example is the four-tiered class labels assigned to college students: freshman, sophomore, junior, senior. One moves through the ranks at a constant rate, competing for honors restricted to class membership (e.g., scholarships, leadership positions). Domains unregulated by class membership, such as romance, would be expected to show greater competition and resentment, as in the case of senior males who are said to "raid" freshman or sophomore classes for romantic partners. In the case of elder and junior generations, generation labels may demarcate domains for noncompetition, so that fathers and sons do not compete for the same marriage partners or resources (Legesse 1973).

Cultural Variation in the Definition of the Lifecourse

Lifecourses are cultural units that may be "perceived, planned for and evaluated as an integrated unit" (Fry and Keith 1982). They may be conceived as having shapes or patterns that can be described, analytically by social scientists or metaphorically by members of the relevant society. These shapes include linear trajectories, a pathway with many branches (representing many opportunities and choices), bundles of intertwined threads or *careers*, or cyclical rounds tied to seasonal tasks or to the larger cycle of human generations. They may be marked by many discontinuities or by strong continuities. Frequently (if not universally) they differ markedly within the same culture for females and males, a form of intracultural variation which is receiving increasing attention in lifecourse research (Cattell 1989a; Rossi 1985).

Whether analytical models of the lifecourse are applicable to all kinds of societies is a matter for empirical investigation (Fry 1990), as are issues such as the extent to which the lifecourse is institutionalized or recognized formally or informally, across societies, in language, in metaphor, or in other ways.

These issues may be fruitfully explored by comparing social science models of the lifecourse with indigenous models. One commonly used social science approach is that of the "life trajectory" used in longitudinal and historical research to detail demographic patterns, for example, changes in the mean age at marriage, widowhood, and other key lifecourse transitions (Elder 1985, Hareven 1978). This view seeks statistical patterns to make inferences about individual lives. An alternative view involves more direct attempts to capture personal lives through biographies and life histories (Cohler 1982, Frank and Vanderburgh 1986). In general, this analytic perspective tends to focus on transitions, conflict, and change, and on individuals as active negotiators of their lives (Fry and Keith 1982; Hareven 1978; Marshall 1985).

Application of the different approaches often results in very different pictures of the lifecourse. The Euro-American conceptualization of the lifecourse, discussed above, is one of linear progression from birth to death, which emphasizes the distinctness of each individual's life. However, the linear view may not truly reflect the full extent of variation in the American understanding of the lifecourse. In one study of lifecourse stages, Fry (1980) found that adult Americans in Indiana (with little difference by gender) actually viewed the lifecourse as a horseshoe-shaped curve, in which varying age-linked changes in the degree of personal independence gave the lifecourse a curvilinear shape. Youth is a state burdened with obligations regarding career and family; middle-age represents the peak of life, and old age is a period of decline that becomes marked by increased frailty and dependence.

LeVine (1978) analyzed the lifecourse of the Gusii in western Kenya and found that three dimensions were necessary to characterize this alternative conception of the lifecourse. In his analysis, Gusii lives are intertwined bundles of interrelated "subjective careers" revolving around reproductive, economic, and ritual activity. For Gusii men and women the reproductive career (having many children) is the most significant. The economic career (including the traditional agropastoral economy and newer wage labor) offers more opportunities for men. And for both genders, the traditional ritual career (in which people serve as diviners, healers, and witches) is important for remediation of economic and reproductive difficulties. LeVine suggests that this subjective career approach could be a useful one for comparing lifecourses in different cultures. Plath (1983) has employed a related approach in a study of aging in Japan.

The Hindu *asram*, a *life script*, codifies a cyclical life plan that ideally leads older family members to transf[er control of resources] to younger family members so that the elderly [may] and enjoy the care and respect of their juniors. This leisure [allows them to] focus more fully on spiritual matters in preparation for [death, afterlife, or re]incarnation. In practice, older persons recogniz[e the features of this c]ultural life plan but usually retire from family [authority rarely, if at all,] apparently because of concerns about whethe[r they will in fact be cared] for (Vatuk 1980).

Thompson (1990), describing [the vernacular Chinese "age by,"] shows how Taiwanese conceive t[his human lifecourse as] analogous to the growth cycle of rice, the sta[ple food ... ing] of human lives, the Chinese link the rice pla[nt's growth, flowering,] and reintegration into the earth as fertilizer for the next season s[i]nce plants to humans' ancestral roots and the succession of generations. A crucial element of becoming completely human involves, for a man, having posterity to continue his connection (as an ancestor or ghost) with his patrilineage even beyond the grave. Thus the linkages between fathers and sons are continuous down the generations. Women, however, are "transplanted" at marriage, breaking the cycle and becoming "useless eaters of rice" (in Ikels's gloss, cited by Thompson). Thus women's lives, instead of being part of an eternal cycle, are marked by disjunctures in their roles as daughters who leave their natal homes, wives who come as strangers into their husbands' homes, and mothers and mothers-in-law who must give up their daughters to be replaced by other strangers, the sons of their wives.

Another example of a cyclical model of human lives is found among the Samia of Kenya (Cattell 1989a). Samia people want to live successful lives, to be human beings, persons who behave properly. In this sense their lives are directed toward achievements as a living person, to culminate in old age with being a respected elder, a person of some material means, someone who is sought out by the young for advice, and who controls the activities of younger persons. This general goal applies to both males and females, with men advancing to lineage elder and perhaps even being chosen headman in their village, and women managing others in the homestead in their roles of mother-in-law and perhaps senior wife. Then, in very old age, when one is frail, it is time to "sit and eat," to bask in the sun's warmth or by a fire and eat the food raised, prepared, and brought by younger persons, usually daughters-in-law or grandchildren, or, for men, wives—a culturally approved (although not desired) late-life dependency, which, in fact, can only happen if one has led a successful life: "Old age is good if you have children to feed you."

At the same time, any individual's life is only one in a long sequence of lives. Samia people speak of "continuing the generations" of their grandfathers, with *grandfathers* referring to *ancestors* in general. For the Samia, the shape of the lifecourse is that of the lineage model of a "line," or lineage of persons related through males. Generational succession, especially for males, is not an abstraction but an everyday reality when you are called by a grandparent's name, uncles and brothers are close neighbors, and grandchildren live in your own home. In this context, what matters in life is to fulfil᾿ ___ duty to replace yourself in the lineage (your own, if a ___ nd's, if a woman) and to pass down to your children ___ the knowledge that you in turn have received from ___ 1se of guardianship and continuity that is important i ___ in spite of changes that have devalued certain kind₃ ___ wledge possessed by older Samia persons (Cattell ___

For Samia females, generat ___ fers, because women are buried on their husband's ___ n be helped, on the land of their own natal lineag ___ own grandfathers (where they might be troubleso ___ omen, this disjuncture may mute their sense of g ___ sion. However, a female ancestor spirit has equal sta ___ male spirit and equal ability to influence the lives of her descendants.

Thus, the Samia lifecourse is a progression through a kinship hierarchy to old age, when a person should (ideally) be respected always and cared for when care is needed, and beyond that to ancestorhood, when one continues to have a role in family affairs. In this concept of the lifecourse as one of generational succession, an individual's being has no end (although we have no ancestors as informants to give us their side of the story).

The Stages of Old Age:
Old People, Ancients, and Ancestors

Indigenous perceptions of the lifecourse vary from culture to culture, but all have in common the fact that they are structured according to a succession of statuses and roles (Fry 1990). For some roles, age is minimally relevant (e.g., membership in a church, civic group, or professional organization). For other roles, age is a critical determinant of one's position in the lifecourse. The minimal set of age categories or stages in the lifecourse consists of "birth," "childhood," "adulthood," and "old age." So far no one has discovered a lifecourse that lacks this minimal set of lifecourse distinctions. Beyond these, there is considerable cross-cultural variation in conceptions of the lifecourse, as we have already seen. We present the case of the "ancestral" stage of the lifecourse to give an idea of just how diverse these stages can be.

Among Marshallese living on the Pacific a[...] site of atomic testing), a person's spirit may t[...] which appears limp and lifeless. So long as [...] son will not be considered to have died, ev[...] spirit does not return to the body, the body [...] tinues to exist, to communicate with the livin[...] tions, or other means. Some living people se[...] spirits continue to play a part in the lives of [...] in traditional Marshallese culture (Carucci 1[...]

ANCESTORS

Spirits

Similarly, in many African societies, anc[...] of the continuum of existence and are "the ul[...]s (and misfortune)" (MacCormack 1985). [...]e power to affect the lives of their descendants, for good or for ill, and continue to play active roles in their families. Ancestorhood may continue indefinitely, as among the Marshallese, and particular ancestors can single out a certain descendant with whom to have a special relationship.

Among the Samia of Kenya, a sense of generational succession and living individuals' continuity with their ancestors continues to be strongly felt in the 1980s, even after a century of social and economic change, including conversion to Christianity. For example, many people, including well-educated young people, claim to receive messages from ancestors in dreams. Children continue to be named for ancestors who are thus remembered for many generations. Namesakes, people who have the same name, have a special relationship. The ancestor who has a living namesake may help that descendant, send messages in dreams, or punish the namesake for misdeeds; the descendant is supposed to offer sacrifices to the ancestor.

A recent innovation among the Samia is the naming of children after living individuals, especially grandparents. Some consider this an invitation to trouble, others say no harm will come of it. One woman in her 60s said, "My son named his daughter after me, and some said she would die. But she is seven years now, and I am the one caring for her." It may be that a parent could have this in mind when naming a child; that is, giving the child the same name as a grandparent should encourage the grandparent to take a special interest in the child. If this is happening with any frequency, grandmothers may be the special targets of this new practice, since grandmothers participate extensively in childcare, and also are more likely to be living than grandfathers. It is a new version of an old Samia custom, which benefits the child namesake and the ancestor-grandmother in important ways (Cattell 1989a).

Formal Models of Life Stages and Transitions

African age-set systems provide special insight on the lifecourse because they represent the most explicit use of the individual lifecourse as a model for more general social organization. The conceptualization of the lifecourse evident in such age-set systems should be contrasted with the definition of the lifecourse that emerges through governmental regulation, as in the case of a nation's tax code or pension system. For the latter, the lifecourse is rigidly divided into fixed stages. One is a "dependent," a "wage earner" (or unemployed), or a "retiree." Short of disabilities that require custodial arrangements, one's "minority" ends at age 18; and one is eligible for social security support, for men, at age 65. In fact, the African age-set systems, so often taken to be gerontocratic ladders in which everyone's position is fixed, may be more flexible than modern bureaucratic states when it comes to structuring the lifecourse.

The centrality of social age or generation in social organization is easy to see in these age-set systems, which are also referred to as "generation-set" or "age-group" systems. Such systems are most common among nomadic pastoralists in East Africa, although they also occur in other parts of Africa, as among sedentary farmers; among a number of societies in South America and Melanesia; and in East Asia (Stewart 1977). Age sets have integrative functions in their societies, including socialization, role allocation, regulation of intergenerational relations, and task allocation (e.g., military, political, judicial, ritual, economic) (Eisenstadt 1954). They also make good ecologic sense in pastoralist societies, which are highly mobile: age sets integrate individuals who range over large territories into a social system that serves the needs of both humans and the livestock on whom the humans depend (Cattell 1982). But age-set systems are not static regulators of a balanced, smoothly running social system. They are also sources of change with both intrinsic causes, especially cohort (age-set) succession, and extrinsic causes, such as modernization and social change (Foner 1982; Foner and Kertzer 1979).

Age sets may be compared to birth cohorts, although there are many anomalies in age sets (including the fact that some age groups are based on genealogical generations, not age), which make the correspondence very rough. Members of an age set move jointly through a series of age grades or formally recognized life stages. Relatively few societies have age sets, but all have age grades or life stages (Kertzer and Madison 1981). In the United States age grades include such categories as infant, toddler, teen, middle-aged, and senior citizen, although there appears to be little consensus among Americans on the number of divisions or life stages (Fry 1976).

In age-set systems, by contrast, age sets are named groups of males (for a discussion of the much rarer female age sets, see Kertzer and Madison 1981). An age set has some degree of internal organization, mutual activities, and certain obligations, rights, and responsibilities toward its own group members and the larger society. Thus, an age set is corporate and membership, following initiation, is lifelong. Ideally, relationships *within* age sets are egalitarian; relationships *between* age sets are hierarchical.

Significant social roles such as warrior, judicial elder, and ritual elder are allocated (or achieved, or even seized by) age-set members as they move jointly through age grades or successive life stages in which, ideally (and often in fact), they become increasingly more powerful and respected. In some societies, there is a retired age set, usually consisting of the last few, often infirm, members of an age set (Sangree 1966).

Spencer (1965) describes what he calls a gerontocratic ladder among Samburu pastoralists in northern Kenya. Males move through the following age grades: uninitiated boys, *moran* (junior and senior: the warrior grades), elders (in several stages: probationary, firestick or patron, judicial-ritual), and finally, retired, or declining elders. *Moran* are on the outside of society, associated more with bush and cattle than with camps and kin; they are expected to be unruly in behavior and to use violence to settle disputes. In contrast, elders are associated with settlements and social order. They are expected to instruct their juniors in proper behavior and to resolve conflicts and disputes through discussion and the moral power of blessing and curse. Thus, the Samburu age-set system establishes an opposition between *moran* and elders. *Moran* have physical ascendancy, elders moral ascendancy. However, elders also have economic power through their control of most livestock and the labor of their wives and children. The Samburu age-set system thus creates a form of gerontocracy that enhances (but does not guarantee) the chances for a successful old age.

While age-set norms of separate life stages and associated statuses and roles seem relatively clear-cut, in reality the distinctions are fuzzy. Gulliver (1963), for example, reports that the Arusha Maasai in Tanzania recognize that "men are individuals whose characters and personal maturation are not equal." The older members of an age set may behave like members of the next age set and share in the senior group's activities long before the formal ceremony that marks their advance to the higher grade. Of course, the formal advance of one group means the advance of every other group, as well as the initiation of a new age set of youths and possibly the retirement of the oldest age set. Thus, there will be some pushing ahead by members of younger sets and holding back by older sets. Gulliver describes conflicts between

Arusha age sets over power and succession to age grades, and Spencer (1965) describes similar stresses and struggles in age-grade transitions among the Samburu of Kenya.

Even in such formal age-set systems, individuals have considerable latitude to develop their own interests and accumulate wealth and status over their lifetime. Thus, the status ascriptions and role allocations derived from the age-set system are guidelines and opportunities, not straitjackets.

In addition, the ideals or norms of behavior may mask very different realities, as in the case of ideals of equality among age peers that mask intense competition and rivalry (cf. Almagor 1978; Bernardi 1952; La-Fontaine 1978). As Foner (1984) has amply demonstrated, systems of age inequality or age stratification exist everywhere—and everywhere such systems lead to intergenerational tensions and conflicts, particularly in the case of cohort succession. Nevertheless, age-set systems do structure intergenerational relationships, channel conflict, and provide a variety of means for dispute settlement.

Finally, based on a study of age-grade transitions in twenty-one African age-set societies, Foner and Kertzer (1978) point out that age-set systems do provide flexibility to accommodate the differential development and capacities of individuals. In their view, age-grade transitions are often prolonged, even though they are marked at some point by rituals. Because of the inherent uncertainty in the timing of such rituals, and because of conflicts between adjacent age sets, transitions are simultaneously structural weak points and sources of flexibility for individuals and change in intergenerational relations. This flexibility, in turn, allows age-set systems to respond to changes in environmental conditions and demography. For example, Legesse (1973) has shown for the Borana of Ethiopia that age-set norms for marriage respond to population pressures. With increases in population beyond the carrying capacity of the land, Borana age-set norms changed to restrict marriage opportunities and reduce the number of births. A similar change was documented by Spencer (1973) for the Rendille of Kenya. When the population-land-livestock equation is balanced again, these restrictions are dropped.

What lessons can we learn from age-set systems? One thing is clear: while an age-set system provides a formal structure for lifelong accumulations of wealth, prestige, and power, particularly for males, they do not guarantee anything. Much is up to the individual, and to changing contexts such as the ecological environment or extrinsic socioeconomic or political situation. Age-set systems are perhaps best regarded as structures of opportunity. Hence we might ask whether such formal structures, which institutionalize life stages and make role continuities explicit, offer important advantages (or disadvantages) to individuals. What are the benefits of ritually marked lifecourse transitions compared to the ambiguities of unmarked transitions? Are those relatively liminal or ambiguous in such systems, such as youths and elders, better or worse off?

In particular, one might ask whether elders in age-set systems derive any particular advantage from the formal structuring of the lifecourse typical of such regimes. The answer seems to be no. Even in such systems, much depends on individual ability and achievement, and also on factors external to the age-set system, such as roles within kinship hierarchies, marital histories, and having the right kind and number of children. Age-set systems make formal and explicit many aspects of social organization and lifecourse patterns that members of a society are expected to follow. The realities of events and behavior are often another story.

Members of age sets are, in a sense, "citizens" of age-set systems, which cross-cut the kinship system and provide alternative sources of statuses and political power over the lifecourse (Fortes 1984; cf. Sangree 1966; Spencer 1965). However, the situation is different in state systems, where individuals are differentiated as citizens and subject to state regulation as individuals rather than as members of collectivities such as kin groups or age sets. The state defines the roles of its citizens and hence the shape of their lifecourse in many ways, through laws and regulations, fiscal policies, and provision of services. Chronological age is a common qualifying criterion in legal and other requirements for citizens—for example, child labor laws, mandatory education, rules for seniority (such as voting age), retirement, and entitlements (Mayer and Muller 1986). For older persons living as citizens in state systems, the state's rationalization of the lifecourse has formalized old age with a chronological boundary and without regard for kinship status. In developed nations, states have made old age the time of life to retire from the work force and claim various entitlements for which only the old (as legally defined) are eligible—although there is great variation among states in their legal requirements (Cain 1976).

Thus, retirement and the pursuit of leisure and pleasure as a senior citizen or golden ager are constructs of the state's rationalization of the labor force. In addition, state pensions can make an elderly family member a desirable occupant of one's home, as among Skolt Lapps of Finland (Ingold 1976), fishing villagers in Newfoundland (McCay 1987), and in the former Soviet Union (McKain 1972).

By contrast, in kin-based economies where the extended family is the production and consumption unit, retirement is not an issue: people work as long as they are physically able to work (Halperin 1987). In this way, the elderly continue to have valued productive roles. This is true today, for example, among Kenyan peasant farmers who participate in both subsistence and cash economies. Many older people retire from wage employment with a small monthly pension or lump sum retirement payment. However, they do not retire from working if they go home (as many do) to the rural area and resume the life of a peasant farmer where the extended family remains to some degree the primary economic unit.

Kohli (1986) describes how, over the past two or three hundred years, European states have institutionalized the lifecourse through processes he categorizes as temporalization, chronologization, and individualization. These refer to the state's utilization of individuals' lifetimes as core structural features (the tripartite life scheme of education, work, retirement) and chronological age criteria, and the state's focus on the individual as the basic unit of social life. He argues that the result is the rationalization or regularization of the labor force and public services and transfers, and also standardization of the lifecourse.

Now, however, Kohli (1986) sees the process of such institutionalization of the lifecourse as being stopped or perhaps even reversed. Individuals have been pushing individualization (in the sense of personal growth) in new directions through changing patterns of behavior that affect the family life cycle (e.g., later marriage and childrearing, and alternative family forms). Discussions of a rigidly compartmentalized tripartite lifecourse, and the obsolescence of age norms in regard to things such as sexual behavior, clothing, and participation in formal education have contributed to this process. Mandatory retirement ages have been eliminated in some cases, although it is much more difficult to regulate age discrimination, which is a real force in the labor market.

As Fortes (1984), Kohli (1986), and others have pointed out, it is imperative to pay attention to the role of the state in shaping individual lives, because the state is such a powerful and pervasive force. However, it is not all-powerful: the actions of individuals have resulted in diminution of the state's effectiveness in standardizing the lifecourse. This result recommends the validity of examining the tension between "the lifecourse as socially ordered reality and biography in terms of individual agency" (Kohli 1986, 292).

Informal Models of Life Stages and Transitions: Implicit Systems of Age Stratification

In any given culture, ideas about the lifecourse provide patterns or models for the way a life should be lived. Shared ideas about life stages and their associated statuses and roles provide a set of expectations or rules about appropriate behavior at different periods in life. These are *oughts*. Individuals can and do violate the rules—by chance, choice, or necessity—and the pattern of any individual life may be relatively congruent with the cultural structuring of the lifecourse, or it may vary considerably. Furthermore, similar events may have different meanings in different cultures. Thus the marriage of a 55-year-old man and a 20-year-old woman may be faintly condoned, or heartily disapproved of, by Americans as a May–December romance, which violates marital age norms, while in many African societies the marriage of an old man to a young woman is a frequent and approved occurrence in polygynous marriage systems.

Transitions between life stages may or may not be marked by ritual. Birth, puberty, and adulthood (insofar as it is marked by marriage) are ritualized in many societies. Rarely is there any ceremonial recognition of entrance to old age, although death (often considered a transition to another life stage such as afterlife or ancestorhood) is everywhere ritualized. Becoming old is something that happens on an individual basis, the criteria for old age tend to be flexible, and the transition may occur over a fairly long period of time. In two cross-cultural samples (with thirty-six and sixty societies, respectively), Glascock and Feinman (1981) found that societies have multiple definitions of old age, with the most common definitions involving changes in work patterns and social roles. Where there are multiple definitions, they are likely to be applied independently of each other, particularly in criteria for men and women (Glascock and Feinman 1981).

One society where we have a good account of the lifecourse, including definitions of old age and the statuses and roles associated with the stages of old age, is that of the Samia of Kenya (Cattell 1989a). Many Samia people, young and old, females and males, were queried about lifecourse issues in a variety of situations, both formal (surveys and interviews) and informal (conversations and participant observation of daily life). People differed to some extent in their definitions of old age, but overall there was a high degree of consensus, that is, many people agreed on major criteria for becoming an old person, and also on differences between women and men.

The chief sign of a Samia man's reaching old age is diminished strength. This can be taken as a physical marker, but its social meanings are more salient to the cultural definition of old age. Mature adults are those who have discharged their reproductive responsibilities by having several children and who work to provide for their families, especially to provide them with food—the quintessential Samia metaphor for parenting behavior. Reduced strength implies diminished ability to work and thus diminished ability to feed those for whom one is responsible. Thus, as a man's strength diminishes, he begins to see himself (and is seen by others) as moving beyond parenting to old age. For Samia women, reduced strength is also a sign of old age and of a reduction in the ability to provide food for others, but the most commonly mentioned criterion is the end of a woman's reproductive career, marked by either menopause or the fact that she has not given birth for some time. As in the case of men, the most significant meanings of these definitions are social: a woman is moving beyond being a mother to new statuses associated with old age, especially the kin roles of mother-in-law and grandmother.

Quite a few people remarked that "A woman gets old quickly," "Women grow old sooner than men," and even, "A man does not grow old." These cultural commentaries on sexual differences in aging are not so ridiculous as they might seem, in view of the fact that the criteria for old age are not so much physical as social. Women marry younger than men (by as much as fifteen or twenty years), and so they become socially old sooner than men. That is, they are likely to be younger than men when their children marry, and they are accordingly younger than men when they become grandparents. On the other hand, because many men take younger wives and continue to father children even into their 60s and 70s, the men retain a younger parenting role (as opposed, or in addition to, a grandparent role) relative to women. Men thus have extended reproductive careers, which allows them to be identified with maturity rather than old age. Furthermore, the criterion of losing strength is not an identifiable event but a gradual process that gives men considerable flexibility in age identity.

What are the social results of entering these age categories? In traditional (precolonial or early colonial) Samia culture, old age marked the culmination of a person's life in terms of status, control of economic and social resources, and moral and ritual power. There were roles for old people that young people could not fill. In general, older persons were leaders and advisors and often, ritual specialists. Old people controlled knowledge in certain ritual settings and to some extent in the making of useful items. They were to be respected and obeyed—an ethic that remains strong today. While some of their roles have diminished in the modern setting, a number continue to be salient, particularly status as parent-in-law and grandparent in the kinship hierarchy, manager of farm and home, and advisor to the young in some areas of knowledge and behavior (Cattell 1989b). Older men become headmen in their villages, although young men are subchiefs, chiefs, and district officers (civil service as opposed to traditional positions). Thus even in the modern setting old age brings enhanced prestige and influence, although undoubtedly less than in the past, and more within the family than in the wider community.

At the same time, old age is a period of losses, losses that increase with time: loss of strength and the ability to engage in productive work; loss of the ability to reason, to be wise and act as advisor to others; and loss of leisure and pleasure. "Old age forces us," as one Samia person said; "we have no choice but to grow old." And the more the years roll on, the more loss and suffering the old person experiences.

The Samia word for an *old person* is *omukofu*. A *very old person* is *omukofu muno*. To be *omukofu muno* is to be in the final stage of life. It is a time of physical weakness and disabilities, inability to engage in productive work, and dependence on others for the essentials of life. It is a time to "sit and eat," as many Samia people phrased it. Quite literally, a person who is *omukofu muno* basks in the sun or sits by the fire, waiting to be brought food that has been cultivated and prepared by others. Their minds also may no longer be "strong," so they are unable even to advise younger people. They are economically and socially useless. Nevertheless they should be respected and cared for, most particularly by their children, especially sons, and by extension, sons' wives and children.

This ethic of filial caregiving is generally found in agrarian societies, where traditional lifecourses tend to be driven by what Caldwell and LeVine (1985) call the "agrarian imperative." This ethic stresses the lifelong loyalty of children to parents and a sense of reciprocity embedded in hierarchical kinship systems, in which elderly parents expect obedience, respect, and support from their children. While today such societies have been drawn into the world political economy, the filial ethic may remain strong. This is the situation in Samia, although the "intergenerational contract" is currently being debated both privately and publicly (Cattell 1989), and actual support of the elderly by their families is under stress from the changing socioeconomic conditions resulting from "modernization" (Cattell 1988, 1990).

Old Age as a New Stage of Life

How might the lifecourse change over time? Relevant changes would include new life stages, statuses, and roles; new divisions of recognized stages and different age markers in the staging of the lifecourse; and changes in the timing and nature of lifecourse transitions. Historical research has shown that conceptions of the lifecourse do change over time, and that it is thus appropriate to think of the lifecourse as an evolving, dynamic component of everyday life.

Aries's (1962) historical study, which demonstrates the emergence of "childhood" as a new stage of life (new sociologically, not new in a developmental sense), is well known. It may be surprising to think of "old age" as a new stage of life that has emerged in the twentieth century, but in a demographic sense old age is new because so many more people are living longer. Far from being rarities in their social setting, older persons nowadays have plenty of age peers with whom to experience old age. This newness of old age as uncharted territory has inspired the view of today's elderly as "modern pioneers" (Silverman 1987a). Yet old people are in a sense strangers (Dowd 1986) or "immigrants in time . . . the bearers of older cultures" (Mead 1978) who may be culturally estranged from younger generations or from the communities in which they have lived for many decades (Cattell 1989a, 1991, 1992a, 1992b). Other consequences of increased numbers of the old and very old are greater health risks and increased economic and caregiving burdens on younger persons and health care facilities—subjects of widespread debate now in the United States in matters such as entitlements and "intergenerational equity" (see chapter 6), and setting limits to health care (cf. Binstock and Post 1991; Callahan 1987).

In the United States, this "new" life stage of old age appears to be fluid, dividing and multiplying itself into young or active old, and the old who are infirm or frail—the "oldest old" (Bould, Sanborn, and Reif 1989), with perhaps still another category beyond the "oldest," or "centenarians" (Beard 1991; Poon 1992a). Poon (1992b) suggests that centenarian is an "exotic status," and so we are back to the most elderly elderly as strangers and pioneers. What next? Perhaps the science fiction notion of elderly entering a cryogenic state, waiting for the next awakening into still another exotic status?

There are many other consequences of increased longevity for the elderly and their families. Riley (1985) points out that greater longevity in conjunction with a host of other factors has prolonged and multiplied older persons' roles. Retirement lasts much longer than it did in the past (Torrey 1982). Families may have four or even five generations living at the same time; marriages may last into very old age, many years beyond the departure of children from their parents' home; widowhood is likely to come later; parents and children share much more time alive, in many cases until the children themselves are approaching old age. In the United States, the numbers of grandparents have increased and grandparenthood roles are in flux. With the modernization of grandparenthood, grandparents (like younger generations) now seek meaning through personal fulfillment (Cherlin and Furstenberg 1986). Familial roles are changing in response to changes in other family events such as increased numbers of divorces and geographical separation (Bengtson and Robertson 1986).

Aside from the demographic revision of old age, and alongside the altered content of old age as a stage of life, we find changes in the mapping of chronological age onto the lifecourse. A number of historical studies have documented the lifecourse as trajectories of sociodemographic states, focusing on average age at key transitions such as marriage and widowhood. These studies have been carried out in nations driven by the forces of industrial production and competition and by conflicts of a global scale. They have revealed both modal patterns and changes in patterns related to such forces as industrial change, war experiences, the Great Depression, ethnicity, and social class (see, for example: Elder 1974, 1982b, 1985; Elder and Clipp 1988; Hareven 1978, 1982; Hogan 1982; Mayer 1988; Uhlenberg 1979).

In peasant societies, the lifecourse has also changed in response to the forces of modernization and social change, which include wage employment, but not necessarily much industrialization, and the development of formal educational systems. For example, among the Samia of Kenya, male youths no longer go on cattle raiding expeditions or engage in wrestling competitions; instead they are warriors in secondary schools and universities where they wrestle with pens and books, and after that go on jobhunting expeditions. Girls also strive for education and employment. Girls are marrying older, men younger, and both are consulting their elders less about this important life event: that is, the elders have less control of marriage and bridewealth. Even widowed older women, taking advantage of their high kinship status in the modern context, are rebelling against forced marriage (Cattell 1992c). Young people are often away from home for schooling and work. Remittances have become a significant element in family economies, but money is not everything in an economy that is still partly subsistence and very labor intensive. As the modern economy intrudes more and more into the agrarian lifestyle of rural Samia, the frail"sit and eat" elderly may find that the privileges and family care of the elderly diminish even further from traditional standards with, thus far, no viable state-supported or other social welfare alternatives. Debates in Samia, and generally in Kenya, about issues concerning the elderly focus on upholding the traditional ethic of filial loyalty to parents and caregiving, rather than on issues of fairness, as in the current American debate on intergenerational equity (Cattell n.d.).

Part II

SOCIAL RELATIONSHIPS, KINSHIP, AND GENERATIONAL TRANSACTIONS

Is it true or a myth that many older Americans live alone and are neglected by their children? Is it true that "in America, you just put your old people in [nursing] homes," as many people in Kenya asked? What are the realities behind the common lament that *the family* or the *extended family* is disintegrating—or defunct—and that old people around the world are being ignored and neglected, left to make their own housing and personal care arrangements? Is there anything left for old people, or do they just have to give up, give over, and move aside to make way for the young?

This section deals with these and related issues, from living arrangements of the elderly to intergenerational and intragenerational relationships, including succession to seniority and the control over resources associated with such seniority.

It is not easy to study social relationships of the elderly. *Social relationships* takes in a vast territory, including transactions with various categories of kin and friends that take place in a variety of institutional and organizational settings, ranging from the work place to health care facilities. To further complicate research on social relationships of the elderly, the *elderly* are a diverse lot within single countries and between countries. They differ from each other along many dimensions, including age, socioeconomic and demographic characteristics, health, and family situations. Their environments vary, both within countries and between countries, with respect to general economic and social conditions, opportunities for retirement and pensions, availability of medical services and prosthetics (made possible by advanced technology), and ethnic or cultural patterns regarding family living arrangements and care of the elderly.

As an example, take the case of living arrangement. The apparently straightforward dichotomy between "lives in own household" and "lives in extended family household" is actually a complicated and elusive concept, even within one nation. The living arrangements of the elderly vary tremendously by age, gender, marital status, and health. Living arrangements are also, in part, the outcome of social relationships with children and others.

In the United Stat___ ~nly about 13 percent of elders reside with kin, most often with adu__ _____ ___ ___se, persons with many children are more likely to _____ _ _____ ____ _ child simply because of numbers; that is, t____ ___ ____ _____ __ ____ e a child who is willing to provide for them (Thomas and Wist_____y 4). However, elders with greater income (_ _____ __ ____ __ re less likely to share residences with chi_____ __ _____ ___ by arranging in-home services when they _____ _____ lose a spouse, but especially women, are mo__ ____ ____ _ house hold with an adult child than are married el____ ____ ___ __ likely to be more limited in functional cap_____ __ ___ ____ ___ __ es, are more likely to co-reside with children ____ _____ __ _____ raphic indicators such as completed fertility, age, g_____ _____ narital status, and health have varying and important impacts u__ _ __ er persons' living arrangements, on whether any given older American "lives in own household" or "lives in an extended family household." Cultural factors are also important. Many Americans espouse the cultural ideals of individualism and independence, and prefer not to depend on anyone, including (or sometimes especially) their children, even when they become frail (Clark and Anderson 1967). In addition to the factors described above, we can expect to see significant variation in ideas about parental dependency and the filial obligation to care for a parent.

Living arrangements, in part the result of social relationships, in turn have effects on social relationships. The social relationships we address in this section are of two main types: intergenerational and intragenerational transactions. Since we are dealing primarily with family relationships, we are using *generation* in its genealogical sense. Hence intergenerational relationships refer to individuals in different genealogical generations, most particularly parents and children; and intragenerational relationships refer to transactions with spouses, siblings, and friends, including age peers or age mates (although, of course, friends need not be age peers). Intragenerational relationships include changing patterns of friendship among aging persons, the importance of siblings in late life, and the effects of living in age-homogeneous settings, such as nursing homes and retirement communities.

The relationships of elderly to their children and grandchildren are difficult to investigate comparatively, first because analyses rarely treat the family as an analytical unit (Draper and Marcos 1989; Handel and Hess 1959; Kenny 1990), and second because relevant measures such as "intergenerational solidarity" (Mangen, Bengston, and Landry 1988) have only recently been developed and assessed. Rather than explore the complicated psychosocial interior of the family with the conflicting and reinforcing behaviors of many actors, survey researchers have found it easier to examine, for example, mother-daughter or mother-in-law/daughter-in-law relationships. Multidimensional measures of the involvement of elders in the lives of their children are similarly underdeveloped.

Nevertheless, researchers from many disciplines have contributed to the study of families and family relationships (e.g., Bott 1957; Handel and Hess 1972; Hareven 1978, 1982; Kilbride and Kilbride 1990; Lancaster, Altman, Rossi, and Sherrod 1987; Nydegger 1983; Oppong 1974; Parkin and Nyamwaya 1989; Rossi and Rossi 1990; Rubinstein and Johnsen 1982; Silverman 1987a; Townsend 1957; Tufte and Myerhoff 1979; Weisner, Bradley, and Kilbride n.d.). In one distinctive approach, Lewis (1967) has relied on the intensive study of representative families inorder to understand cultural patterns.

In this section we will combine these approaches—the strictly comparative quantitative approach and the ethnographic approach of anthropologists, historians, and others who have examined families as structural and interactive units, as we consider the elderly and their social relationships.

In chapters 5 and 6 we examine family relationships, centering on cross-cultural variation in living arrangements and intergenerational transactions. Chapter 7 pays particular attention to social exchanges among age peers, especially as they may be modified by age-homogeneous settings. Chapter 8 returns to intergenerational relationships, but this time beyond the family setting, in an exploration of conflicts around issues of succession to authority and control over resources.

5

Family Relationships of the Elderly: Living Arrangements

Being without a home—whatever kind of structure constitutes a home—is not a popular option anywhere in the world. Whether it is the temporary brush-and-grass huts of the !Kung San (bushmen of the Kalahari Desert in southern Africa) or the vast and elegant estates of the wealthy and palaces of royalty, nearly everyone wants a house, a room, a place to call one's own. Even the homeless of America have particular street corners or spots under bridges that they feel belong to them.

When we talk about the dry-sounding topic of living arrangements, we are in fact dealing with issues basic to physical and emotional security. *Home* entails deep feelings revolving around roots or a sense of attachment to place and continuity with ancestors and others, personal identity, and, of course, practical matters of everyday living having to do with such fundamental aspects of life as eating, sleeping, social interaction, and personal care.

Living arrangements matter tremendously to all people throughout their lives, but they are particularly important to the maintenance of general well-being, and even life itself, for those who need care: infants and children, persons with physical or mental impairments, or people who are physically frail because of illness or senescence. People invest much effort in assuring their living arrangements throughout the lifecourse and particularly in old age. The living arrangements of the elderly are not something that just happens at the end of life but are, rather, the outcome of lifetime strategies of individuals with differing characteristics who seek secure housing in a variety of socioeconomic and cultural settings.

There is an extensive body of findings from cross-national survey research in the industrialized or developed world on living arrangements of the elderly. Here we present some of these findings in order to indicate characteristics of the aged and the factors that are commonly associated with their living arrangements. While there is little such data from the developing world, we use what there is to make broad comparisons of older persons' living arrangements in developed and developing nations along these sociodemographic and economic dimensions.

However, even with similar data from every nation in the world, the picture would be incomplete. Living arrangements are outcomes of a complex of economic, social, cultural, historical, and personal factors. They are also integral aspects of intergenerational and intragenerational relationships. A discussion of living arrangements of the elderly based on data from cross-national surveys provides a broadly comparative view that can be enormously enriched by the introduction of ethnographic data.

Anthropological research findings, because they tend to be qualitative (although anthropologists also use surveys), have great descriptive value. They provide a sense of differences and similarities, of cultural variation and common humanity, with regard to ideologies of filial care; traditional housing arrangements; the meanings of home; lifetime strategies to assure housing and often, thereby, a place in kin or other social networks; and the effects of modernization and social change on shared living arrangements of the elderly. Juxtaposed with cross-national data, these cross-cultural findings flesh out the social, cultural, and personal meanings embedded in living arrangements considered as household composition.

The wealth of research findings from the world's "cultural laboratory" also has explanatory value and can suggest alternative hypotheses for investigation. Recognition of cultural variation challenges concepts derived from single-culture research (see chapter 1). One such challenge in this chapter is to examine living  (whether with family or independently) to see just how reliable it is as a predictor of social isolation among elders and family members. We see that living arrangements is an excellent point of entry for exploring economic transactions, intergenerational relationships, and what has been called "the household production of care" for elders (A...

Living Arrangements of the E... The More Developed Coun...

Perhaps the most striking variation in family relationships of the elderly is visible in the case of living arrangement. In the developing countries, clear majorities of the elderly share residences with children and other relatives, although this varies by gender and marital status of the elder, type of household, and gender of the target child in the elder's "re-formed" household. In the more developed countries, sharing a household with a child is the exception and is linked mainly to health limitation in the elder or, less remarked, to the economic dependency of the child. The latter is currently quite common in the United States, largely because elders are more likely to own their home (Crystal and Shea 1990). Roughly 70 percent of elderly in the United States own their own home (Kinsella 1990).

We may best begin to explore this divide with a more careful look at residential patterns in the United States. The vast majority of elderly do not share households with adult children. Excluding the 1.5 million elderly in nursing homes (National Center for Health Statistics 1989), the most recent U.S. census figures show that 31 percent of the elderly live alone. An additional 54 percent are married, with the two elders forming a distinct household of their own. Of the remaining 15 percent, 13 percent share households with relatives, most with their own children. The remaining 2 percent live with nonrelatives in noninstitutional settings (Saluter 1990).

The desire of U.S. elderly to live apart from their children is clear. The goal, as often remarked, is "intimacy at a distance": having one's own household but living in close enough proximity to children that contact is frequent (Shanas, Townsend, Wedderburn, et al. 1968). An additional slant on U.S. patterns is provided by Crimmins and Ingeneri

(1990). The U.S. census figures do not control for completed fertility and the vital status of such children, that is, whether an elder has living children or not. If we restrict the analysis to elderly with living children, is the proportion of elderly sharing households substantially higher? Crimmins and Ingeneri (1990) performed this analysis and found that, in fact, only 18 percent of elders with living children share households with a child, a proportion only slightly higher than the figure reported for all elderly. Thus, even when children are available, U.S. elders on the whole do not share residences, and the percentage of elderly sharing households with children continues to decline (Smith 1981).

Is the lack of shared households a result of children's rejection of the elder? Quite the contrary. Research on adult children and elders' preferences for living arrangement consistently reports that elders wish to reside apart from children for as long as possible, until health declines make independent living impossible. If anything, adult children are more likely to want the elder to co-reside, because they fear for the elder's welfare in the face of health limitations (Brody 1985, 1990). Thus, adult children may go to elaborate lengths, scheming, one might say, to convince an elder to give up an independent residence and move into the adult child's home. For example, an adult daughter may form a quasi-household with the parent, moving the parent into her home for limited periods of time until the elder simply does not return to an independent household (Albert 1990b). When health limitation is _____ adult children prefer that a parent move in with them an_____ _____ _____ ___ _ t in a nursing home (Schorr 1980; Brody 1_____ ____ _____ ult children are more reluctant than elders to _____ _____ ___ ___ the parent (e.g., home health care, adult day _____ _____ _____ caregivers) (Brody, Johnsen, Fulcomer, and _____ _____

An imp_____ ___ __ _____ rominence in recent research in the United St_____ __ ___ ____ _h of elders plays a relatively small role in the _____ ____ _____ _ult children to co-reside (Aquilino 1990; Crim_____ ____ _____ _awton, in review). When elder and adult chil_____ _____ ____ he house usually belongs to the elder, not t___ ____ _____ ___ __out half these cases, the households represent cases of long-term co-residence, that is, situations in which the adult child never left home (Crimmins and Ingeneri 1990). Albert (in review) reports that among ethnic Italians in South Philadelphia, for example, one adult child of a sibling set comes to be designated care-giver to the parent and the one who will ultimately inherit the elder's house. These sons or daughters either do not leave home or move back into the parent's home in midlife; and they are selected for the caregiver-inheritor role as a result of their own economic need. Adult children are also likely to move into a parent's home as a result of divorce. Divorced adult children, strapped for money, find that joining the parent's home is a convenient transitional arrangement. Once co-resident, they may discover how infirm the parent is and decide to remain.

Thus, lifelong residence arrangements or the economic need of adult children accounts for most co-residence of elders with adult children in the United States. In these cases, resources, including a place to live, flow from elder to adult child, rather than the reverse (Lawton, in review; Morgan, Schuster, and Butler 1991). The poor health of the elder motivates re-formation of households in only 12 percent of such households (Crimmins and Ingeneri 1990). Lawton (in review) concludes that shared residence with adult children is typical only of the most frail elderly.

It should be said at once that the developed countries do not all follow the U.S. pattern. The proportion of elderly living alone in developed countries, for example, ranges from a low of 9 percent in Japan to 40 percent in Sweden (Kinsella 1990). With 31 percent of its elders living alone, the United States tends toward the pole represented by Sweden. Even in Europe, the proportion of elderly living alone varies. The less "gray" countries, or countries with a lower proportion of elderly (see chapter 3), tend to have fewer elderly living alone. Thus, Spain, Portugal, Ireland, and Greece tend more toward the pole represented by Japan.

Living Arrangements of the Elderly: The Less Developed Countries

Developed and developing countries differ most in elder living arrangement with respect to the proportion of elderly living alone. While a large majority of elders live apart from kin in the developed countries (with the exceptions noted above), the reverse is true in the developing countries. The proportion of elders living alone, for example, ranges

from 2 to 8 percent in Southeast Asia, and from 5 to 11 percent in Latin America. African nations for which data are available also follow this pattern, with o~~nly~~ ⌐ ~~~~ rcent living alone. African elders do not want
t⌐ ~~~~

tr⌐ ~~~~ oportion of elderly living with kin, the con-
a~~~~ d developing countries becomes even more
a~~p~~ t in the United States only 13 percent of the
el~~d~~ th relatives. This figure contrasts sharply
wit~~~~ leveloping nations, which typically range
fro~~i~~ s intermediate in this distribution; in 1980,
60 ~~p~~ lived with a child, the majority residing
with~~~~ n to the Japanese case below for an ex-
tend~~~~ it is instructive to look at living arrange-
ment~~~~ ountries to see how they contrast with
those ~~~~ States and other more developed nations. We ex-
amine African data because a series of detailed ethnographic studies are available for the region. We then turn to other regions, combining cross-national and cross-cultural data sources.

Housing in traditional West African towns consists of walled family compounds with many rooms, often quite old and with too few rooms to accommodate all who might wish to live in them. Persons may spend decades away in migrant labor or cash cropping, as among Ashanti cocoa farmers in Ghana; but individuals want to spend their later years in their hometown so they can participate in kin networks and religious ceremonies and be buried there. When these cocoa farmers return home, their living arrangements will be determined in large part by their lifetime exchanges in family networks, or their failure to participate in these networks. Inheritance of houses (male property) is matrilineal, with men inheriting houses through their mothers. Ashanti men are responsible for their matrikin, people related to them through their mothers and sisters. Hence many Ashanti women leave their husbands in late middle age in order to get a room in a brother's compound; and among Ashanti, these older divorced women tend to live in their brothers' compounds (Stucki 1992).

Among the patrilineal Temne people of Sierra Leone, Dorjahn (1989) conducted a series of five surveys in a rural area and in a town from 1955 to 1976. Here, in contrast to the matrilineal Ashanti, elders (age 60 and over) were more likely to be living with patrikin (people related to them through their father and brother), especially sons, although the brother-sister tie was utilized by some women. Among 393 older women, one-third lived with sons, about one-fifth with husbands (most elderly women were widows), and 15 percent were themselves household heads. Most of the rest lived with a variety of other kin. Only a few (6 percent) had no relationship to the household head. The majority of the 256 men were household heads; most lived with spouses and married or unmarried children. Of the sixty-two men who were not household heads, half were the head's father (n=7) or brother (n=24). These relationships are shown in Table 5.1.

Living arrangements of Temne elders in both the rural and the urban area, and in the different time periods, were quite similar in that the elders were able to draw on a wide range of kin ties in establishing residence in a family compound. Women, however, had a greater variety of ties to households, which was not surprising because men were likely to be heads and thus did not have to make claim to a room through others. Very few elderly Temne lived alone. Also in West Africa, Peil (1985) surveyed elderly residence patterns in The Gambia, Nigeria, and Sierra Leone (n=264 men, 206 women aged 55+). These surveys, like Dorjahn's among Temne, indicated that the most common situation of elderly women was to be living as a dependent in multigenerational households headed by a son; a substantial propor-

Table 5.1 Residence Patterns of Elderly Temne of Sierra Leone: Kin Ties Establishing Claims to Residence

	Women (%)	Men (%)
Household head	15	76
Relationship of Elder to Household Head		
Head's wife	18	—
Head's parent	33	3
Head's brother	—	9
Head's sister	10	—
Other relationship	18	5
No relationship	6	7
Total	100	100
N	393	256

Source: Adapted from Dorjahn (1989)

tion (about one third) were widows and heads of households of their children and grandchildren. Most men (91 percent) were household heads, as among Temne, and they most commonly lived in a one- or two-generation household with children and with one or more wives; roughly a third lived in three-generation households. Only 3 percent of the 470 elderly in her surveys lived alone, although living alone "may mean different things to different people. . . . While living alone means that [elders] have not attracted any dependents to share their room, few are actually isolated from their relatives" (Peil 1988).

Two studies in East Africa report similar patterns of living arrangements, with few elderly living alone (and even then, generally not being "really" alone), and most living with kin. Both studies were done in rural Kenya, where the common residential pattern is a family compound that consists of one or several houses occupied by spouses (including co-wives), unmarried children, married sons, daughters-in-law, and grandchildren. While the houses are separate dwellings for sleeping and other purposes, the entire compound is the family unit characterized by joint decision-making and sharing of resources, including labor, money, and material goods.

In Kenya the critical element in getting a house is access to land, either through inheritance (from fathers to sons) or through women's claims (through marriage) to land for cultivation, a house, and a burial place. People usually build their houses on farm plots, so housing is dispersed over the landscape, not concentrated as it is in West African towns. There are growing land shortages in many areas of Kenya, and some people move away to try to obtain land elsewhere. But a person who owns or has claim to land can build a house (actually men's work, so w_____ _____ _____ _____ [husband, son, or others] to build their house

A s_____ _____ ns (age 55 and over) in Meru, central Kenya, _____ _____ ercent of these elderly lived alone and that m____ _____ r at least one of their sons and often grandcl_____ _____ 992). Nearly one-third of the elderly men we__ _____ ndent children in their households; most oth_____ _____ ent to adult children. Few women (only 6 p_____ _____ nen) lived with spouses and dependent chil_____ _____ cent to adult children. Among the people of l____ _____ ally means in the same family compound. Thus while older persons may have their own houses, they live very near their actual or potential caregivers, most often their children, and may in fact be said to co-reside with these children.

Cattell (1989a) found a similar pattern among the Samia people of western Kenya, where she surveyed 200 women and 216 men age 50 and over. Like the people of Meru, the Samia live in family compounds that often consist of two or more houses. Only fourteen people (3 percent) said they lived alone, and even these fourteen lived near kin. Eight of these "loners" were known to us outside the survey, and all had kin living nearby: five of the six men lived near a brother's compound, one near the homes of a son and an adult grandson; one widow lived near two co-wives, and the other woman (also a widow) lived near a nephew and got help from two married daughters living nearby. She was fortunate because daughters, who go to live in their husband's village when they marry, often live some distance away.

Living alone does not have the same meaning in Samia as it does in an American city. Year round, life is lived outdoors and publicly. The many footpaths go right through the compounds, and passing by, greetings, and impromptu visits are numerous. Of course, such activity does not guarantee care when it is needed. For that, most elderly Samia depend on kin who live in their compound.

Some elderly Samia women and men lived with their spouse only, in homesteads that included grandparents and one or more grandchildren, or in nuclear family or parent-child compounds. Table 5.2 is a breakdown of these elder living arrangements among the Samia.

The majority of older Samia women (78 percent) and men (70 percent), however, lived in extended families, three-generation compounds, often including married and unmarried children, daughters-in-law, and grandchildren, all likely caregivers for older women. Most elderly women (67 percent) and men (75 percent) had sons in their compound; many, especially men, still had daughters at home (the proportion decreased with age, as daughters married and left). For women, in terms of work companions and care when needed, daughters-in-law often replaced daughters; and 64 percent of the women had at least one daughter-in-law living in their compound (older women were more likely to have a resident daughter-in-law). Grandchildren, who often do chores for their grandparents, lived in the homes of about two-thirds of all respondents.

Table 5.2 Residence Patterns of Elderly Samia of Kenya: Co-residence in Family Compounds

	Women		Men	
	N	%	N	%
Lives alone	7	4	7	3
With spouse only	6	3	15	7
With grandchild*	13	7	7	3
In nuclear family**	19	10	36	17
In extended family	155	78	151	70
Total	200		216	

*Includes one or both grandparents.
**Includes 10 women, 1 man in single-parent homes.
Percentages rounded.
Source: After Cattell (1989a: 454)

Most older women (56 percent) were widowed; most older men (92 percent) were married. While both men and women are likely to receive care from co-resident children, daughters-in-law, and grandchildren, men also depend heavily on wives for care when it is needed. Obviously, for the oldest women, a husband is not likely to be on the scene; almost all women aged 70 and over were widows. Thus for Samia women, the presence of sons, sons' wives, and grandchildren becomes increasingly important as they age.

We can supplement these intensive ethnographic studies with cross-national survey research to round out our areal survey of elder living arrangement. These cross-national data confirm findings from ethnographic research and show that living alone or in a truly independent household is not typical of elders outside the developed nations.

In 1975 the United Nations Fertility Survey examined household composition in probability samples from six Latin American nations (Colombia, Costa Rica, the Dominican Republic, Mexico, Panama, and Peru). The survey found that 60 percent of those aged 60 and above lived in "complex families," that is, extended households characterized by more than one conjugal bond. In these households, single or married elders were living with a married child or another married relative (such as a niece). However, an additional 20 to 25 percent of the elderly in the six countries were residing in "simple families," that is, married or single elders were sharing households with unmarried children.

Combining the complex and simple family types shows that fully 80 to 85 percent of the elderly across the six countries were living with kin; only 5 to 11 percent were living alone (De Vos 1990; Kinsella 1990).

Unfortunately, it is not clear from this survey if elders reside with daughters more than sons, or vice versa. This is significant for a related contrast among developing and developed countries. In the United States, for example, elders are more likely to reside with adult daughters than with sons; adult daughters are viewed as the appropriate caregivers (Ikels 1983). However, in Pacific rim countries, the preferred household for co-residence is the adult son's, preferably a married son.

A 1984 World Health Organization survey of Malaysia, the Philippines, Fiji, and Korea found similar results. Between 72 and 79 percent of elders aged 60 and above shared households with children (Andrews et al. 1986). In Korea, the majority of elders were co-residing with sons. Thus, regardless of age, gender, or marital status, the majority of elders resided with kin in extended family households.

Research from South Asia supports these high levels of co-residence, although samples are smaller. Here the choice of a son's household for co-residence is quite clear. In a survey in Bangladesh, Cain (1986) found that 62 percent of those aged 60 and above reside with a married son, 16 percent with an unmarried son, and only 2 percent with a married daughter. Similarly, a survey in Nepal showed that 70 percent were co-residing with a son or daughter-in-law (with the son temporarily away), and another 11 percent with daughters (Nag, White, and Peet 1978). For high-caste Nepali Hindus, co-residence with a married daughter is considered unsuitable (Goldstein, Schuler, and Ross 1983). A survey of elderly Sherpa villagers, however, found relatively low rates of co-residence (under 50 percent), which the authors attribute to a preference to live with the youngest son. Since many of these sons are away from villages in pursuit of employment, a higher proportion of elderly are not living with kin. Finally, Vatuk (1982) reports high rates of co-residence in India across caste and rural-urban divisions. Older men appear to co-reside with sons at higher rates than do older women, perhaps attesting to the greater economic resources of men.

Finally, research on the living arrangements of the elderly in China offers an important potential qualification on the reported high rates of shared households in the developing countries. Goldstein, Ku, and Ikels (1990) initially found equally high levels of elder co-residence with kin but, upon more careful inspection of ethnographic materials, were led to question these findings. In the two Chinese villages they surveyed, roughly half the elderly were clearly sharing residences with kin in extended households; another 20 percent were eating and sleeping "by turns," that is, rotating between children's households for food and shelter. The "by turns" arrangement is widely distributed in Taiwan and China. The authors make a good case for considering the "by turns" relationship as an example of separate households, rather than extended household co-residence. We return to this point below.

Thus, it is clear that variation in the living arrangements of the elderly broadly follows development status. The more developed nations have high proportions of elderly living alone and low percentages of elderly sharing residences with kin. When households are shared, a mother–daughter household is most likely, owing to the late stage in which such households form. That is, by the time parent and adult child share residences, the parent is likely to be quite infirm and the daughter accordingly assumes a caregiver role (see chapter 6). However, it is worth noting that a major element in the formation of joint parent–adult child homes is also the economic need of adult children, and this typically is responsible for the shared living arrangements in cases in which the elder is younger and less infirm. The pattern in the developing countries (or countries about to join the ranks of the developed nations) is quite different. In these countries, an extremely small number of elderly live alone; the great majority reside with kin; and the preferred relative for the joint household is usually the son, sometimes the oldest (as in Taiwan and Japan), sometimes the youngest (as with the Sherpa).

Determinants of Living Arrangements

What determines whether an elder will share a household with kin, and do the factors that promote such shared living vary across cultures? In cross-national research, a number of factors have been identified as predictors of shared living arrangements. Putting aside the obvious, such as the availability of locally resident children or other kin (primarily grandchildren), these predisposing factors include the elder's age, marital status, and sex; the rural or urban status of the elder and his or her kin; and the degree to which children or other kin adhere to traditional ideology regarding care of aged parents. We can examine the relative salience of these factors by returning to the research cited above.

The cross-cultural perspective is especially valuable here because it shows that demographic facts, by themselves, are often inadequate to explain living arrangements of the elderly. For example, since elderly women are more likely to be widowed than elderly males (because men marry women younger than themselves and have more opportunities to remain married through polygyny or remarriage), we might expect elderly women to co-reside with children at greater rates than elderly men; for those elderly men who are still alive are more likely to be married and maintain a separate household in late life. In this scenario, elderly women would receive caregiving support from their children, while elderly men would receive such support from wives. Yet cross-cultural research shows that this intuition is often incorrect. In many developing countries, the elder's sex has little to do with co-residence in late life; elderly males and females are equally likely to co-reside with kin. Likewise, we might expect widowed status to be a major predictor of co-residence, but it is in fact only a minor predictor of living arrangement, once we examine the position of the elderly outside the developed countries. As the prior section has shown, in most of the developing countries the vast majority of elderly, married or not, co-reside with kin, primarily children, in extended families. In such cases, ideological factors, such as ideas about what is appropriate in the relationship between elders and their descendants, and economic considerations may be more important as determinants of living arrangement. This must be kept in mind because most cross-national research is relatively limited and remains restricted to analysis of demographic predictors alone.

Data collected in the United Nations World Fertility Survey are instructive on this topic. Overall, for the six Latin American countries included in the survey, De Vos (1990) reports that marital status, not sex, is the most important predictor of shared living arrangements for the elderly. The widowed co-reside with kin at greater rates than married elderly. However, sex exerts an effect in that widows are more than twice as likely as widowers to live in extended families. Age, on the other hand, is not a strong predictor of shared households. Finally, the

United Nations data show that rural, as opposed to urban, residence has no significant relationship to the likelihood of an elder sharing housing with kin. While one might expect to see fewer shared households in the urban setting (as would be consistent with the claims of modernization theory: see chapter 8 and below), in fact, the likelihood of sharing households is not affected by rural versus urban residence. This may reflect economic demands and shortages of living space in the urban setting, as well as the economic advantage households gain by having a co-resident elder.

These results from the World Fertility Survey represent an aggregation of data on the elderly from Colombia, Costa Rica, the Dominican Republic, Mexico, Panama, and Peru; a total of about 7,000 households. However, the aggregate figures mask important variation between countries, which points to more subtle differences in cultural attitudes governing co-residence in late life. For example, the Dominican Republic differs from the other countries in that *married* males are actually more likely than unmarried males to live in extended households. Yet the reverse is true for elder women in the Dominican Republic: they follow the overall pattern of the six countries, with unmarried women more likely to co-reside with kin than married women. De Vos (1990) explains the anomaly in terms of the high rate of divorce and separation in late life in the Dominican Republic and the more central role of women in households. That is, the unmarried male in late life may be marginal in a relatively matrifocal society such as that of the Dominican Republic.

More generally, De Vos (1990) suggests that the relative similarity of the Dominican Republic, Panama, and Colombia in the determinants of elderly living arrangement may reflect a Caribbean culture, which stands apart from Peru's pattern, which in turn may reflect an Andean culture. But the World Fertility data set unfortunately does not allow further investigation of these differences; nor have we been able to identify ethnographic studies that would allow us to explore the issue (although see Kerns 1983 for a perspective from Belize).

The minor role of age as a predictor for elderly living arrangement evident in the World Fertility Survey should remind us that generalizing from the U.S. experience to that of other populations is often unwarranted. Cross-national data force us to abandon our intuition that increasing age, and hence greater frailty and need for support, should best predict living arrangement. In fact, data from Mexico show a much more variable pattern. Christenson and Hermalin (1991) report that while widowed women do co-reside at greater rates with increasing age, for widowed men the pattern is in fact *bimodal*. Younger widowed males (those in their early 60s) are likely to co-reside with adult children, as are older widowers (late 70s, early 80s). But between these age extremes, widowers are likely to reside in independent households.

Christenson and Hermalin (1991) explain the bimodal pattern in terms of lifecourse transitions. At age 60, the widowed male is likely to be economically active and working with adult children in a family-run business. When the elder reaches the late 60s and early 70s, adult children are likely to move and establish their own households, leaving the widower in an independent household. The adult child–elder shared household re-forms later, when the elder becomes infirm. Thus, age, by itself, cannot be viewed as an indicator of the increasing need of elderly for family support and hence shared living arrangement. Likewise, living arrangements of the elderly may be determined by the resources elders can bring to a family as well as their need for support in late life. Once we recognize the more complex setting in which people age, such as lifecourse transitions within families and the increasing command of resources associated with greater age, we should not be surprised that in some settings the young-old may co-reside with adult children at greater rates than the old-old, or that men may co-reside at greater rates than women.

For the island nations examined in the Western Pacific survey (Andrews et al. 1986), it is striking how minor a role age, sex, and marital status play in determining the living arrangements of the elderly. In Fiji, the Republic of Korea, Malaysia, and the Philippines between 75 and 85 percent of the elderly reside with kin in extended households, regardless of the elder's age and sex. Being widowed increases the likelihood of co-residence only slightly. Thus, a strong cultural prescription appears to be at work, in which adult children are enjoined not just to provide for elders in late life, but also to share households.

Reports from south Asia, especially India, show that living arrangement varies by region, caste, and socioeconomic status (Vatuk 1980, Martin 1990). Still, as mentioned above, the vast majority of Indian elderly reside with married sons, ranging from 62 percent in urban Delhi to 73 percent in rural villages near Lucknow (Vatuk 1982). Co-residence with married daughters is roughly 5 percent in both rural and urban surveys, and independent residences for the elderly appear to be around 7 percent in both settings. However, Martin (1990) summarizes research that shows a subtle differentiation according to the sex of the elder. In the case of elderly residing with married daughters, admittedly a minority of elders, older women predominate. Also, of the small number of elderly living alone, women are again over-represented, perhaps because of the low status of women and the greater number of widows as opposed to widowers. Elder unmarried women may simply be less welcome in the household of an adult child.

Research by Evans (1990) on Javanese households (see chapter 2) may be relevant here. He found that older men and older women have quite unequal control over income and resources, even *within* Javanese households, so that it is simply a mistake to speak of "household income." Men command a great deal more wealth and are free to use it as they wish. By extension, it may be that elderly Indian women offer less wealth to a household than do elderly men and are thus viewed as more of burden to the adult child's household. Elderly widowed Indian and Javanese women are evidently at greater risk for poor health as a result of their inferior economic status. Evans (1990), for example, reports poorer nutrition for elderly Javanese women. It may be that these widowed elder women are aware of their poor position and unwelcome status and thus prefer independent living.

The last point is interesting in light of data reported for the "by turns" living arrangement typical of China, described above. In a careful study, Goldstein, Ku, and Ikels (1990) found that differences in the frequency of the "by turns" arrangement between a relatively poor and rich village could not be explained in terms of differences in age composition and marital status of the elderly, or by differences in the availability of sons for co-residence, or by differences in cultural attitudes regarding filial obligation to the elderly. Despite overall similarity between the villages on these measures, elders in the poorer village were four times as likely to live in the "by turns" arrangement (i.e., four times as many people, in this case widows and widowers, were rotating between adult sons' households for food and shelter).

The explanation for the disparity lies in a combination of sociocultural and economic factors, with the latter being more significant. In both villages, elders reported a decline in the traditional ideology regarding filial piety and care for the aged in late life. Even elders living in the traditional elder-son household reported that they received less support and respect than they had given to their own parents. They said their sons were more interested in their own conjugal relationship and in gaining material goods than in honoring the elder. One consequence of the decline of this traditional ideology has been more tension between elders and adult sons. Accordingly, independence is now valued more highly by the Chinese elders in the sample. Widows and widowers who can maintain an independent household now do so, and those who cannot prefer the "by turns" relationship because of the relative independence it affords. Thus, the greater frequency of the "by turns" relationship in the poorer village follows from the poorer economic position of these elders. Elders in the wealthier village maintain truly independent households; they have greater incomes and housing is available for purchase. Elders in the poorer village maintain their freedom in the absence of such wealth by resorting to the "by turns" arrangement. Needless to say, sons in the poorer village prefer the "by turns" relationship as well because it frees up more wealth for their own household use. Goldstein and colleagues (1990) conclude that "selection of the 'by turns' alternative . . . therefore appears to be an artifact of the differential impact of the new economic system, not [a result of] different value orientations."

Japan offers perhaps the most vivid case of a cultural prescription as a determinant of living arrangement. As we mentioned earlier, Japanese elders co-reside with children, primarily sons, at extremely high rates (between 60 and 70 percent in recent surveys), yet Japan is otherwise similar to the more developed countries in its demographic and socioeconomic profile. Palmore and Maeda (1985) show that attempts to explain the high co-residence rates as a function of economic difficulty or housing availability are simply inadequate. The Japanese pattern of co-residence follows from a culture-wide emphasis on age and seniority, which appears in family life as an extreme code of filial piety. Devotion to parents is an unconditional and absolute duty. Thus, in a comparative study of women in Philadelphia and Tokyo cited by Palmore and Maeda, the Japanese women were more favorable toward living with parents and leaving their jobs to care for mothers; the Japanese women were also more likely to rely on their own caregiving efforts than to use formal sector services, such as adult day care or home health aides. For the minority of Japanese elders who live apart from children, it is notable also that fully 85 percent see a child daily or nearly daily. Also, Japanese filial piety is evident in low rates of institutionalization of frail elders. The rate of nursing home utilization in the developed countries is between 5 and 9 percent; for Japan it is less than 2 percent (Palmore and Maeda 1985).

It should be said, however, that while the code of filial respect promotes joint residence, in most Japanese households shared residence usually takes the form of distinct living quarters for the elder or elderly couple. Elders usually live in a separate part of the household, with separate cooking facilities (Palmore and Maeda 1985). In the rural sector, elders may even reside in a small house set behind the family house.

Palmore and Maeda (1985) explain the predominance of the shared living arrangement not only as a product of the tradition of filial responsibility, but also as a function of the important role elders play in their sons' households. The elders are *rusuban*, caretakers of the home, and are also quite active in childrearing and other components of the household economy. They are charged with religious instruction of children, and they serve as senior advisor in the case of family problems. Japanese elderly recognize this responsibility. The most common response among elders when asked why elders should live with children was not "to hand down customs and tradition," but rather "to share in the housekeeping and child care" (Palmore and Maeda 1985). Thus, the high rates of co-residence among elderly Japanese should be seen not simply as an expression of a particular cultural pattern centering on filial respect, but also as a distinct type of household organization or household economy. The tradition of filial respect has helped maintain this household form despite the vast changes associated with Japan's postwar modernization.

Position of the Elderly within Households

A fundamental tenet of what has come to be known as modernization theory is the claim that the status of the elderly "tends to be high in societies in which the extended form of family is prevalent and functions as a household unit" (Cowgill 1972). Since the less developed countries are characterized by higher rates of elder co-residence with children, it follows that the status of the elderly in these societies should be higher than that of elders in the more developed countries. We have already seen that elder co-residence with children, either as an extended family (an unmarried elder living with a married child), as a stem-family (an elderly couple living with a married child), or as a joint-stem family (two or more adult married children living with parents), is built upon cultural traditions of filial obligation as well as the often important economic contribution of elders to a child's household. Can we say with modernization theorists that the position of the elderly is likely to be better in societies in which elders share households with adult children?

Critics of modernization theory have rightly pointed out that shared living arrangement by itself says nothing about the *position* of the elder within the household. And an allied line of research has shown that modernization does not necessarily entail the "nuclearization" of extended households, as we have seen in the case of Japan and South Asia. Finally, data presented above show that lack of co-residence does not imply lack of concern for the elderly. For example, in the U.S. a high rate of separate living arrangements is perfectly compatible with considerable contact and emotional involvement between adult children and their parents. Nydegger (1983) considers the modernization theory claim an unwitting expression of nostalgia for a "golden age" of intergenerational harmony that has in fact never really existed. She points out that rates of co-residence were never very high in the historical past of Western societies because of the short life expectancy of elders and the high mobility of adult children; likewise, high rates of co-residence in developing countries often represent the failure of elderly and their children to live as they would like: that is, apart, to allow greater independence on both sides.

Thus, two questions need to be addressed in this section. First, does the shared living arrangement typical of the developing countries imply higher prestige for elders, and by implication, greater well-being, relative to the elderly in the developed countries? And second, to what extent does modernization, as defined by increased education and literacy, increasingly urban households, and greater participation in wage labor, dissolve the extended- and stem-family household associated with elder co-residence?

For the first question, research by Goldstein, Schuler, and Ross

(1983) among high-caste, middle- to low-income Nepali households is valuable. As might be expected from the prior section, elderly co-residence was nearly universal, following the canonical South Asian pattern. Of the forty-six high-caste elderly interviewed (representing 87 percent of the high-caste elderly in the town), 61 percent lived with at least one married son, 96 percent lived with a relative (including a spouse), and only one elder lived alone. However, Goldstein and colleagues show that the co-residence figures actually give a false picture of intergenerational relations. For example, of the eighteen elders not co-residing with sons, half did in fact have married sons in the town. Even more significantly, in more than half of the households in which elders were living with married sons, the elders were essentially supporting themselves and not receiving economic support from sons. The authors conclude that "the economic situation of elderly adults differs from what one might infer from Hindu ideals (norms/values) and actual household composition" (Goldstein, Schuler, and Ross 1983). This is poignantly illustrated by the case of a 79-year-old male living with one of his three sons who reported that "old people must have their own money; otherwise they will not have a one rupee note [US–0.08] even to purchase poison [to kill oneself] if it is needed."

The Nepali data offer an important qualification to the claims of modernization theory. The increasing education of sons and their new participation in wage labor employment has come hand in hand with the end of a primarily agrarian economy, an economic order in which an elder's ownership of land was central to his ability to command deference and economic support. Having lost this source of authority, the position of elders in households has changed, despite the shared living arrangement. Adult sons are now free to invest time and resources in their conjugal relationship, often to the exclusion of filial obligations. The elderly perceive their newly weakened position and have taken steps to ensure security in late life. Many have invested in property as a source of income; others threaten not to pass valued goods on to their sons after their death. Goldstein and colleagues (1983) point out that living in such circumstances may be more difficult for Nepali elders than independent living: "Several elderly respondents actually commented that they were like strangers in their own family; no one talked to them or paid them any attention. They were taken care of, but only in a manner they perceived as both demeaning and alienating." The culturally prescribed obligation to care for parents, still largely followed so far as co-residence is concerned, has taken on a different meaning with the loss of a parent's control over household land.

These data do not invalidate the claim that modernization results in poorer status for elderly. In fact, the position of the Nepali elder has worsened with modernization, by any measure. The Nepali data, however, do show that shared living arrangement and high status for elders do not always go together.

Turning now to the question of household nucleation and modernization, we must first stress the paucity of data available for assessing the claim. Second, Martin (1990) points out a number of confounding demographic processes that make assessment of the claim difficult even when such data are available. A change in the proportion of nuclear households in a population may result from a number of processes; as a result, change in this proportion is not always an accurate indication of cultural ideals about the value of shared living arrangements. For example, members of joint families pass through stages in which they live in nuclear households. With the death of an elder, nuclear households form; but these in turn may become stem or joint-stem households as people age. Household formation is inextricably bound up in lifecourse transitions, and separating this normal fluctuation from secular trends in shared living arrangements is quite difficult.

Another source of demographic confounding involves changes in fertility and mortality associated with the demographic transition (see chapter 3). A decrease in fertility by itself results in fewer nuclear households, even if the rate of shared residence is constant. The decrease in nuclear households at the population level in this case would result from there being fewer siblings of the child with whom the parents co-reside. On the other hand, decreases in infant mortality might mean greater survival for siblings and a corresponding increase in nuclear households. Martin (1990) concludes that the gross rate of nuclear households is not a reliable indicator. A better approach is to examine change in the proportion of elderly living alone, with a spouse, or with children.

Martin (1990), in a thorough review of South Asian research, has identified only one data set that contains such information for the same community in two time periods. The value of these data is clear, and we present Martin's tabulation here as Table 5.3.

Table 5.3 Living Arrangements of the 60 and Over Population in 13 Villages in Bihar, 1960 and 1982

	Males		Females	
	1960	1982	1960	1982
Alone	10.6%	2.7	2.7	3.9
With spouse only	4.5	13.2	0.0	8.0
With son	83.3	80.9	78.1	80.1
With daughter	0.0	0.0	5.5	4.5
With grandchildren (but not children)	0.0	0.8	11.0	0.6
With sibling	1.5	2.3	2.7	3.0
(n)	(66)	(257)	(73)	(337)

Source: Recategorized data from Biswas (1985:246).

These data on living arrangements were collected in a study of thirteen villages in Bihar, India (Biswas 1985), first in 1960 and again in 1982. Examining the table makes clear the lack of any major change in elderly living arrangements over this twenty-year period of modernization. The proportion of elderly males and females living with sons, the culturally prescribed pattern, has remained more or less constant. A small proportion of elderly women continues to live with daughters. No males at either time reside with adult daughters, in accord with the high-caste Hindu proscription on receiving assistance from a married daughter (Goldstein, Schuler, and Ross 1983). The proportion of males living alone has decreased, while the proportion living with a spouse has increased. The most significant change involves an increase in the proportion of elderly females living with a spouse only (from 0 to 8 percent), and the corresponding decrease of those living with grandchildren (from 11 to less than 1 percent). Martin (1990) concludes that the overall pattern of change and stability reflects lower mortality in late life (greater co-survival with a spouse, greater probability that children are alive in addition to grandchildren), rather than a change in cultural attitudes toward shared residence.

To conclude, then, shared living arrangement is a function of demography as well as culture. Also, even when shared residence is modal, the status and well-being of elders may be poor. We can generalize Martin's conclusion about South Asian elderly to the elderly at large: "status of the elderly . . . appears not to be guaranteed by virtue of their age or co-residence with offspring. Rather, status more likely is a function of sex, health, and economic resources." If the research on living arrangement and elder well-being supports any firm conclusion, it is that the poor status and compromised well-being of the elderly has most to do with lack of services and poverty (Goldstein, Schuler, and Ross 1983; Martin 1990). To the extent that modernization has impoverished the rural sector of many developing countries, it has indeed led to poorer outcomes for elders.

6

Family Relationships of the Elderly: The Flow of Intergenerational Transactions

Sokolovsky points out that "only human societies have developed systems that require high levels of prolonged material and social interdependence between generations" (Sokolovsky 1990). The long postreproductive survival of humans means greater opportunity for differentiation of roles based on age (elder or senior, as opposed to adult) and the emergence of more or less explicit codes for assistance and exchange between parents and adult children. In addition, an increased life expectancy makes it likely that younger descendants will provide some degree of caregiving support for elderly parents and grandparents when health limitations make such support necessary. Finally, in the developed countries, increases in life expectancy mean new late-life relationships between parents and adult children, as these adult children can expect to age along with their parents and share as many as fifty or sixty years together as adults. For example, compared with women in nineteenth-century America, women in 1980 will live four times as many years with both parents alive (Bengston, Rosenthal, and Burton 1990). The contours of this relationship, with an adult child aged 65 or 70 and a parent 85 or 90, are still unclear, as such long-term

joint survival is truly a new feature in human rel⋯ new
opportunities for strain and intimacy (M⋯

Accordingly, in the developed cou⋯ has
emerged as a lengthy component of the l⋯ m
parenthood than ever before (Hagestad an⋯ d
Furstenberg (1986) point out that aging⋯ -
creased opportunity to observe their grandc⋯
as infants, children, and adults. Increased lo⋯
portunity for contact, and greater opportunit⋯
evolve over time. In the developed countrie⋯
family members per generation as a result of i⋯
uals have a longer time to invest themselves in⋯ ups
of kin (Bengston, Rosenthal, and Burton 1990)⋯ developing countries, opportunities for long-term relationships such as these are limited because of shorter life expectancy; also, kin groups are larger. Patterns of exchange and assistance are thus likely to differ between
generations as a result of demographic variation in addition to cultural
differences.

We propose to examine family relationships involving the elderly
from the perspective of transactions, exchanges in which parent and
adult child may each provide or receive some kind of good, which may
range from material assistance to less tangible expressions of relationship, such as deference or other aspects of filial obligation. One virtue
of this approach is its explicit recognition of the bidirectionality of the
flow of support in the family relationships of the elderly. In examining
intergenerational transactions within families, it is important to keep in
mind the central lifecourse transitions of late life that affect family relationships. These include the transition to grandparenthood, the transition to widowhood, and the condition of childlessness, all discussed
previously in chapter 4. Also to be kept in mind are the coordinate
changes in living arrangement that may follow such lifecourse transitions, which are discussed in chapter 5.

Because of its increasing significance in the lives of adult children,
we single out one particular form of family support, informal caregiving
to the impaired elder, for separate analysis. Such caregiving is particularly important because it accounts for the vast preponderance of care
provided to impaired elderly, in developed countries (Horowitz 1985,
Doty 1986) as well as in developing nations. Front-page newspaper

headlines about neglect of the elderly by affluent children make good copy but give a poor picture of the extent of family caregiving to frail elders (Brody 1985, 1990). Even in the United States, where laments about family dissolution and increasing neglect of aged parents are often heard, it is important to note that for elders aged 65+, only about 5 percent reside in nursing homes at any given time (National Center for Health Statistics 1989), and that nursing home utilization has declined for elders in the oldest age groups (Manton and Soldo 1985). However, it should also be noted that the likelihood that a person will spend time in a nursing home in late life is quite high (43 percent for those turning 65 in 1990; see Kemper and Murtaugh 1991), which indicates that recourse to skilled nursing care is often the culmination of family caregiving. Given the extremely high prevalence of dementing disease in late life (as high as 50 percent for those aged 85+), use of skilled care as the culmination of family caregiving may, in fact, be appropriate; but the resistance families feel in using such services, and the continued contact they have with an elder following a decision to institutionalize an elder, all point to the undeniable commitment of families to care for the aged (Shanas 1979; Nydegger 1983).

Finally, we begin this chapter with a discussion of cultural variation in the construction of generational ties. We have already seen in chapter 4 that age transitions can be more or less discontinuous. The transition from child to youth to adult to elder can be drawn sharply and marked with ritual or it can be downplayed. Likewise, contact between people of different points in the lifecourse can be restricted and couched in manners or relatively unmarked. In drawing these distinctions we must remember that generational relations consist of different pieces and that the degree of formality or contact may vary from dimension to dimension. For example, among the Lak of New Ireland (Papua New Guinea), while children and youths do not shy away from asking a father's brother for betel nut, the most common daily transaction, they would never presume to overstep a number of restrictions regarding his position as owner of a men's house, the central ritual place of the matrilineage (Albert 1988).

More broadly, and more relevant for family relationships, ties between the generations can be made a central feature of family experience, in which conjugal ties and personal self-expression are overridden by the centrality of generational relationships; or generational relationships can be relatively neglected in favor of a nuclear family organization that excludes the elder. Caldwell (1982), as we have mentioned in chapter 3, makes the historical transition from such multigenerational extended kin units to nuclear families the central determinant of fertility decisions, as the intergenerational flow of goods reverses with such a transition. That is, in the ___ ___tional extended kinship regime, which is the m___ ___zation in the rural sector of the developing w___ ___ildren to parents in late life, and parents there ___ ___centive to have as many children as possible. ___ ___me, on the other hand, wealth flows from par___ ___ late life, and having children becomes far mo___ ___th variation in the cultural order bound up ___ ___ amily regimes and the ways such variation a___ ___ s in families.

Cultural Variation in the
Construction of Generational Ties

Simic (1990) provides a rich description of such variation in cultural order in his discussion of Serbian and Croatian households on the one hand, and American households on the other. He conducted research within a wide variety of Yugoslavian households, both urban and rural, and both abroad and among recent immigrants to the United States. Simic draws a broad distinction between two cultural ideals, the individualism characteristic of white, middle-class America and the Yugoslav ideal of kinship corporacy. The distinction, stated so starkly, is perhaps overdrawn; yet the systematic influence of these overarching cultural ideals on family function is brought out well in Simic's analysis.

The American orientation toward self-fulfillment and individualism has a number of notable behavioral correlates. First is a division of household space. Rooms and household goods are personal possessions, not family objects; and privacy, individual space, is a central American ideal. Thus, early on, children are given their own rooms, both for sleeping and for play. A consequence of this division within households is a sense that individual expression is superior to family ties: "Underlying this are the beliefs that each child's uniqueness transcends the commonality of the family group and that brothers and sisters will inevitably develop divergent interests, values, and extrafamilial ties that will not be shared with other members of the household" (Simic 1990). For example, American children must earn their "own" money as a sign that they are growing up properly.

Contrast this orientation toward personal expression with the Yugoslav ideal. Simic points out that the word *privacy* simply cannot be translated into Serbo-Croatian and that the closest cognates (*secrecy, loneliness, withdrawal*) all have negative connotations. In contrast to the American ideal, personal social engagement in southern and central Yugoslavia revolves around family and kinship. Personal space, that enduring feature of the American adolescent, is so alien to Yugoslav college students that, when asked if they would like their own apartments, virtually all of Simic's Yugoslav informants rejected the idea as strange. A typical response, Simic reports, is "What a strange idea! It would be so lonely without my parents."

A second consequence of the American ideal is an emphasis on peer-group solidarity. Extrafamilial ties compete with, and perhaps even subvert, family ties. Thus, parents are on the sidelines at children's birthday parties and may even be banished from teenage gatherings in the home. Children are expected to spend most of their time outside the home and to develop friends apart from siblings and even distinct from their own siblings' friends. This, too, stands in extreme contrast to Yugoslav ideals. For example, during school holidays, Yugoslav children are packed off to spend time with cousins, who may live some distance away, just because family is seen to be the most appropriate venue for companionship. Children's birthday parties, a recent innovation in Yugoslavia, also emphasize family relationships; it is an occasion to strengthen kin ties, rather than an opportunity for extrafamilial socialization.

An additional consequence of the American ideal of individualism is a kind of family-level democracy. Each family member, within bounds, has equal voice in family decision making; and each has equal claim to respect of his or her wishes. The result is de-emphasis of hierarchy and a consequent devaluation of age as a principle of such hierarchy. Birth order confers no special rights, either to inheritance or command over siblings or responsibility for parental well-being in late life. This democratic ideal extends beyond the household, so that merit, rather than kin connection, is seen to be the most important factor in regulating relationships between people. One should not hire a kinsman just because he is a kinsman. Likewise, parental involvement in a child's choice of spouse would infringe on a son's or daughter's freedom. The Yugoslavian ideal inverts these principles. Even with the decline of the *zadruga* and *bratstva*, patrilocally extended households in which related males and their families would jointly hold land and livestock, kinship solidarity is still paramount and lends a fundamentally different cast to intergenerational relationships. Children continue to reside near parents, and patrilocality in marriage is still the rule in the countryside (Simic 1990). A bride joins a husband's household and lives with his family until a house is built, and the new house typically stands next to the groom's father's or grandfather's farm. Sons and brothers work the plot of their father in common. Even when an adult child lives apart from a parent, as in urban settings, contact between adult children and parents is a daily occurrence. Simic (1990) concludes that the transition between generations "is not usually punctuated by abrupt separations, as is so commonly the case in the United States. Rather, the transition . . . tends to be an imperceptible and gradual one."

Other contrasts with the American ideal follow from these premises. The stress on intergenerational ties leads to a greater role for grandparents in raising young children and hence greater cohesion across generations (Hagestad 1985). Conjugal affection is neglected in favor of attachment to children and kinsmen. Thus, couples do not openly display affection, cannot demand "time to themselves," do not typically have a strong confiding or self-disclosing personal relationship (one goes to a sibling or parent for that), and usually do not even address each other by first names, preferring instead affinal terms such as *my husband, my wife*).

Economic individualism is similarly downplayed. The family is the economic unit, and one's good fortune is not separable from one's parents or siblings; they can make strong moral claims on it. Thus, rural households in Yugoslavia typically show the influx of wealth provided by kinsmen serving as guest workers elsewhere in Europe, or as new immigrants to the United States. Finally, age is central to family authority. Elders command deference, and their influence in the choice of a sibling's or child's marriage partner is a matter of course. Age as a principle of hierarchy is given a cosmological significance in ritual feasts that celebrate a lineage *slava,* or patron saint, an elder founder of the lineage.

Finally, and relevant to the discussion of family caregiving presented below, the stress on corporate kin units and intergenerational ties is consistent with designation of one child to be a caregiver to parents in late life, the so-called sacrificial child syndrome (Simic 1990). The sacrifice involves an adult child who forgoes marriage, economic independence, and perhaps complete psychological separation from his or her parents in preparation for assuming the role of caregiver to parents in late life. In cases where postmarital patrilocal residence is strong, as in rural Yugoslavia, one sees less of the sacrificial syndrome; here daughters-in-law reside near the groom's parents and assume the role of caregiver, along with their husbands. In America, on the other hand, the sacrificial syndrome is more common, as Simic (1990) points out, because daughters-in-law are unwilling to take on the role, so that parents must ensure support for themselves in late life through designation of one of their own children as a caregiver.

The evidence for such a sacrificial child syndrome bears examining. Simic (1990) reports that "in many cases mothers deliberately select a particular child to be socialized for this role." He reports that in a sample of 119 California Serbian households, fifty-seven consisted of married couples with adult children living in the home, and that of these fifty-seven, twenty-four contained an unmarried son or daughter. "Thus, in almost half of all those instances where it was possible, the sacrificial child syndrome occurred" (Simic 1990).

In fact, Simic's claims appear to be too strong. It is unclear how many of the adult children in the twenty-four households were middle-aged, and it is also unclear what the appropriate denominator was for the claim that "almost half" of the eligible households showed evidence of the sacrificial child syndrome. The appropriate denominator would be *all* households consisting of elderly parents, and not the households with adult children already co-residing with parents. Finally, the distributional data on residence patterns does not provide evidence for parents' selection of children as sacrificial caregivers. Adult children in these households evidently do become caregivers and forgo marriage and economic independence, but the question of motive and explicit selection of a particular child as caregiver remains unclear.

Evidence from research with Italian-American caregivers offers an interesting contrast with the Yugoslavian data on the sacrificial syndrome. As mentioned in chapter 5, actual selection of a child to be caregiver is the exception. In most cases, a number of circumstances converge to lead a particular child to remain in the elder's household or to co-reside with a frail parent in late life. These circumstances include the adult child's economic needs relative to his or her siblings' economic status, the personal competence of the sibling in establishing his or her own household, divorce or childlessness of the adult child in midlife, and lifelong processes of attachment between a particular child and his or her parents. Actual selection and grooming for the role was not observed among these ethnic Italians in South Philadelphia; and when such a selection mechanism was mentioned to informants in the research, respondents denied any such explicit determination of late-life roles (Albert 1992b).

The Yugoslav–American contrast is valuable, less for the broad and perhaps overdrawn contrast between such competing ideals regarding the place of the individual within family than for the concrete ways in which these alternatives are worked out in family life. The corporate ideal of the Yugoslavian household and the American ideal of an individual-centered world represent one approach to the range of possibility in family form. In the one, ties between generations are central; in the other, they are more or less peripheral. We turn next to the ways such variation in the preeminence of generational linkages matters in the daily transactions of life, and how it matters for the provision of support for elders in late life.

Generational Transactions within Families

In surveying variation in generational transactions across cultures, it is perhaps best to begin with the case in which we have the most extensive data, American culture. In summarizing the literature on intergenerational relationships in the United States, we draw heavily on the excellent review of Bengston, Rosenthal, and Burton (1990).

Bengston and his colleagues (see also Mangen, Bengston, and Landry 1988; Roberts and Bengston 1990) have developed an important measure of parent–child relationships, which they designate "intergenerational solidarity." Excluding measures relating to the opportunity for interaction and support, such solidarity can be assessed according to five dimensions: association, or the frequency of contact; affect, or joint subjective assessments concerning the warmth and quality of contact; consensus with respect to beliefs or values; patterns of exchange and assistance; and, finally, attitudes toward filial obligation. The five domains of intergenerational solidarity offer one productive approach to the characterization of family relationships and an important, although still unexplored, avenue for cross-cultural assessment of intergenerational ties.

Taking first association between adult children and their parents, we note four important predictors of variation in this domain of solidarity that have been reported for American families. The first predictor is gender. Daughters have more interaction with parents than sons, in accord with daughters' roles as "kin-keepers" (managers of social calenders and extended family relationships; see Rossi and Rossi 1990) and as "care managers" for parents (Archbold 1983). The second predictor is marital status. With widowhood, adult children see more of their parents; also, unmarried children see parents more often than married children (Lopata 1973). The third predictor is social class. Higher income is associated with less frequent parental contact, partly because of the increased mobility of high-income children. The fourth predictor is ethnicity. Hispanics see more of their parents than do Afro-Americans and white Americans (Mutran 1985).

With respect to affectual solidarity, parents and adult children both typically report high levels of positive feelings about intergenerational contact. With greater age of the parents, however, available evidence indicates divergence between generations: adult children characterize interaction with older, more frail parents less positively, while older parents tend to view interaction in more positive terms, perhaps because they come to have a greater investment in intergenerational bonds as they themselves decline (Bengston and Kuypers 1971; Rossi and Rossi 1990).

Consensus in beliefs and values is an especially important indicator of solidarity because of our intuitive sense that parents and child are likely to see the world through the same lens; also, transmission of much of what we consider culture, or at least the exoteric features of culture, occurs in the setting of parent–child contact and informal teaching of values and beliefs. In fact, available data show that with age, adult children and their parents grow farther apart on such consensus (Bengston, Rosenthal, and Burton 1990). On such matters as religion and political ideology, parents and adult children diverge. Also, in late life children begin to have a greater impact on a parent's attitudes (Glass, Bengston, and Dunham 1986).

The domain of exchange and assistance has received perhaps the most attention, and we have already reported that elders are often donors of aid and support, as well as recipients of such assistance. Data from the 1985 Survey on Income and Program Participation (SIPP), an ongoing survey of about 20,000 American households and their economic condition, are valuable in this regard for allowing a clear sense of the extent to which elders are on the giving and receiving end of these intergenerational transactions. The 1985 SIPP contained a supplement specifically geared to assessing financial support between related individuals living in different households. The SIPP data are limited in two ways: such financial assistance between the generations represents only a small part of the transactions linking adult children and parents (Cafferata, Stone, and Sangl 1987); and the SIPP supplement is limited to inquiries regarding people who do not share households, again restricting the domain of intergenerational involvement. Adult children in college are excluded in this definition of support transactions (i.e., they are considered to reside with their parents).

Even with this delimitation of intergenerational transactions, it is notable that elderly family members, those aged 65+, provide 16.8 percent of all the financial support provided by family members in the United States. These elders provide financial support to 427,000 adults, of which 114,000 are adult children aged 21+. A total of 495,000 such adult children are receiving financial support from family members, Thus, elders aged 65+ provide the bulk of family support to 23 percent of adult children receiving financial support from their families, and this amounts to a mean yearly sum of $4,658 in assistance. On the other hand, of the 2,726,000 individuals receiving support from their families in the United States, 918,000 (or 33.7 percent) are parents receiving support from adult child providers. Significantly, a small group of elders (59,000) provides financial support for their own parents, so that 6.4 percent of American parents receiving support from their families receive such support from adult children themselves aged 65+ (U.S. Bureau of the Census 1988; Tables 1 and 2). In sum, elder Americans constitute one-third of those receiving family support, *and* one-quarter of those providing such support.

Finally, with respect to the norm of filial obligation, research has found great heterogeneity, with adult children showing greater support for the norm in some cases than their parents (Bengston, Rosenthal, and Burton 1990; Mancini and Bliezner 1989). Ethnic variation in adherence to the norm is also apparent, with Hispanics reporting a greater sense that they must provide for their parents than either whites or Afro-Americans (Becerra 1983).

Albert (1990a) found that the norm of filial obligation really consists of two divergent understandings of obligation: an exchange orientation, in which adult children feel they must pay back the parent for the support the parent provided to the caregiver when he or she was young; and a communal orientation, in which the bodily bond between parent and child is seen to motivate the obligation to provide for a parent in his or her infirmity. In a small sample of caregivers, the exchange orientation was the more common. Caregivers holding the communal orientation in filial obligation were more likely to "infantilize" the parent (i.e., view the changes in the parent resulting from infirmity as a regression to childhood) and more likely to characterize the caregiving relationship as a case of role reversal, in which they now stand as a parent to their own parent.

Comparative Research on Intergenerational Solidarity

The dimensions of the intergenerational solidarity construct are useful, then, for examining variation in intergenerational ties within American culture. Less research has been conducted on intergenerational relationships outside the United States, although in principle the same set of dimensions should be useful for such research to see if intergenerational solidarity emerges in similar form (but see Roberts and Bengston [1990] for a qualification on the structure of such solidarity in the United States). It was shown previously that outside the developed countries large extended family households are typical. The most common pattern is separate nuclear households of parents and children, who reside next to one another and jointly cook, provide childcare, and undertake subsistence activities. These households extend horizontally within generations, so that siblings may reside near one another and cooperate economically, as well as vertically, so that parents and a set of children and their spouses reside in the same village or compound.

A first difference between the developed and developing nations in the case of intergenerational solidarity involves the influence of social units larger than the family. Descent group organization (i.e., whether children are classified as belonging to a mother's or father's line of descent) and allied postmarital residence rules may bind households into more extensive political units, such as clans (which are considered matrilineal or patrilineal according to the way descent is reckoned).

In Melanesia, for example, the Lak of Papua New Guinea prefer that at least one adult child reside in the same village as his or her parents. Total completed fertility for Lak women is roughly seven children, and one of these children is encouraged to remain in the parents' village following marriage. The adult child and his or her family reside in the village but maintain a separate household and garden; ultimately they look after the parents when they need care.

Whether Lak elders have adult children residing near them depends to a great degree on the "big man" status of these elders. A big man, or matrilineage leader, attempts to keep as many of his own sons and daughters in his village, with their spouses, as possible, to supplement the labor of his nieces and nephews (who belong to his clan and have an obligation to provide labor and resources for his execution of clan feasts, such as those necessary in mortuary rituals). In this way, he builds a great pool of labor he can draw upon. Spouses of his children, then, are pulled into his orbit and away from their own parents' villages. In this way, preferred extended household arrangements are modified by the larger social organization of Lak villages (Albert 1988). This effect on families may be typical of descent group systems.

A second difference in family relationships between developed and developing countries involves the relative priority of biological connection. *Fictive kin* and *classificatory kin* relationships are extremely important in clan-based societies, not just because they make kinship the idiom for all social relationships (and hence establish kin-based norms of behavior that extend to all personal contact), but also because the boundaries of *family* are made less distinct. Children in such societies clearly understand that they have a single biological mother, even though they call a wide variety of women mother (such as the mother's sisters in bifurcate merging classificatory systems). Yet it is striking how little is made of biology in the behavior between these children and their "mothers." To take the Lak case again, fosterage is common, so that a childless woman typically receives a daughter from her more fortunate sister (Albert 1987). Daughters in this circumstance may live next door to their biological parents and recognize the fact, but also find no difficulty in being a daughter to a mother's sister and her husband. The classificatory mother and father see to the daughter's schooling and may even arrange a marriage; the daughter assumes domestic duties and gardening tasks for her classificatory parents. Such fosterage builds upon a classificatory system, which in some sense encourages it; but fosterage occurs even in the absence of kin relationship and may be explicitly undertaken with elder support in mind. Bledsoe and Isiugo-Abanihe (1989) describe such a system for the Mende of Sierra Leone in Africa, and Donner (1987) describes a related arrangement for a Solomon Islands society in Melanesia.

Thus, cultural variation is likely to affect intergenerational relationships most dramatically in societies in which large extended families are the rule and in which the boundaries governing the extent of the family are less distinct. The effect of large extended families on the dimensions of intergenerational solidarity becomes clearer in research conducted in Israel. Weihl (1983) was able to compare monogenerational Israeli families with an Askenazi origin (immigrants from Europe and North America) to those of a Sephardic origin (immigrants from the Middle and Near East), and both to Israeli Arab families. This represents an ideal design for testing the relative role of culture and other factors in determining the form of intergenerational relationships because Askenazi families typically adopt the nuclear form of family organization, as opposed to Sephardic and Arab families, who have more extensive family ties and who typically reside ingreater propinquity.

Differences between the three groups were less marked than one would expect. Comparing the two groups of Israeli Jews, Weihl found that contact between elderly parents and children was equally frequent, with 73 percent of the elderly in each group having seen a child at least once in the prior week. Differences in family structure were significant only in the *location* of such intergenerational contact: intergenerational contact for the Sephardic group was more likely to occur in the elderly parents' homes, while Israelis of European origin were equally likely to see parents in their own home or the parents' homes. Weihl reports that a quite marked breakup of the traditional joint household among Israeli Arabs (because of increased education and greater economic freedom of adult children) has not been accompanied by a decline in intergenerational contact or erosion of norms regarding affection, deference, or filial obligation.

An important point brought out in the Israeli research is an unexpected relationship between elders' feelings of dependence on children and living arrangement. Elders' sense of dependency on children was *greater* among those living in multigenerational households than among those who lived apart from their children, even when differences in health and functional capacity between the two groups of elders were controlled. Weihl (1983) concludes that the multigenerational household may in some cases be an overprotective living arrangement, in that it fosters such feelings of dependency. One would expect this consequence of shared households to be more frequent in developed countries, where the norm is independent living and the governing ideal of life is independence. In developing countries, on the other hand, multigenerational households are a more acceptable feature of late life, and thus one might conclude that feelings of dependency would not be associated with this type of living arrangement. However, we have not identified comparative research that has investigated this issue directly.

More generally, Weihl's research shows that cultural differences may be less significant than socioeconomic factors in predicting features of intergenerational solidarity. For example, comparing the "modern family" European Israelis to the "traditional family" Middle Eastern Israelis, one would expect greater intergenerational support among the latter. After all, greater assistance and more extensive affectual bonds, it would seem, should occur in households that are more closely knit as economic units. In accord with such cultural differences, the Middle Eastern Israelis were twice as likely to provide financial support to parents living in separate households as were the European Israelis. But in the case of support in the instrumental activities of daily living, such as help with shopping and running errands, and in the case of emotional support, income level seems to be a much better predictor than cultural origin. In both cultural groups, higher incomes predict more of this type of support between adult children and their parents.

Weihl's concern about the relative role of culture and socioeconomic factors in predicting features of intergenerational ties is important in another sense as well. We are surprised to find cultural variation less salient than socioeconomic differences because of a "golden age" or "golden isles" myth, the false sense that intergenerational ties were once—say, in the past, or perhaps still in some far-off primitive place—better than they are today and as they should be, that is, warm, satisfying, and without strain. Nydegger (1983) has shown that this expectation bears little relation to reality and yet continues to haunt contemporary thinking about the nature of intergenerational relationships. Thus, we find it hard to believe that hunter-gatherer elders are unhappy with the care they receive, or that intergenerational relationships in extended families, where members live in close proximity and share economic activities, are characterized by their share of strain, dependencies felt to be illegitimate, and unequal allocation of resources, rather than by affection, mutual support, and sharing. In fact, Nydegger (1983) has marshaled evidence that systematically removes support for just about every component of these myths.

Taking the "golden age" myth first, she points out that multigenerational households were not more common in the past and not more desired then by adult children or their parents. Old age was devalued in nineteenth-century America and England, as it is now. If anything, adult children are more involved in the lives of their parents today than they were in the past. The "golden isles" myth fares equally poorly when subjected to close scrutiny. Nydegger (1983) points out that "critical inspection of the least modernized societies suggests that many claims are indigenous versions of the Golden Age [myth]." True gerontocracy is rare and is usually associated with great competition for power between sons and fathers (Foner 1984; see also chapter 8). Too often ethnographers report cultural ideals regarding deference to elders and filial respect rather than the actual relationships between adult children and their parents. We saw in chapter 4, for example, how even culturally normative support arrangements, such as shared living arrangements in Nepal, can mask great variation in the economic security and status of the elderly.

Nydegger also reminds us that if elders command respect in Africa or Melanesia, it is likely because of the power they have accumulated over their lifetimes, and not just because of their age. We might also note a striking parallel between elders in developed and developing nations in securing support in late life, "the strategic bequest" (Bernheim, Shleifer, and Summers 1985), in which elders use the threat of disinheritance to motivate adult children to fulfill obligations to parents (Nugent 1990). If adequate support were modal, it is unlikely that elders would resort to such a strategem, which is described so well, and with all its complex psychological overtones, in *King Lear*.

We saw above that consensus in beliefs between the young and old is an additional component of intergenerational solidarity. Comparative research investigating this issue has concentrated on consensus with respect to one particular social norm, that of filial obligation as it bears upon old age support. Nugent (1990) presents a cogent game-theoretic analysis of the pressures that threaten this norm in developing countries and the potential mechanisms available for shoring up the norm. He begins by examining the economic advantages of intergenerational transfers in the traditional family system. Parents invest in children through their fertility and perhaps selective investment of food, schooling, and health care. In later life, children transfer goods back to parents, including personal attention and care, in this way substituting for poorly developed markets for the types of goods required by the elderly and disabled, such as insurance and home health care. In fact, in some cases the traditional system is economically more efficient than the modern regime of pensions, insurance, and purchased services. Nugent (1990) points out that the extended family household is a setting in which "every member can closely observe the actions of every other member, and where reputation, sanctions, and social norms combine to limit the extent to which anyone would want to misreport the extent of a disability." In the traditional system, feigned disability is at a minimum and support in this sense is more efficient: "within the traditional system, transfers and other sources of support need be provided only when they are absolutely necessary, thereby greatly reducing the costs of such support."

The traditional system is threatened by the same forces at work in developed countries: decreased fertility reduces the number of children available to care for aging parents; and the greater mobility, schooling, and economic opportunity available to adult children leads them to settle away from parents and thus compounds the problem by depleting further this reduced pool of resources for old age security. Nugent (1990) points to two factors that counteract these trends.First, elder household heads can enforce cooperative behavior between generations; and second, social norms of filial care appear to persist in the face of modernization, even with major changes in family organization.

The most important means by which parents can enforce cooperative behavior from adult children has already been mentioned. The threat of disinheritance by the father is a credible deterrent to noncooperative behavior by sons, especially in societies in which fathers own land, livestock, and other basic necessities of daily living. That the threat is credible only if the father has substantial bequeathable assets goes without saying. Economic analyses also assume that a credible threat requires that the father have another son or potential heir to whom the assets can alternatively be bequeathed. In this way, the father can enforce cooperative behavior from the one who stands to inherit the estate according to convention (say, the firstborn). This, however, does not always appear necessary. In Melanesian societies, at any rate, fathers may bury wealth and threaten not to give it to any of their children or clan relatives. Elders attempt to enforce cooperative behavior by threatening to carry the secret of the location of such wealth to the grave. And, in fact, stories of buried, rotting wealth irretrievably lost are common (Albert 1987).

Unfortunately, detailed accounts of the bequeathment process in traditional societies are lacking, perhaps because disinheritance is rare, and perhaps also because it is not the kind of social event that is casually revealed to outsiders. It is perhaps the clearest example of the violation of the social norms that link generations. What seems more remarkable is the persistence of such norms in the face of major changes in family structure. For example, increased geographic mobility and dispersion undermine social norms by making such defaults on the intergenerational contract less visible; reputations are not as threatened. Yet Nugent (1990) points out that even with increased geographic mobility, frequent communication and close relationships between city and village are typical. Villagers moving to cities tend to settle in a common enclave; and village institutions, such as clubs and churches, are transferred to such enclaves, so that city neighborhoods become satellites of villages. In this way, the communication that enforces normative behavior is maintained even with geographic dispersion.

Another source of norm reinforcement is evident in ethnographic reports. There is ample evidence that elders make a concerted, and often public, effort to make their children adhere to such social norms. While elders may threaten disinheritance, it is more likely that they will simply go public with gripes about poor care and neglect. The "complaint discourse" of the !Kung elder (Rosenberg 1990), like the "discourse of norm reinforcement" among the Samia of Kenya (Cattell n.d., 1992b), all represent conscious attempts by elders to shame adult children into fulfilling their obligations to support parents in late life. Foner (1984) points to the strategic aspects of such complaining to ensure support, so that elders are expected to complain and feel entitled to do so. For the !Kung, in fact, these complaints are a sign of vitality in old age.

This process, of course, is not limited to band societies or villages in the developing nations. However, the way one complains about perceived neglect takes different forms. Going public with complaints about poor care is not an acceptable strategy for the American elder because it is too frank an admission of dependence and family stress. Myerhoff (1978), for example, presents wonderful case material that shows the subterfuge elderly Jewish women engage in to shame their children for neglecting them, without actually *saying* they are being neglected. However, in the United States the norm of filial support in old age is so strong that such public complaint may not be necessary. A common refrain nicely shows the degree to which the social norm of filial obligation has been internalized. When asked whether adult children fulfill their end of the intergenerational contract, it is surprising how often an adult child, even someone providing quite extensive caregiving support, will shake his or her head and remark, "How do you like that: a parent can care for three or four children, but three or four children can't even care for one parent." As we will see, adult children do provide such care but still feel they are not doing enough.

The last domain of intergenerational solidarity involves exchange and assistance. We have already shown that the flow of exchange and assistance between generations is reciprocal, both in the developed nations where the number of elders receiving assistance from adult children is only slightly higher than the number providing assistance to such children, and in the developing nations, where the norm of filial support is part and parcel of the domestic economy of the extended family. What remains undiscussed are data showing that the norms of intergenerational reciprocity themselves vary cross-culturally. Here the best source is research by Akiyama, Antonucci, and Campbell (1990), which compares the experience of Japanese and American women. They point out that "the concepts of exchange and reciprocity are vital parts of the lives of these women, but operate in strikingly different ways in the two societies."

The first major difference in the norm of reciprocity across the two societies involves the commensurability of exchange items. In America, an exchange good should be reciprocated with a good of the same type: gift for gift, service for service, affection with affection. In Japan, by contrast, "expressive resources such as love and status are granted a much broader range of exchangeability," so that affectionate behavior is seen as an acceptable reciprocation for such material gifts as money and goods. Thus, in Japan love is seen as the appropriate response to any sort of material support, while Americans seek to repay in kind. An implication of this difference in exchange rules is that dependence of the elderly on adult children is more acceptable in Japan. That is, the elderly accept their inability to reciprocate in kind (because of weak physical condition or few resources), just as their children are willing to accept affection from elders as an appropriate discharge of an exchange obligation.

Another major difference between the American and Japanese in intergenerational exchange involves an important distinction between mother-daughter relationships and relationships between mothers-in-law and daughters-in-law. American elderly women make no distinction in exchange rules, whether one is dealing with a daughter or a daughter-in-law; in both cases, the appropriate response to a gift or aid is a similar gift or aid, in accord with the symmetric reciprocity typical of American intergenerational relationships. In Japan, on the other hand, a different rule of exchange governs mother-daughter and mother-in-law–daughter-in-law relationships. Exchanges between mothers-in-law and daughters-in-law are characterized by the asymmetric reciprocity described above, in which affection by the elder can be considered an appropriate return to a daughter-in-law who has provided some sort of material assistance. On the other hand, the mother-daughter relationship does not show this latitude in the perceived commensurability of exchange goods. Here the rule is more akin to the American rule of symmetric reciprocity. This difference in exchange rules is a consequence of the Japanese preference for stem families, in which parents live with their oldest son and his wife. The daughter-in-law, as a result of this living arrangement, is part of the family and hence falls under the asymmetric reciprocity rule. Daughters, on the other hand, live with their own husbands and may reside in the husband's stem family, so that they are incorporated into his family. Along with the symmetric reciprocity rule governing relations between the different "families" comes a more general increase in formality. Married daughters do not commonly provide assistance to mothers; that is the domain of the co-resident daughter-law. Akiyama and her colleagues (1990) go on to report that "the daughter is expected to maintain a certain distance from her parent's 'family' as a measure of her respect for the wife of the brother with whom her parents live." In their sample of co-resident mother-in-law–daughter-in-law pairs and separately living mother–daughter pairs (n=254 pairs), they found that only 9 percent of the daughters living with their husband's parents were visited by their mothers, compared with 31 percent of the daughters who were not living with their husband's parents.

Which exchange rule is best for ensuring adequate support for the elderly in late life? The Japanese rule has the advantage of allowing elderly to reciprocate assistance with a resource that does not diminish in late life, that is, affection and love. They thus remain equals in exchange, in the sense that the inability to reciprocate in kind and the dependency it implies are downplayed. American elderly do not have this option: losing one's ability to reciprocate in kind means dependency (Dowd 1986). On the other hand, American elders are able to draw on the assistance of daughters and daughters-in-law, while Japanese elderly women must rely on the aid of a single co-resident daughter-in-law. The American–Japanese contrast shows clearly that the content of exchange rules varies cross-culturally, and that these differences are tied to variation in household structure. It would be

valuable to have additional data on the correlation of household structure with norms of inter___ ____ional exchange, but little such cross-
cultural ____ _____.

_____ to the Frail Elderly

Through____ ____ ____ ___ _____ essed that most elders are healthy
and highl_ _____ _____ 's are, in the aggregate, likely to be
providers ___ _____ __ _____ ilies as well as recipients of such
support. Y_ _____ __ _____ ure of late life (see chapters 2 and
9); accordi__ _____ ____ ___ _____ with an increase in the prevalence
of impairm___ ____ _____ competence and make independent living _____ _____ for a subset of the elderly. Estimates
of the size of this subset of functionally dependent elderly vary according to definitions of *functional dependency*, a point discussed at length in
chapter 9. Using a need for assistance in one of the instrumental activities of daily living (IADL: e.g., going shopping, using the telephone,
managing money) or one of the activities of daily living (ADL: e.g.,
feeding oneself, using the toilet, getting around inside the home) as a
measure of functional dependency, about 19 percent of the elderly non-
institutionalized U.S. population (aged 65+) is unable to live independently. Ninety percent of these functionally dependent elders receive
the bulk of their assistance from family caregivers (Lawton, in review).

Comparable estimates of functional dependency and the prevalence
of family caregiving outside the developed nations are for the most part
unavailable (see chapter 9). This reflects the difficulty of surveying
morbidity in late life but also, to some extent, the general merging of
old age support and family caregiving in the developing nations. We
have already seen (in chapter 5) that co-residence in late life between
elders and an adult child is the rule in most of the developing nations.
For example, in the People's Republic of China, upwards of 70 percent
of elders reside with adult sons and their families (Liang 1985), a proportion that is typical of East Asia (Chow 1988; Kwan 1988). Similar
percentages, or greater, have been reported for Southeast Asia, South
America, and Africa. As Hermalin and his colleagues (1990) point out,
living arrangements must be seen as a kind of intergenerational support, and such residential-based support, we might add, often shades

into caregiving as well. The transition from general old age support to caregiving may be less marked in such circumstances, unlike the case in the United States, in which an elder's hospitalization or functional loss often precipitates a change in living arrangements and clear demarcation of the beginning of caregiving.

One clear cross-cultural source of variation in family caregiving involves norms regarding which child should assume the role of caregiver when a parent beomes infirm. We restrict our discussion of family caregiving to this process of *caregiver selection* because it offers an important perspective on cross-cultural variation in intergenerational transactions. Also, cross-cultural data have recently become available in this area. On the other hand, a literature search on cross-cultural variation in family caregivers' perceptions of burden and satisfaction was less productive. Such research would clearly be valuable and these topics can only be approached indirectly here.

Variation in norms for caregiver selection mainly involves the gender of the caregiver child, and, not surprisingly, norms for caregiver selection follow norms regarding the preferred living arrangement in late life. Thus, in the United States, co-residence with daughters is the preferred living arrangement for the elderly, and daughters also provide the vast majority of informal care to impaired elders. In Japan and mainland China, on the other hand, co-residence with sons, rather than daughters, is the preferred living arrangement, and, accordingly, *daughters-in-law* are the primary caregivers.

In fact, as Ikels (1983) points out, the process of caregiver selection is largely invariant across cultures except for this variation in norms regarding the gender of the adult child expected to assume the caregiving role. In a sample of Irish and Chinese elders living in Boston (n=242), she found that ethnicity otherwise mattered very little in "determining whether, how, and why someone in a family assumes responsibility for the well-being of a particular older member." Caregiver selection in both groups was determined for the most part by demographic considerations, family history, and personal factors, in that order: "The process of caretaker selection appears to follow rules that transcend cultural differences." Cultural values exerted an effect only in determining whether a son or daughter was considered the appropriate source of caregiving support, and thus whether a daughter or daughter-in-law would become caregiver.

Demographic factors are the most important predictor of caregiver selection. Being an only child or the only child of the preferred sex clearly makes it far more likely that a particular adult child will assume the caregiver role. In cases in which there is more than one child, residing near the parent (i.e., being the only proximate child) is next in importance in predicting who will assume caregiving responsibilities. Finally, if more than one child is proximate, or if not all the adult children are married, being single increases the likelihood that one will be selected as caregiver.

The salience of these "demographic imperatives" in caregiver selection seems obvious, as does the hierarchical, nested order presented by Ikels (1983), but it is worth investigating why residential proximity or not being married increases the likelihood that one will become a caregiver. As Ikels notes, residing near the parent in many cases reflects an adult child's anticipation that he or she will accept the caregiver role. The same may be true in the case of remaining single. Thus, demographic factors are not easily separable from other predisposing factors, such as family history and personal characteristics, because these factors have demographic consequences: they may lead adult children to reside near a parent or to delay (or even forgo) marriage. Likewise, a delayed marriage is more likely to result in childlessness, where childlessness is an additional factor increasing the odds that one sibling will be selected as caregiver over another. Research assessing the salience of demographic factors, while controlling for these other predisposing factors, has not yet been undertaken.

A related issue regarding these demographic factors has to do with their relation to family behavior. Are the demographic regularities identified by Ikels's *rules*, in the sense that elders limit their requests for assistance to proximate children or consciously choose single children over married children? Or are they simply *regularities* in the caregiver selection process that can be observed, say, in retrospective research? The former implies conscious intent on the part of elders and their adult children, and also greater order in the allocation of family members to caregiving responsibilities. The latter suggests more drift in the process, with less intent by parents and children and greater scope for countervailing predisposing factors.

The latter is the more likely. As Ikels suggests, caregiver selection is heavily affected by contingencies that force the issue of selection. Also, the allocation of caregiving responsibility within families often shows a great deal of trial and error, more or less explicit negotiation between siblings, attempts to work out joint caregiving arrangements between siblings, family crisis, and in many cases plain lack of clarity. Having a family meeting to discuss elder care is the exception; likewise, assumption of caregiving duties often proceeds in a halting, tentative way, as adult daughters attempt to integrate tasks relating to their role as wife and mother with more specific parent-caregiving tasks. Thus, in the U.S. context it is striking how often caregiving daughters first form a "quasi-household" with the elder, either by having the parent move in with the daughter for limited time periods or by spending nights at the elder's house (perhaps over weekends), before the elder and caregiver formally co-reside (Albert 1990b).

Caregiver selection is forced when an elder's status changes dramatically, as in a health crisis that prevents a formally independent elder from living on his or her own, or when an apparently competent elder is widowed, only to reveal that the deceased spouse had been providing far more caregiving support to the surviving parent than anyone knew. Family history variables have the greatest predictive role in the case of such crises. In this case the onset of such crises at an early age is likely to catch an adult child, most often the youngest, still at home. This child, as Ikels's (1990) informant so aptly put it, is "caught holding the bag" for caregiving: "If there is only one child in the area at the time of the crisis, that child has no choice but to step forward." If more than one child is in the area, other family history factors emerge to increase the odds that one child over another will assume caregiving responsibilities. Ikels identifies two such factors: a special debt on the part of a child to the parent, which may bring a particular child to step forward as caregiver, and having the fewest competing obligations of any sibling. The former, such as a debt to the parent for help the parent provided in the past, acts to single out a child as having a special obligation to step forward and provide care; the latter give other siblings an opportunity not to step forward. Thus, the adult child who is not working, or who does not have children of her own, or who has the most marginal labor force participation has the least excuse not to assume caregiving.

An important additional point brought out by Ikels (1983) is the relative insignificance of affection for the parent in predicting who will step forward as caregiver. In assuming caregiving duties in the American context, for example, affection is rarely mentioned. The implication is that filial duty overrides the presence or absence of affection. Indeed, research conducted by Horowitz (1985) has shown that while affection helps reduce the perceived burden of caregiving for adult daughters, such affection is clearly not a prerequisite for caregiving: quite a few caregivers in her sample professed clear dislike for the parent, a finding replicated in other research (Albert, Litvin, Kleban, and Brody 1991). The *unimportance* of affection for the parent in the case of late-life caregiving may be an important feature of intergenerational relationships that transcends cultural differences, but more research is needed on this point.

To help put this research on caregiver selection in focus, it may be useful to examine findings from a large study that asked specifically how adult children assumed caregiving responsibilities. In research conducted at the Philadelphia Geriatric Center, 688 daughter or daughter-in-law caregivers were asked "how it happened that you were the one in the family who became the main caregiver."[1] Open-ended replies were sought, transcribed verbatim, and coded for salient themes. Caregivers spontaneously produced a variety of reasons, in many cases more than one, and these were all recorded. Thus, in the results reported here, percentages will total more than 100 percent. The major selection factors mentioned by the caregivers in this sample included the following, listed in descending order:

- The inability of other siblings to assume caregiving responsibilities was mentioned by 70 percent of the caregivers. The majority of such explanations involved other siblings' competing obligations, lack of proximity to the impaired parent, or poor health (33.3 percent). Another 23.2 percent of the caregivers were only children and had no siblings who could assume the role. Lack of interest or frank refusal to assume caregiving duties by siblings was mentioned by 13.2 percent of the caregivers.

- Family history factors were mentioned by 24 percent of the caregivers as the reason for their caregiving. These included a sense of obligation based on what the parent had done for the adult child (8.9 percent), the gradual development of a parent's dependency on the child, perhaps through past illness (6.1 percent), and an assessment by caregivers that they, unlike other siblings, were the "caregiving type" (9 percent).

- Proximity to the impaired parent was mentioned by 21 percent of the caregivers: they lived with the parent before the parent needed such care (8.3 percent) or lived nearby when caregiving needs became apparent (12.8 percent).

- Explicit social norms as selection factors were mentioned by 20 percent of the caregivers. These included the gender (11.2 percent) and birth order (8.4 percent) of the caregivers (although first born and last born were equally prominent).

- Situational factors, such as absence of competing obligations or access to particular resources that would make caregiving easy or appropriate, were mentioned by 15 percent of the caregivers. These caregivers were not working (2.6 percent) or not currently married (5.3 percent); alternatively, they had a spare room in their house (3.6 percent), or free time (3.9 percent).

- Finally, an emotional bond was mentioned by 14.4 percent of the caregivers. These caregivers mentioned love, closeness to the parent, their desire to be caregivers, and, significantly, the parent's choice of them as caregivers over other siblings.

In the American case, then, selection to caregiving is primarily a matter of default, but also an obligation strongly felt. The majority of explanations involves the inability of other siblings to step forward; less common are predisposing factors that lead a particular child to step forward, although we have seen that certain demographic factors, such as proximity or remaining unmarried, may be a consequence of an adult child's *advance* selection to such caregiving. Social norms, particularly regarding the appropriateness of women as caregivers and birth order as a selection factor, are not trivial in the American system. In accord with Ikels's (1983) research, family history and situational factors again emerge as important determinants of caregiver selection. Finally, affection is important in only a minority of cases.

Caregiver selection outside the United States has not been extensively investigated.However, two detailed studies, one involving Taiwanese elders (Hermalin, Chang, Lin, et al. 1990) and the other Yoruba elders in Nigeria (Peil, Bamisaiye, and Ekpenyong 1989), offer an excellent opportunity to observe cross-cultural variation in processes governing the recruitment of family caregivers.

The Nigerian case shows quite marked variation in caregiver selection according to the gender of the elder. In the United States, we have seen that family caregivers are largely adult daughters, whether the impaired elder is a father or mother. If these daughters are more likely to be caring for a mother, the asymmetry reflects the fact that women typically outlive their husbands and also provide caregiving support to older husbands in late life. Among the Yoruba, on the other hand, elderly men are more likely to be receiving caregiving support from adult children than elderly women. An elderly woman's source of support, in contrast, is likely to come from *grandchildren.* This variation in caregiving support by gender of the impaired parent exists, it should be noted, in the presence of a well-articulated ideology of parental support, in which all adults are expected to help parents, and which leads to acute censure for those who fail to uphold the obligation. Unfortunately, most reports on elder care report only such ideology and do not follow Peil, Bamisaiye, and Ekpenyong (1989), who go further and explore the ways elder support is actually distributed.

For the Yoruba, elder men are about three times more likely to be under the care of adult children than are elder women. This follows from the greater likelihood that an elder man will have adult children residing near him or in his household in late life. Fathers are more likely to have children nearby for a number of reasons. First, men are typically older than their wives, so that an infirm father is likely to have unmarried adult children in his household. The children and his wife are thus available for caregiving support until, perhaps, his death. By the time the wife is of comparable age, the children will be older, more likely to be married, and less likely to co-reside or live nearby. Second, the Yoruba are organized in patrilineal clans. Children have an incentive to live near the father, and there appears to be some postmarital patrilocal residence. Finally, Peil, Bamisaiye, and Ekpenyong (1989) point out that among the Yoruba, as in many African populations, marriages tend to dissolve in late life. In these cases, women move away from husbands and the children who have settled near them. The older women leave the husband's household and settle with an adult child, usually a son. They then help to raise their grandchildren and ultimately receive caregiving support from these grandchildren.

Unfortunately, we know little about the factors leading an elderly Yoruba woman to select one adult son over another outside of such residence considerations. More than likely, the elder's relationships to her daughters-in-law are critical, as is the presence of grandchildren, which serves as both a justification for the move and an investment in future caregiving support. In any case, Peil and her colleagues (1989) show that in a sample of 1,004 Yoruba elders, distributed across rural and urban settings, 50 percent of the elder men have children in their households, while 12 percent of the men have grandchildren in their households. For elder women, by contrast, 20 percent have children in their households, while 30 percent have grandchildren in their households. Caregiving for elder Yoruba women, then, follows an alternate generational pattern, so that granddaughters are likely to care for grandmothers. Daughters, on the other hand, are likely to care for fathers. Not brought out by Peil and colleagues (1989) is the lifespan developmental quality of caregiving among Yoruba women, for granddaughters caring for grandmothers ultimately become daughters caring for fathers. A lifespan approach to caregiving and the longitudinal perspective it implies, then, would be extremely valuable for further research among Yoruba elders.

Turning now to the Taiwanese case, Hermalin and colleagues (1990) show that even with high fertility, the availability of caregivers for Taiwanese elderly is not assured. First, as in mainland China, Hong Kong, Japan, and Nepal, sons are the preferred providers of old age support. This pattern, as we have seen, reflects the patrilineal organization of settlements, in which sons would traditionally remain with parents to take control of family lands, while daughters would marry out of such settlements and take up residence with their husband's patrilineal kin as wives and daughters-in-law. Ikels (1990) points out that Chinese aphorisms expressly characterize sons and daughters in terms of old age support: "The conventional wisdom is succinctly expressed in the aphorism 'rearing a son for old age is like storing grain for a famine' and in the pejorative description of daughters as 'goods on which the capital invested is lost.'" Thus, only sons are appropriate sources of old age support.

Second, such sons should be married so that a daughter-in-law is available for any hands-on care required by elders. Thus, the pool of appropriate caregivers shrinks further, and shrinks further still if the preference is for firstborn sons, as in Japan. Hermalin and colleagues (1990) show that even with five children, most elders have fewer than two appropriate caregivers available to assume such duties. Given the decreased fertility of more recent cohorts of Taiwanese, the availability of traditional married son caregivers is seriously imperiled. For if each generation has only two children, then 25 percent of the couples (assuming random mating) will only have daughters. They will simply not have the option of a traditional old age support relationship, a matter of some consequence since levels of satisfaction with old age support are highest in the traditional arrangement (Hermalin, Chang, Lin, et al. 1990). Also, the traditional arrangement for old age support carries with it a particular division of labor, which distributes the burden of caregiving across a number of individuals and relationships: daughters-in-law provide assistance with the tasks of daily living, sons with financial support, and daughters with food, clothing, and other material goods. Decreased fertility is likely to have a major and negative impact on old age support.

Of course, such a negative impact would be mitigated if the norms for appropriate caregiver changed as well. Hermalin and colleagues (1990) point out that those families with two daughters (25 percent of the married couples) would significantly improve their chances of having family-based caregiving support if one of their daughters married a second son in another family, that is, a son whose older brother has already assumed caregiving duties, and if they were willing to receive old age support from a daughter and son-in-law. Again, assuming random mating, among these two-daughter families, 75 percent of the daughters will marry into a family with two sons. Thus, if a daughter in these families married a second son, the 25 percent of married couples lacking caregivers would shrink to 6 percent (i.e., $.25 \times .75 = .19$; $.25 - .19 = .06$). These relationships are shown in a simplified kinship diagram in Figure 6–1.

In the figure, family caregiving units are enclosed in a circle. The outer family units follow the traditional married-son caregiver pattern. The inner family unit represents the alternative pattern, in which daughter and son-in-law assume caregiving duties. So long as one

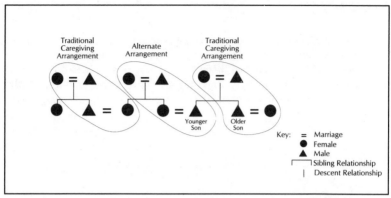

Figure 6–1 Alternate and Traditional Caregiving Arrangements in Taiwan

daughter in this family marries a second, or noncaregiving, son, she is available for caregiving. However, if both daughters marry first sons, the parents are at risk of having no direct old age support. Hermalin and colleagues (1990) speculate that mating patterns may change in accord with such old age support considerations, so that women from daughter-only families will favor second sons who are not responsible for support of their parents. Such a change in mating patterns would clearly show the centrality of old age support needs in domains far afield; indeed, in such a case, old age support needs would lead to an extensive alteration of the Taiwanese system of marriage and family. It will be interesting to see what happens in the Taiwanese case, and by extension, in the other Asian societies that specify married sons as the normative source of old age support.

To conclude, while we have restricted our attention to only one aspect of familial caregiving, that is, caregiver selection, it should be clear that a great variety of allied issues has emerged. Given the worldwide reduction in fertility, the increased life expectancy of elders, and the unavailablity of formal sector support for elders in most of the world, it is likely that family caregiving will become a focal point for more extensive changes in social organization and family relationships. Additional cross-cultural research in this area is truly imperative because so much of elder care is provided by adult children, and because changes in this system are likely to drive further alterations in social organization.

Notes

1. The caregiver selection data reported here are drawn from the Philadelphia Geriatric Center program project, "Family Caregiving and the Dependent Elderly," National Institute of Mental Health, MH–43371 (M. P. Lawton, E. Brody, and R. Pruchno, principal investigators). We thank Miriam Moss for making available the descriptive statistics presented here.

7

The Aged and Intragenerational Relationships

The study of elder intragenerational relationships is well established in social gerontology, and has been quite fruitful in research conducted in the more developed countries. Researchers have taken great interest in the ways older adults make friends, develop social networks, and develop a "we feeling" as members of distinct communities (Keith-Ross 1977) because these relate directly to issues of immediate policy interest, such as housing design, social service delivery, and community mental health programming. In societies outside the developed world, by contrast, researchers have paid far less attention to the intragenerational relationships of older adults. The focus, instead, has been intergenerational, vertical relationships, that is, the position of elders within families and the institutional form given to elder–junior relationships as a principle of social organization or political order (see chapters 5 and 8). The elder–elder horizontal component of daily experience has been slighted, and consequently we know less about cross-cultural variation in this component of old age. Yet further information on such horizontal relationships would clearly be of immediate value for a cross-cultural perspective on lifespan development and the psychology of aging, and ultimately would be useful in policy contexts as well.

The gerontological literature on elder intragenerational relationships is vast, while the cross-cultural ethnographic literature is quite limited. Given this imbalance, the preponderance of research summarized here involves research conducted in the United States. We take up three areas of investigation that have emerged in recent research on elder intragenerational relationships, all of which merit further investigation in cross-cultural research. These include (1) reciprocity and interpersonal exchange among elders; (2) variation in rules and rule-keeping in different interpersonal contexts, and (3) the claim of psychological *disengagement*, or alternatively, active social exclusion, that has been advanced to account for the lower rates of social participation typical of late life.

For the last, we will see that Fredrickson and Carstensen (1990) have advanced a far more satisfying explanation for the reported trend of reduced social participation in late life. Their "selectivity theory" of partner choice in friendship offers an important perspective on the ways old age acts as a psychological constraint on certain types of social behavior. If true, the theory implies a clear limit to cultural variation in the intragenerational relationships of the elderly. It thus offers an important hypothesis for cross-cultural examination.

Reciprocity and Interpersonal Exchange among Elders

Before analyzing the functions of reciprocity in relationships between older adults, it is important to report more general findings regarding cross-cultural variation on the role of reciprocity in interpersonal transactions. We know from Mauss (1967) that the flow of goods has symbolic properties as well as material significance. The way goods are exchanged makes a statement about the form, or value, of a personal relationship. Thus, gifts carry messages of great variety and convey information about the intentions of a giver and receiver and the status of the relationship itself. Take, for example, the role of a gift in conveying insult. Not accepting a gift can convey disrespect to the giver and result in great insult; by contrast, giving too large a gift can assert the giver's superiority and insult a receiver; finally, returning a gift too soon can show formality in a relationship and once again insult to the giver. In each case, the meaning of the gift is quite variable, covering the full range of complexity in interpersonal exchange; yet the material properties of the objects exchanged remain constant.

Gift-giving, then, demonstrates certain properties about relationships. Even with market mechanisms to determine the price of goods, a great deal of social life involves just this use of goods to establish, maintain, qualify, and ultimately sever personal relationships. One reason the exchange of goods has such massive social significance is that the act of giving is bound up with the establishment of personal identity relative to some alter, or partner. Exchanging objects implies recognition of another person as someone distinct but comparable to oneself. Thus, in exchange one is indebted to another. In a tradition that stretches back at least to Rousseau, theorists have recognized that the exchange of goods is not simply an economic fact, but is rather a fundamental social relationship to which economic features can be variably appended. Thus, Levi-Strauss (1969 [1949]) makes the institution of the incest prohibition the origin of society, for it implies the interdependence of human groups and the insufficiency of the individual, who, in his formulation, must give up a daughter to receive a wife.

The psychological correlate of receiving a gift is obligation. Givers are superior to receivers until a debt is cancelled. This idea is expressed clearly in an Inuit aphorism cited by Sahlins (1972): "Gifts make slaves like whips make dogs." It is also evident in the relative superiority of descent groups that have given wives to other groups, as in the asymmetric marital exchange systems typical of Southeast Asia and Indonesia. The recognition of such dominance relationships in the exchange of goods and services is central to the claims of "exchange theory" (Dowd 1975), in which aging is linked to the progressive loss of the ability to meet exchange obligations, so that elders can no longer hold their own in social transactions. The result is marginalization of older adults and a kind of generalized contempt: not respected by others, they also lose respect for themselves because their only resource is "the humble capacity to comply" with the wishes of others (Dowd 1975). However, we have seen in earlier chapters that this conclusion from exchange theory is clearly not applicable to societies in which late-life dependency on adult children, for example, is not a contemptuous state but is rather expected, desired, and modal. Or rather, as the Japanese case shows, we must recognize that what appears to be a disparity in exchange in one society (and which would therefore fail to cancel a debt) may not be so in another. Thus, Japanese daughters-in-law provide extensive instrumental support to their mothers-in-law, but receive in return "only" public affective demonstrations of love and gratitude (see chapter 6). Yet for the Japanese, the exchange is evidently viewed as balanced.

An additional feature of the Maussian paradigm involves the different evaluation of a donor according to variation in the indebting quality of a gift. This accords with our daily experience of the "gift economy" (Cheal 1988; Gregory 1982). Donors who have little and yet give a gift are likely to create a greater obligation in the receiver than donors who have a lot and give the same gift. The first is seen to have made a greater sacrifice, and the indebting quality of the exchange is correspondingly greater, even though the gift in each case is identical. This sort of indebtedness is not necessarily preferable to a receiver, who now faces a great obligation to sacrifice to an equal degree (and this may involve a larger gift to establish parity of sacrifice). But receiving a gift from the resource-rich donor (who has made comparatively little sacrifice and may insist that no return is required) is also unsettling to the gift receiver. The gift is "hollow," the claim that the gift need not be returned an assertion of the giver's superiority.

Consistent with these observations, cross-cultural research has shown that receivers are most attracted to donors when the level of obligation attached to a gift is roughly equal, that is, when donors and receivers show rough parity in resources and when a gift is understood to require a return gift (Gergen, Maslach, Ellsworth, and Seipel 1975). More formally, the relationship between level of obligation and degree of attraction to a donor assumes a curvilinear form: receivers are most attracted to donors when the obligation to return the gift is understood to be equal; a low or high obligation to return the gift (because of lack of parity in resources) is associated with less attraction to the donor. Comparing samples of Swedish, Japanese, and American studies in an experimental study, Gergen and colleagues (1975) found that this relationship was valid across all three cultures, although to a variable degree.

When we turn to older adults and their experience of reciprocity, we find an important qualification of this relationship between gift-giving, obligation, and attitudes toward a donor. Because of health limitations (and often restricted income as well), older adults are at risk for asymmetric exchanges in which they are unable to discharge obligations incurred to donors. They are likely to be "overbenefited," that is, they are likely to have received help or support that they will be unable to repay. Even at relatively high levels of physical function, elders may be unable to shop on their own, for example, or they may require aid in home maintenance. In such cases health limitations prevent them from upholding their end of an exchange relationship. In such circumstances, reciprocity is not possible in all domains, even though equal exchange is the preferred relationship. Elders thus risk being overbenefited in some domains, with the attendant loss of face and power it implies.

The response of older adults to this threat of asymmetry in exchange is still somewhat unclear. Some research has found no special variation on the theme of reciprocity in exchange among older adults. Rook (1987), for example, examined three different types of exchange relationships (companionship, emotional support, and instrumental support) among older adults and found that social exchange imbalances, whether of the underbenefited or overbenefited type, were each associated with poorer mental health. Satisfaction with friendships depended strongly on the presence of reciprocity in social exchange. Yet other research shows that older people prefer *underbenefited* relationships with friends, exchange relationships in which they provide more than they receive. In another sample of American elders, Ingersoll-Dayton and Antonucci (1988) found that elders who anticipate receiving more instrumental support from friends than they expect to provide feel that their social networks are too demanding and report greater negative affect.

Additional insight on the significance of reciprocity in late-life friendships comes from a series of studies conducted by Roberto and Scott (1986a, 1986b). They found that equal exchange was not important in the case of best-friend relationships, but concern for equality played quite an important role in secondary acquaintance relationships. However, in the case of such secondary relationships, elders in this sample preferred the underbenefited condition because it offers a measure of superiority that may counterbalance dependency in other relationships. It may also be a way to invest in future social support, as in a bank where one deposits credits that can be withdrawn at a later date. Antonucci (1985) has used this metaphor to describe intergenerational relationships, but it may apply equally to intragenerational behavior. Wentowski (1981) has explored the ways older adults tactically invest in support relationships both to ensure aid when necessary and to maintain a degree of independence and authority. These elders are skilled in making the overbenefited condition seem *more* equal than it truly is: "When they can no longer reciprocate fully, they send token returns as a way of maintaining the appearance of reciprocity."

Old age may alter friendships, then, in that elders seek the underbenefited position in exchange relationships to counterbalance other transactions in which impairment or poor resources necessarily puts them in the overbenefited position. Is this a cross-cultural universal of late-life experience? We have not been able to identify studies that have explicitly addressed this issue, but there is indirect evidence that this is indeed a universal social response to impairment or disability (see also Scheer and Groce 1986). For example, we have seen in earlier chapters how childless African women invest in unrelated kin and raise them as foster children, assuming the underbenefited position in support transactions so that they will be able to secure support in late life. A study of elder black Caribbean women in Belize (Kerns 1983) similarly shows how strategic use of generosity bolsters personal autonomy among otherwise dependent elders. More research on this issue would be extremely valuable.

Variation in Rules and Rule-keeping in Interpersonal Relationships

Apart from the general significance of reciprocity in friendship and its likely alteration in late life, it is also worth asking whether the "rules" of friendship change during the lifespan, that is, whether the informal conventions that govern friendship formation or dissolution change with age. Cross-cultural research has shown that social relationships are highly rule-bound. This research has also examined variation in the salience of such rules across cultures. For example, in comparing rule endorsement across four cultures, Argyle (1986) found that rules regarding obedience to authority, saving face, group harmony, and restraining emotional expression were more highly endorsed and were also seen as relevant to a greater variety of social relationships in Japan and Hong Kong than in Italy and England. An additional study examined age differences in rule endorsement. Argyle and Henderson (1984) compared college students to older adults aged 60+ on the relevance of forty-three rules of friendship. While they did not find significant differences by age in rule endorsement, they found an intriguing difference in the rules of friendship dissolution. Older adults placed more importance on lack of privacy and importunate requests for personal advice as causes of disaffection in friendships; younger people singled out public criticism as the major rule violation leading to the dissolution of friendships. This difference is consistent with hypothesized age-related changes in affective experience: older adults appear to be less likely to be concerned with public opinion and more interested in privacy (Lawton and Albert 1990).

Unfortunately, we have not been able to identify cross-cultural studies that have explicitly investigated variation among elderly in rule endorsement for different types of social relationships. However, a series of studies have investigated the "interaction styles" of ethnic minorities in the United States. Additionally, research has explored gender differences in friendship experience in late life. Finally, a number of studies have explored the effect of certain housing environments on the social relationships of the aged. While these are not strictly cross-cultural studies, they are worth reviewing because they point to hypotheses that ought to be explored in cross-cultural investigation.

Myerhoff's (1978) study of elder Jews is worth particular comment because it introduces an important qualification about cross-national research on friendship rules described above. The elder Jews of the senior center that Myerhoff investigated have adopted an extremely aggressive and demonstrative approach in interpersonal relationships; they say, "we fight to keep warm." Mitchell (1978) found a similar interaction style in his study of *mishpokhe*, Jewish family circle organizations in New York; and Zborowski and Herzog (1952) report such an interaction style among east European Jews living in the tightly knit *shtetl*, or peasant communities, of Poland and Russia. Myerhoff's research suggests that this interaction style, if anything, may be heightened in old age and in the age-homogeneous setting of the Jewish senior center.

In commenting on an extraordinary public fight in the center (complete with an "evil eye" accusation), Myerhoff points out that these frail elders "experienced their connectio[...] ingly through the expression of ang[...] style in elder relationships serves a [...] to experience autonomy and perh[...] l, Myerhoff stresses the way such negative identification emphasizes how different one is from senior center peers, who app[...] nd lonely. Finally, Myerhoff makes a convincing case for the greater psychological danger of friendly ties as opposed to oppositional ties. "Ties could be eradicated at any moment. Each week and day, people were snatched away. It was safer to quarrel with one's friends, denying the fullness of their mutual needs, yet remaining together, linked by intense emotional ties." Other studies in settings geared to frail elders, such as nursing homes (Shield 1988), have found a similar aggressive interpersonal style, again linked to low investment in friendship relationships.

This last point is highly significant. In research conducted in Continuing Care Retirement Communities (CCRCs), communities in which complete health care services are made available in an age-homogeneous setting, it quickly becomes apparent that close friendship ties are the exception, despite a vast variety of planned activities and clubs. Residents are quick to point out the superficiality of the personal relationships they do have, and they explain this lack of involvement by citing the temporary character of their stay in the CCRC: deaths are a feature of daily life, lifelong ties to other residents are lacking, and the community is "artificial." As one CCRC resident of a Quaker community pointed out, "my real life is not here" (Albert, in review).

The proximity of death, made inescapably real with the loss of close friends and associates, then, may reduce the likelihood that older adults will make *new* friendships in late life. This, then, is an additional hypothesis for an age-related cross-cultural universal in intragenerational relationships. The null hypothesis would be a claim of a lower likelihood of making new friends in late life, relative to younger years, irrespective of culture. How much of this reduction involves psychological processes related to perceptions of social closure with death, and how much reflects a decreased opportunity to meet new people, remains an open question; yet the senior center and CCRC research suggest the former explanation, a point we return to below. In any case, if the perception of social closure related to death leads to such a contraction in interpersonal behavior, it may be worth comparing friendship in old age to friendship in other settings that are temporary, either because of death (such as the friendship patterns of soldiers in combat), or because of other sorts of community instability (such as the temporary communities that emerge to house refugees, the elder populations in skilled nursing institutions and in licensed board and care homes [Eckert 1980], or the semitransient population of the skid-row Single Room Occupancy hotel [see Cohen and Sokolovsky 1989]).

Turning next to gender differences in friendship experience in late life, Albert and Moss (1990) examined consensus about the characteristic features of relationships with friends and relatives in a sample of 220 elders. In the American context, it appears that lifelong gender differences relating to friendships are accentuated in late life (but see Gutmann [1987] for an alternative view). This gender difference is significant because women's generally greater self-disclosure, expressiveness, and intimacy in personal relationships appear to have an adaptive quality in late life (Hess 1979). Older women are more likely than men to have close friends apart from a spouse, and they are accordingly better able to make the transition to widowhood than men. Given these differences in friendship behavior, Albert and Moss (1990) sought to explore how similar men's and women's perceptions of friendship were. They also asked whether deviance from such common perceptions of friendship carried different mental health costs for older men and women.

Using the consensus methodology pioneered by Romney and his colleagues (Romney, Weller, and Batchelder 1986; Romney, Batchelder, and Weller 1987), Albert and Moss (1990) had the older men and women in their sample rank ten attributes of appropriate behavior for four different types of personal relationship: relations with a closest friend and friends in general, and relations with a closest relative and relatives in general. Overall, the older women showed greater levels of agreement about what is important in personal relationships; also, consistent with research on younger adults, the older men placed greater emphasis on "convivial" attributes, while the older women placed greater emphasis on "intimacy" attributes. An important unexpected finding involved the different mental health consequences of deviating from consensus judgments about the characteristic features of personal relationships. Women whose rank orders deviated from the women's consensus judgment were at greater risk for depression, while men whose rank ordering differed in this way were at greater risk for poorer personal mastery. Thus, the different interpersonal cultures of older men and women appear to carry with them different patterns of mental health risk. This is an important finding in need of replication and extension, both with other U.S. samples and in cross-cultural research.

An additional significant factor for elder intragenerational relationships is the suprapersonal environment (Lawton 1990a), most notably the relative age-heterogeneity of a residential environment. Adequate discussion of this topic would have to include a survey of research on elder housing environments, a topic that we cannot take up here. However, for the purposes of cross-cultural investigation, research on the effects of age-homogeneous environments is immediately relevant, especially because age-homogeneous long-term care institutions are now appearing in the developing nations (as in Western Samoa [Rhoads and Holmes 1981]).

In a synthesis of research on age-segregated communities, Silverman (1987b) reports that approximately 6 percent of American elders reside in such communities; an additional 5 percent or so reside in nursing homes or other skilled nursing facilities (National Center for Health Statistics 1989). We find that most research on age-homogeneous communities (which include age-segregated apartment complexes, CCRCs or "life-care" communities, congregate housing, and retirement communities without medical facilities) has found a positive effect in the case of intragenerational relationships. Rosow (1967), for example, has shown a correlation between the number of friends an elder reports and the proportion of elders living in close proximity. Homogeneity in age concentration promotes friendship. Morale of elders also appears to be higher in such age-segregated communities (Lawton 1980). This is especially significant in light of research by Cutrona and Russell (1987) and Rook and Pietromonaco (1987), who argue that larger friendship networks and increased social contact may have a health-protective effect. The increased interaction typical of the age-segregated community may prompt people to function more effectively, either because of an increase in social support or because of the high-quality self-care and reduced risk-taking that follow from close social integration in a community.

Yet it should also be said that an alternative line of research has questioned these claims. Jacobs (1974) has found that elders in an age-segregated community were for the most part "underchallenged"; the age-segregated environment did not demand enough of its residents, which led to boredom and poor morale (see also Lawton [1980]). Also, an alternate line of research has raised questions about the presumed supportiveness of increased interaction. An "upset" in social interaction may carry more weight than positive daily interactions (Fiore, Becker, and Coppel 1983; Pagel, Erdly, and Becker 1987); therefore, increased interaction and a greater number of interaction partners may also mean increased risk for negative interaction. This finding is important for the light it sheds on reports of the small and typically nonsupportive networks of elder Americans. Hirsch (1980) and Coyne and Delongis (1986) have argued that reports pointing to a deficit in elder supportive interactions may actually indicate efforts on the part of elders to *avoid* negative social involvements. The jury, then, is still out on the benefits and costs of the age-segregated environment for intragenerational relationships.

The age-segregated nursing home should probably not be evaluated on the same grounds because elders entering such institutions are for the most part severely impaired. In the nursing home of the Philadelphia Geriatric Center, for example, the mean age of residents is 84, more than half suffer severe cognitive impairment, and high mortality reduces the average stay to about a year and a half. This represents the more extremely impaired segment of the spectrum of nursing home patients. Yet for the more functional resident, friendships are formed, social participation is valued, and daily life is characterized by the struggle to maintain reciprocity in interpersonal exchange. Savishinsky (1991), in particular, has shown how some nursing home residents take pains to remain active, going so far as to serve as helpers to staff or companions to those more impaired than themselves. He has also shown the resourcefulness of more impaired residents in securing privacy or claiming a piece of a public space as their own, despite often extreme institutional pressures that chip away at these elements of personal autonomy. Tactics to achieve these goals include displays of aggression, putting on a false show of disorientation or null behavior, and finding ways to be involved or left alone, as mood and situation allow. The retreat within or dialogue with one's own body should also not be overlooked as a strategy for involvement or control for elders in such a position of extreme dependence. As Savishinsky reports of two residents in a New York nursing home, "Frank . . . could curse his legs and praise his bladder, Stavros swear at his spine but bless his mind." Here we have left the domain of interpersonal relationships proper, but we must also recognize that for the extremely frail nursing home resident, the dialogue with oneself may also be a form of engagement, perhaps subsocial, but engagement nonetheless.

We know very little about elder intragenerational relationships outside the developed countries. Yet the rise of age-segregated institutions in these countries and the increasing concentration of elders in urban areas makes knowledge of such intragenerational relations important. A first step in this direction is research by Moller (1992) on the leisure activities of South African blacks and by Rhoads and Holmes (1981) on daily life in a Samoan nursing home. Moller (1992) shows that leisure outings by South African elderly black women, made possible through senior luncheon clubs and social service agencies, are of great significance as perhaps the first opportunity these women have to leave black townships and mix with people of other races. In South Africa old age may carry certain advantages in overcoming the bonds of apartheid.

Rhoads and Holmes (1981) point out that nursing home life in Samoa differs from that in America. The design, organization, and daily round of life in the Samoan nursing home are quite similar to that of a Samoan village, something that could not be claimed of an American nursing home. Thus, Samoan families drop grandchildren off at the nursing home for an elder to watch, and families on occasion may move in with the elder. The residents of the home are organized into a council similar to the ones that govern villages. In such ways, the difference between nursing home life and village life is reduced to a minimum. The authors feel that this environmental similarity is the only way to account for a "cultural enigma," a full nursing home with an extensive waiting list in a society that prizes its elderly and which places great emphasis on family care for the frail elder.

Of course, the relevance of this model of nursing home care to the American case is not clear. American elders enter nursing homes in a much more impaired state, and the nursing home in America is the epitome of dependence in a society that virtually worships independence (Johnson 1987). The American nursing home could profit from examination of such alternative models of care and organization.

Disengagement, Activity, and Selectivity in Social Participation

In late life, rates of social interaction decline from levels typical of younger years. This finding has been established for American elders in both cross-sectional (Cumming and Henry 1961) and longitudinal (Field and Minkler 1988) research. The latter research also shows that old age is associated with an overall decline in the need for friendship; thus, Field and Minkler (1988) report declines in "the subjective sense of commitment" to such interpersonal exchange and "a lessening of feelings of involvement outside the family." The meaning of this decline in social participation, however, is less clear. A great deal of research has been conducted to determine whether such declines represent a self-initiated retreat from social life, in short, psychological *disengagement*; or whether such declines are the consequence of social exclusion of elders from activity or social life.

Proponents of "disengagement theory" have viewed the declines in social participation as a more general process by which elders divest themselves of connections to the world in preparation for death. Thus, reductions in social participation in this view are one with loss of interest in current affairs, divestiture of belongings, and increased recognition of the inevitablity of death. All are linked by a psychological process consistent with preparation for death. The theory has some plausibility, at least for the very frail, but founders in failing to recognize that elders do maintain *long-term* friendships late in life. It also cannot explain why elders who do report intimate friendships score higher in measures of psychological well-being than elders who lack a confidant, for example.

These faults in the theory have led to a rival "activity theory," which claims that reductions in social participation are imposed on the elderly by health limitations and lack of opportunity. Maddox (1963), responding to Cumming and Henry (1961), argued that reductions in social participation were not self-initiated, but rather resulted from barriers to interaction, which increase with age. These barriers include health problems, which limit mobility and hence interfere with social activity, and the loss of social partners through death. One consequence of this "activity theory" of social withdrawal has been an attempt to increase rates of social activity for elders. Yet, as Fredrickson and Carstensen (1990) point out, increasing social activity through special programming has not had the unequivocal beneficial effect on elder well-being one would expect, given the claims of activity theory.

An important advance in accounting for the decline in social activity typical of late life has been proposed by Carstensen (1987), which she terms *selectivity theory*. Carstensen claims that, with age, people become more selective in choosing social partners. Such increased selectivity serves two important purposes: it allows elders to conserve limited physical energy, so that elders exert themselves only in the most valued activities; and it contributes to the regulation of emotional experience. In the latter case, "because most emotions occur in the context of social relationships, maximizing contact and investment in one's closest relationships and minimizing interaction with less familiar social partners is an adaptive mechanism for affect regulation" (Fredrickson and Carstensen 1992, 335). An important virtue of selectivity theory is its use of a particular socioemotional process, rather than aging alone, to explain the reduced rates of social activity observed in late life. That process is the perception of social closure ("perceived social endings"), which is made more pressing with death, but which can also operate independently of age. Thus, from the perspective of selectivity theory, the reduction in social activity visible in late life, which begins in earlier years and gradually increases, is not evenly distributed across all types of relationships (even the frail elderly prefer to have close friends), and is not simply a function of the availability of partners.

The reduced rate of social participation evident among older adults, then, is not a result of general disengagement from life; nor is it simply a consequence of barriers to social interaction. Rather, the reduction in social activity reflects greater *selectivity* by elders in the choice of social partners. Fredrickson and Carstensen (1990) show that older adults prefer the familiar partner over the novel partner; consequently, they are less likely than younger people to make an effort to meet new partners. Elders choose the familiar partner because contact with this kind of partner is more reliably linked to positive interchange. In this sense, elders are not "affective risk- takers." With a more limited reserve of physical and emotional energy, they choose partners and occasions to conserve such resources. More generally, old age represents a social ending; thus, the 80-year-old understands that developing a long-term relationship with a new partner is unlikely; he or she will accordingly avoid such emotionally risky involvements. If the perception of social endings is the critical factor in the reduction of social participation, we can also expect that younger people, when placed in situations of social closure, will also avoid making new friendships as they come to prefer familiar partners. Finally, because conservation of emotion is a more important determinant of partner choice for elders, elders can be expected to give greater importance to the affective features of friendship.

Fredrickson and Carstensen (1990) explored these issues with a sample of teenagers, middle-aged people, community elderly, and nursing home residents. A striking finding in this research was the far greater salience that the older adults gave to the emotional quality of relationships. In a multidimensional scaling analysis, the "anticipated effect" of a particular social interchange was the major dimension by which elders judged choice of partners. The salience of this dimension increased with age and infirmity, so that it was most central in the nursing home sample. Additionally, the desire to meet new or unfamiliar social partners decreased with age and level of infirmity.

Comparing the healthy elderly who live in their community with the sample of elderly who live in a nursing home reveals that selectivity is more a matter of perceived social endings than age per se. The nursing home sample was far more likely to restrict social activity to partners with whom they were already familiar, which maximizes pleasurable social contact in the short run and appears to be directly linked to the short horizon of life in the nursing home. Moreover, when social endings are anticipated, younger people are likely to behave in the same way. For example, young people who are planning to move and leave familiar circles appear to wish to spend their remaining time with familiar partners rather than with novel partners.

In short, increased selectivity in partner choice, based on a condition of perceived social endings, seems best to account for the reduction in social participation typical of late life. Cross-cultural research is required to assess whether such selectivity operates in the same way in other societies. The Carstensen theory is a plausible candidate for a universal feature of aging, but even here cross-cultural variation may obtain. It would be valuable to know if perceptions of death as a social ending (and hence as a motive for restricting partner choice) are equally salient in societies in which death has a less absolute meaning. Also, we might expect the *strength* of the correlation between age or infirmity and partner selectivity to vary from society to society, even if the general association does obtain. Investigation of these issues would be extremely valuable for cross-cultural research on the intragenerational relationships of the elderly.

8

Succession to Seniority

Every culture has developed processes for transferring control of valued resources such as knowledge, material goods, and property from elders to younger successors (Maxwell 1986). The process may be more or less explicit, the timing of such transfers more or less fixed, and the willingness to relinquish authority more or less forced; but as leaders age and lose the capacity to manage community resources (losing as well their credibility as competent stewards of such resources), they face increased pressure to hand over control of goods or skills they have controlled in their seniority. Thus, an important component of generational succession is *resource control* by elders and the mechanisms by which elders relinquish such control and transfer it to those junior to them in status.

With such transfer of control, elders face a potential loss not just of influence, but also of necessary goods and services that they may no longer be able to obtain on their own. This is because control over important cultural resources makes juniors dependent on elders and thus ensures that juniors will provide elders with the care they require as part of the general deference due to them. As Amoss and Harrell (1981) point out, "through control or access to resources, the old, although physically dependent on others, can make others legally dependent on them." Control over such resources allows otherwise dependent elders a measure of power because they have something juniors do not. By threatening not to transfer control, or by delaying such transfer, or by threatening to transfer control to one adult child rather than another (see the "strategic bequest motive" described in chapter 6), elders can use their rights to land, movable property, title, or ritual knowledge to "compel others to support them or provide them goods and services" (Amoss and Harrell 1981).

However, elders face a delicate balance in the timing of such transfer of control. Clearly, if they relinquish control too early, they face potential neglect and dependency with no power to enforce juniors to provide for them. This is the position of King Lear. On the other hand, as Glascock (1986) points out, "if no resources are transferred to children until after the parents' death, the result is often intergenerational conflict and the lack of support when the aging parents need it most—when they are ill or physically dependent." This is the position of a number of less famous literary figures, such as those in the novels of Balzac and Dickens. Thus, elders must negotiate a delicate balance between giving up control too soon and giving up control too late, and discussions of resource control must inevitably take up issues relating to *resource transfer* as a way of ensuring old age security.

Control over valued resources and the degree of latitude elders have in specifying how and when they will relinquish such control are broad measures of elder authority. So long as elders have such authority, those junior to them have good reason to defer to them. Under such conditions, the status of the elderly will be high. Is there, then, a regular relationship between the degree of elder control of resources, a measure of elder authority, and the status or esteem accorded to the elderly? The claim of such an association lies at the heart of a great deal of cross-cultural research on aging, much of which has been directed toward validation or refutation of the set of hypotheses associated with "modernization theory" (Cowgill and Holmes 1972, Cowgill 1986). If elder authority and status are uniformly high in less modern societies (such as hunter-gatherer bands or nonintensive horticulturalists) and uniformly low in modern industrial societies, then the null hypothesis of no association can be rejected, and one can infer, as did Cowgill, that "modernization" is responsible for the decline in the authority of the aged.

In fact, modernization theory is probably not the best label for the claim of association between resource control and elder status. Virtually *none* of the *cross-cultural* studies addressing this association has examined secular trends in particular societies to see how resource control and elder status change over time. Far more common is cross-sectional comparison of a range of societies at different "levels" of modernization and inferences about longitudinal change based on such cross-sectional differences. Thus, for all the talk of modernization, change, in fact, is conspicuously absent from virtually all the research purporting to support or refute the theory.

This stress on modernization with very little data on actual historical change is puzzling. In fact, Cowgill's choice of the term modernization reflects a general philosophical orientation, summarized in the Weberian "rationalization of the life-world." In this view, societies move from "a relatively rural way of life based on animate power, limited technology, relatively undifferentiated institutions, [and] parochial and traditional outlook and values, toward a predominantly urban way of life based on inanimate sources of power, highly developed scientific technology, highly differentiated institutions ... and a cosmopolitan outlook which emphasizes efficiency and progress" (Cowgill 1974, 127). *Why* societies "modernize" is unclear: for Weber it appears to be a consequence of contingent historical events that give human rationality a chance to transform the world (for good and bad); for Cowgill modernization appears to follow demographic processes, namely the decline of fertility (Cowgill 1986, 175). Thus, Cowgill draws attention to modernization as part of a philosophical commitment. It is the "black box" process that links societies characterized by high status–high authority elders, such as those studied by the traditional field anthropologist (societies relatively peripheral in the world economy), to societies in which the aged have low status and low authority, as appears to be the case for the more developed nations.

If we strip modernization theory of this philosophical bias, we are left with a more humble, but more researchable, hypothesis: greater control over resources predicts higher status for the elderly; lack of such control is associated with poorer status. We might call it "resource theory." And for this hypothesis we find strong support, particularly in the research of Maxwell and Silverman (1970), Silverman and Maxwell (1978), and Silverman (1987). Reducing the claims of modernization in this way is valuable for forcing one to return to the data that are in fact available. It also spares one the ordeal of all at once stretching and restricting the meaning of modernization, as critics and supporters of the theory have done, when even Cowgill admits that the concept of modernization has no clear content or measure.

Thus, for cross-cultural comparison of the relationship between resource control and the status of elders, we are limited to a more restricted hypothesis and cross-sectional comparison. For longitudinal investigation of the ways elder status has changed with changes in control over cultural resources, we are fortunate to have ethnographic studies that have examined the position of elders in traditional societies now facing increased contact with the more developed societies. These, however, are single-culture (and typically single-village) ethnographies that offer little opportunity for valid generalization. Still, they offer insight on the diverse ways in which elders may lose or retain resources, or even gain control of new resources, as these peripheral societies are incorporated into larger economic and social spheres. In this chapter, then, we also take up a particular corrrelate of resource control—elder status—and examine as well a number of case studies that show how social change may alter the association between resource control and status.

Finally, it is natural to conclude a chapter examining elder control over resources with a discussion of *generational equity*, an increasingly common, and unfortunately loaded, phrase in the popular press. *Generational equity* refers to the commonly expressed view that the young and the old should have a roughly equal claim to the wealth of a society. Policies that favor one generation to the exclusion of the other would, in this view, be illegitimate. Concerns about generational equity have become topical recently because taxation policy and income maintenance programs, it has been claimed, favor the old at the expense of the young. In fact, the situation is more complex. We raise the topic here because in many ways it expresses in modern idiom a more widespread tension between elders' control over resources and the desire of juniors to gain such control and assume positions of authority.

The Aged and Resource Control

To what extent are resources concentrated in the hands of the elderly? By dint of long life, the aged clearly have greater opportunity to accumulate resources; they are also likely to receive support in late life through such redistributive mechanisms as Social Security in the United States, or through community and family support in societies lacking formal mechanisms for old age support. Such late-life support appears to follow from a deeply felt sense of filial obligation within families (see chapter 6). In the developed countries, old age security provisions built into taxation systems codify a kind of veneration for the aged by making younger wage earners contribute to the economic well-being of the aged. But this opportunity for accumulation of wealth by elders is offset by loss of current sources of income and influence (e.g., with retirement or transfer of productive resources) and new expenditures (e.g., in assuring health care and obtaining help with tasks beyond the capability of a possibly impaired elder).

In the more developed countries, concentration of resources can be assessed by comparing the household income of different age groups after adjusting for a variety of confounding factors, such as differences in household size, income reporting patterns, and variation in assets. Using data from the Survey of Income and Program Participation (SIPP) for the United States (see chapter 6 for details on this important survey), Crystal and Shea (1990) were able to show that elder households, in the aggregate, do show a modest concentration of resources or wealth when compared with nonelderly households. Elderly household income in this analysis was 124 percent that of nonelderly household income. However, it is important to recognize that this aggregate figure masks considerable variation in the economic well-being of the elderly in the United States. In fact, Crystal and Shea show that economic inequality increases throughout the lifespan and is *greatest* in late life. Income inequality increases substantially after age 40, so that disparities in adjusted income within the 65+ age group are the most glaring for any age group. This inequality is only minimally offset by government programs, such as Social Security and Supplemental Security Income (SSI), because the greatest proportion of income in late life is from pensions and investments that reflect lifetime earnings and employment opportunities. Accordingly, a substantial proportion of U.S. elders are actually quite badly off; and, as one would expect, these poorer elders are likely to be female, widowed, living alone, poorly educated, and nonwhite.

Thus, while not all elderly in the United States enjoy the concentration of resources evident in greater household income, available data suggest that increased concentration of resources does come with age. The same trend is evident in nonindustrial societies, although with important differences in the kinds of resources that are concentrated in the hands of elders. Also, we must immediately point out that the ability of resources to be concentrated in *anyone's* hands varies across ecological conditions. As Foner (1984, 31–32) points out, among hunter-gatherers, "economic resources are largely open and there are generalized rights to exploit a territory, so that the young are relatively independent of older men for acquiring rights in productive resources. And there are few valuable possessions in such societies that anyone, young or old, accumulates or waits to inherit." Sahlins (1972), for example, describes in striking terms the irrelevance of accumulation under hunter-gatherer conditions, where bands are continually on the move (so that possessions must be carried) and rights to ownership, if there are any, are almost impossible to enforce.

We might add that accumulation of resources by elders outside the developed world depends less on control of material goods than on access to *people*, that is, control over other people's labor. Control over resources, such as land, does not always entail control over people. For example, in low-intensive horticultural economies (the shifting, slash-and-burn horticulture of the tropics) where there is a surplus of land, elders are unlikely to exert great control over juniors and are thus partly prevented from concentrating control over resources in late life. In such cases (e.g., among the coastal dwellers of Papua New Guinea) young people "vote with their feet" if a landowning lineage elder is felt to be too overbearing; that is, they simply return to their own clan lands where they are assured a plot simply by asking (Albert 1988). Likewise, pressures on the elderly to disburse resources are likely to be greater in regimes that depend on continued mobilization of juniors as sources of labor. An elder seen as greedy or as one who oversteps traditional rules of competition in accumulating resources is a target for witchcraft (or outright murder; see Oliver 1955), which should be seen as an important leveling device in such regimes (Albert 1988).

Concentration of resources in elders' hands appears to be most marked in the more intensive, sedentary farming economies and among agropastoralists. In these societies, elders control land and livestock; and "the young are thus often beholden to old men for their very livelihood, especially when the resources under men's control are in

scarce supply" (Foner 1984). Control over such productive material resources allows elders to regulate the marriages of those junior to them,
for elder men are the fathers in patrilineal systems, and the uncles in
matrilineal systems, who provide the bridewealth young men require if
they are to wed. In polygynous regimes, access to such wealth also
means that elders can take additional wives and father additional children, all of which enhances the amount of labor elders may control and
the number of clients they are likely to recruit and harness to their am-
bitions as community leaders. Control over material resources and
other people's labor ultimately means freedom to participate in expressive realms such as rituals, which confers further prestige and power.

An excellent example of the ability of elders to concentrate resources in their hands is evident among the Tallensi, an agropastoralist
population of Ghana intensively studied by Fortes in the 1940s. Fortes
(1949) reports that elders could successfully exert control over a son's
labor and the son's independently acquired livestock even after sons
had married and left the father's homestead. First sons, who were
slated to inherit a father's possessions, must have particularly felt this
burden because fathers held control as long as possible. The strain between the two was clear to Fortes's Tallensi informants, who articulated
a wide-ranging theory of intergenerational conflict to explain senior
privilege in allocating resources. Older Tallensi say, "Your oldest son is
your rival," and they report an inborn antagonism between the personal
destiny, or *Yin*, of a father and that of his eldest son: "The son's *Yin*
wants to destroy the father's *Yin*; but the father's *Yin* desires the father
to live and be well and remain master of the house. . . . It will try to
destroy the son's *Yin*, and if it is the stronger *Yin* it will cause misfortune and perhaps death to the son" (Fortes 1949, 227).

The Tallensi case shows how command of resources in an
agropastoralist setting reinforces paternal authority. Glascock (1986)
reports a similar connection between concentration of resources and
paternal authority among East African Somali pastoralists. In research
conducted in the early 1980s, Glascock found that even when sons receive sufficient land and animals from their fathers to become independent household heads, they do not in fact operate as independent
heads of households so long as the father is alive and retains control of
resources that a son stands to inherit. Sons prefer to link operation of
their households to the households of their fathers, deferring manage-

rial decisions to the father. In this way, they show loyalty and respect as good sons, which, it should be stressed, is well recognized by fathers. Such sons are rewarded with better land and animals even in a system prescribing equal birthrights for all sons.

Such domestic concentration of resources by elders and the control over others that it entails leads to a powerful position in the community sphere, for concentration of resources at the household level is the typical route to command of a descent group, and descent group leadership puts a man at the forefront of community leadership and even regional politics. Thus, the "bigmen" of Melanesia build personal followings around their extended households and in this way take on the exchange obligations of a lineage, the mark of lineage leadership. Such bigmen will provide bridewealth not just for close kinsmen (such as sister's sons, nephews, in a matrilineal system), but also for classificatory nephews more distant genealogically (e.g., distant collateral kinsmen who are also reckoned "sister's sons"). These bigmen will assume the obligation to host mortuary ritual for all lineage kin, a typical measure of lineage leadership and a concrete illustration of a senior's ability to mobilize a following behind his efforts, for such ritual involves large displays of food, often massive transfers of wealth, and great efforts to organize entertainment for those who attend the feast. The successful discharge of such responsibilities is crowned finally with an elder's unchallenged claim to control important ritual emblems bound up with clan identity. This concentration of wealth, or more accurately, ability to mobilize and manipulate wealth, is the hallmark of lineage and community leadership; and it emerges from the successful expansion of one's own household to subsume a descent group or even village.

Melanesian bigmen who achieve such authority often leave their stamp on village life in quite noticeable ways. A leader among the Lak of coastal Papua New Guinea was able to populate an entire village with the families of his sons, daughters, and clients. His leadership allowed him to put a conservative stamp on social life in the village that stood in stark contrast to the social change that had transformed surrounding villages. For example, every woman from his village gave birth in the village, without recourse to hospital or aide-post obstetrical support because the elder encouraged such home deliveries. Likewise, this village made little use of the schooling available. No house in this village had a corrugated tin roof because the younger adults of the village did not think they could take this step in advance of the elder, and the elder preferred to apply his resources and command of labor to more traditional efforts.

Such command of resources and the political career it allows are by and large beyond the reach of elder women. Yet the relationship between resource control and age for women is worth noting, for aging generally allows greater latitude for women to exercise control, and elder women may also reap certain benefits from access to the enhanced labor pool associated with an elder man's household. Gutmann (1977) has argued that this greater access to influence in late life follows from a more general psychological feature of aging, in which women become more like men with the onset of menopause, and that this masculinization is recognized by a wide variety of societies. Thus, Gutmann speaks of "a late-life women's liberation," which is the cross-cultural expression of a lifespan developmental process. Some support for Gutmann's claims comes from Melanesia, where elder women are at least partly privy to men's cult secrets, which are rigidly kept from younger women.

Whatever one thinks of such psychological claims (see Rubinstein 1990 for a challenge to Gutmann), it is clear that women do gain influence in late life. Ethnographic reports from a variety of regions support assertions of an expanded role for women in late life. Elder women are able to arbitrate disputes and appear to have some influence in the political arena. However, such reports of political influence for elder women must be separated from reports of elder women who occupy senior positions in royal or priestly lineages (such as the West African Ashanti "Queen Mother"). These women are powerful because of their ascribed political office more than their age. Likewise, the ethnographic literature is scattered with references to older women who are atypical, who arrange their own remarriages or settle a major dispute; but these cases are exceptions. One impressive case of elder women achieving power, however, is visible in the Shahsevan *aq birchek*, a term denoting a postmenopausal woman with significant authority in nomadic bands in Iran (Tapper 1978). Women who rose to this political office played major and powerful roles in community affairs, where such influence was clearly denied to younger women. Still, we must recognize that cross-cultural evidence speaks more to the pervasive asymmetry between genders, which appears to be only slightly attenuated with age.

Male control of most heritable resources places an upper limit on the ability of elder women to achieve positions of community influence. Instead, as Foner (1984) points out, women gain authority in later life less in community affairs than in the domestic arena, and, in particular, in their control over *younger women*. Control in the domestic arena is most clear in the authority older women have over their married sons, and in their ability to draw upon the labor of daughters, daughters-in-law, and grandchildren who may co-reside in an extended household or compound. In Kenya, Gusii elder women are able to exert control in their husband's lineage, to which they are attached, through their adult sons (LeVine 1978). Such an enhanced position in the lineage results in marked alteration of interpersonal behavior, and these Gusii senior women show greater assertiveness and confidence than they did as junior women.

Elder women's control over young women outside the domestic arena is most salient in women's organizations, including age sets, secret societies, and local political organizations, all of which are most common in Africa. Senior women control the initiation of young women into secret societies such as the Sande society among the Mende of Sierra Leone (Little 1960) and the Kpelle of Liberia (Gibbs 1965). Paralleling male elders' control of junior males, older women regulate women's sexual, business (trading), and public behavior in women's village associations (Leith-Ross 1939; Okonjo 1976) and through age sets (Kertzer and Madison 1981), especially in West Africa. For example, Ottenberg (1971) describes how in Afikpo Ibo (Igbo) villages in Nigeria, younger women prepared a major feast for elder women, with a distribution of money, while elder women were able to command the labor of junior women.

The ability of elder men and women to concentrate resources in late life and in this way enforce a measure of control over their juniors has declined to some extent as children become educated, gain independent incomes from wage labor, and begin to center production and consumption activities around a nuclear household rather than an extended family or descent group. This transformation has been discussed earlier in a number of contexts, from demography to inter-generational relationships, especially as it bears on the "wealth flows" theory of Caldwell (1982). In summary, with this reorientation of production and consumption, wealth begins to flow more from parents to children than from children to parents. Nuclear households become the central economic unit, displacing larger kin-based units; and husbands and wives show greater affectual solidarity (and affective investment in their own children) at the expense of clan-based obligations.

One result of this transformation in the flow of wealth is loss of elders' ability to concentrate resources and greater equality across age groups, if not a decline in elder authority. In fact, the challenge to such authority cannot be separated from larger transformations of the cultural order. For example, in a report from American Samoa, the decline in elder authority is only one component in the transformation of an entire social economy, the replacement of the traditional Polynesian redistributive economy, in which commoners gave their economic surplus to chiefs who continually redistributed such wealth, by an entrepreneurial system revolving around wage labor and individual or family consumption.

> It used to be that everybody in the family would work and give their whole paycheck to the chief, and he would distribute the money to the members of the family.... Maybe fifty years ago, if somebody went fishing, he would come back and give all the fish to the chief. And the chief would distribute them. But now, if I want to go fishing, I don't give any [fish] to the chief. If I want to eat them all, I eat them all. (Maxwell 1970, 144)

Clearly, then, changes in the ability of elders to concentrate resources are linked to the more general process of social change, which may affect an indigenous economy in different ways. It is thus difficult to make blanket statements about the effects of social change on elder authority. For example, one is tempted to conclude that the dissolution of the descent group as the unit of production and consumption must adversely affect the status of elders. After all, elders are "apical" figures in such units, founders and leaders all at once, whose influence is carried down the generations and outward through collateral lines headed by their children. In fully developed lineage systems, current apical leaders are merged with ancestral lineage founders; indeed, there is some evidence that lineage leaders are elevated into such ancestral status in very short timespans (Albert 1986). But if social change dissolves such units and leads to their replacement by nuclear households, social change may also carry with it offsetting, compensating changes that in some cases promote the position of elders.

Amoss and Harrell (1981), for example, report increased authority for Coast Salish elders in British Columbia and Washington state. These elders initially suffered a loss of their position in the community when newly introduced technology displaced their expertise in subsistence activities and hence younger people's dependence on them for such knowledge. Introduction of mission-based religion further eroded the authority of elders, who were central figures in traditional religion. Thus, the first wave of contact did in fact break the authority of elders in Coast Salish communities. However, the position of Coast Salish elders as authorities in the community has evidently improved because juniors in the community now recognize the value of ethnic identity, and recognize too that the current generation of elders holds title to that ethnic inheritance, which may be irretrieveably lost if it is not cultivated and respected. Thus, elders find themselves superior to juniors once again, but on different terms.

This reintroduction of elder authority as part of a general revitalization of ethnicity may be a more widespread process, and worth additional study. For it means that one feature of elder authority in less developed nations may survive quite radical changes in economy and society, and may even be enhanced in the face of such change. Such stewardship of ethnic identity, while not a direct control of material resources, is still control of a valuable resource, and this control may be used to ensure material well-being.

It should also be noted that elder authority in aboriginal populations may be enhanced by the presence of government support that links income maintenance payments to the presence of an elder in the household. Native American elders, as has been reported among the Navajo, maintain a measure of authority through control over such disbursements, where government support also appears to bolster extended family units and thus counteracts other pressures that challenge the sources of elders' traditional authority (Kunitz and Levy 1991).

To summarize, inasmuch as increasing integration into the global economy erodes the traditional basis of elder control over resources, elders are likely to suffer a decline in their authority over juniors. To this extent, modernization means a decline in the position of elders, as predicted by modernization theory (see below). However, as the Coast Salish and Navajo cases show, modernization in some cases may favor the position of elders.

The Aged and Resource Transfer

We have already had occasion in prior chapters to describe the significance of the bequest as a strategy by which elders retain control over juniors in late life. As an extreme example, we saw in chapter 6 how Melanesian elders bury shell currency wealth and threaten to take the secret of its location with them when they die to ensure that they are treated properly. In chapter 5 we saw how Nepali elders may construct a ruse about stored wealth to promote a similar end. Goldstein's Nepali informant insisted that elders need such a "money box" in the modern age to ensure proper care (Goldstein, Schuler, and Ross 1983). Finally, we mentioned the "strategic bequest motive," a facet of household economic organization that has been the subject of formal economic analysis (Bernheim, Shleifer, and Summers 1985). The threat of disinheritance is a powerful weapon in the hands of elders who have accumulated resources or who hold title to such resources because of their seniority as lineage leaders or family heads. The strategic manipulation of this threat is perhaps an even more potent weapon, for by dangling such an inheritance in front of rival sons or other potential providers of old age support, the savvy elder may recruit a wide range of support.

The ability of elders to manipulate bequests is obviously limited by norms of inheritance. Too severe a transgression of such norms, as when an elder leaves his wealth to a relative stranger to spite his neglectful kin, is likely to be challenged in court and resolved in favor of the claim of kinsmen. There is a deeply felt sense among Americans that wealth should flow downward and be roughly proportional to degree of consanguinity. For example, kin of similar degree, say, a set of children, should all receive equal portions of an inheritance. The status of a child as a "black sheep" or incompetent steward of wealth may disqualify him from receiving his portion, but on the whole the American system favors equal distribution according to consanguinity.

Other systems of inheritance are obviously quite different. The principle of primogeniture, in which only an eldest son receives the inheritance, challenges the American sense of equality or at least the principle that merit be rewarded. It may also mean less freedom for an elder to make use of the strategic bequest to ensure late-life support. Does the presence of such a stricture on resource transfer significantly work against the power of the aged to maintain their position in late life?

This is a broad question and a proper answer can only be outlined here. Once again we are limited by the absence of data. Two general points should be noted. First, even in primogeniture regimes it is likely that elders exercise more latitude in resource transfer than the norms would lead one to expect. Sons could be disinherited, for example. Second, regimes with strict inheritance stipulations may force fathers and eldest sons into a particular kind of intergenerational relationship. The son who knows he stands to inherit and the father who knows he must transfer control to this son are bound to be rivals, as the Tallensi case makes clear, but they are equally bound to be *partners*. While the ethnographic literature stresses rivalry, partnership is also, and perhaps more, significant (although less dramatic). The inheriting son has good reason to help his father preserve the estate, for he will assume control of it. A long apprenticeship to his father may also be in his own best interest, as he is likely to learn from the father valuable skills and knowledge associated with effective management of the estate. He will also, by necessity, co-reside with the father, both to safeguard the inheritance and to profit from the apprenticeship. Thus, while primogeniture regimes limit the ability of elders to manipulate resource transfer, they also have built-in mechanisms by which elders receive old age support from eldest sons.

A case study worth examining in some detail is Glascock's research on inheritance among Somali agropastoralists (Glascock 1986). Inheritance in southern Somalia does not involve primogeniture, but rather "hard and fast religious and cultural rules" that mandate equal transfer of land and livestock to children. Transfer of resources from fathers to children is staged in a graduated fashion across the lifespan, so that fathers set aside animals upon the birth of a son, which are transferred upon the son's marriage; additionally, animals are transferred when the son becomes a father. Finally, upon the elder's death, his property is divided among surviving children. The rules of inheritance require that fathers make these transfers to all children, including daughters, and in equal measure; a governing village council is supposed to validate the fairness and timeliness of the transfers. However, Glascock found that the rules are systematically broken. Taking the transfer of animals at birth as an example, it appears that in a random sample of over 800 households, only 5 percent of daughters received their portion. The village council, which consists of elders, ratified this exception on the grounds that herd animals given to daughters are likely to be assimilated to the daughter's husband's herd and are thus likely to be lost to the elder's patrilineal descent group. This gender asymmetry is consistent with what we have seen earlier and contributes to the restricted capacity of elder women to concentrate resources in late life.

More remarkable is the way elders bend the rules of inheritance to favor "good sons" over "bad sons." While the rules of inheritance mandate equal portions to all sons, fathers systematically favor good sons by giving them qualitatively superior land that is closer to settlements and easier to clear. Good sons also receive superior livestock that is younger, more fertile, and healthier, even though all sons receive the same number of animals. Once again, the village council validates these transfers in accordance with Koranic law.

Glascock (1986) points out that this distinction between good and bad sons represents an important contract between a father and a particular son, an often explicit agreement by which a father nominates a particular son to be his support in old age and the son accordingly agrees to leave his inheritance in his father's hands essentially until the father's death or incapacitation. Good sons, then, are not just good workers who cause little trouble to fathers; they are also sons who decide to live adjacent to the father even after they marry, who continue to work on the father's plots even when they are free to start their own households, and who allow the father to manage *their* rightful inheritance of land and livestock. In return, they receive the choicest part of the father's estate at some later date. The result is that "the father, through reserving the best land and animals for the sons who have shown a willingness to work with and for him, gains leverage in his quest for a secure old age" (Glascock 1986, 64). Although Glascock hints that this pattern is typical of Somali elders, he does not present data showing how many Somali elders actually practice the strategy. However, an upper limit on the proportion of Somali elders who practice the strategy must be about 80 percent, for Glascock reports that 12 percent of elder males were impaired to the point of being completely dependent on sons, and that an additional 6 percent were either childless or living alone.

The Somali case is valuable for showing how inheritance rules can be manipulated in ways that favor elders even when the rules mandate strict accounting of all resources and equal transfers to all children. The Somali data also point back to the complexities of caregiver nomination described in chapter 6. Children, in this case sons, step forward and defer their inheritance to become parental caregivers for economic as well as other reasons.

Resource Control, Elder Authority, and Modernization

As described earlier, the premises of modernization theory are fairly straightforward. The theory hypothesizes a direct association between resource control and elder status. Accordingly, since "modernization" challenges the ability of elders to control resources, a society's "degree of modernization" will be inversely associated with elder status: thus, low modernization will be associated with higher elder status, and high modernization with lower status.

Testing the hypothesis is another question entirely. Studies attempting to assess the theory have been faulted for their concepts, measures, and sampling procedures. The concept of modernization has been challenged as a coherent predictor because it is not clear to what *modernization* should refer. It would seem to reduce all social change to a single process of "Westernization," which is also impossible to define. Yet we know that change occurs in traditional societies in the absence of contact with more developed nations, and it is likely that such change also affects the position of elders.

Whatever we mean by *modernization*, it is clearly a multidimensional construct whose components have a variable relation to resource control and elder status. It is likely that some of these components affect elder status directly (as in the decline of traditional religion) while other components more than likely affect elder status indirectly through a change in the control elders exert over resources (as in the removal of young adults' labor power from a community with the introduction of wage labor). As mentioned earlier, it is also unclear whether modernization is a process internal to all societies (as implied by the philosophical tradition invoked by Cowgill, who first suggested the theory) or simply a theory of the effect of culture contact on traditional societies. The comparisons used to support the theory compare nations high in modernization with traditional societies (or aboriginal societies within modernized nations), implying both a linear scale of modernization linking all societies and modernization effected through culture contact.

An additional problem with the concept of modernization concerns inferences about individual attitudes and experience that are drawn from a set of society-wide indicators. The "modernization" of a society and the "modernity" of individuals in that society need not coincide perfectly and probably do not. Assuming a perfect correspondence is too simple and leads to an ecological fallacy. Thus, highly modernized societies may still contain a large proportion of individuals who retain traditional attitudes about the authority of elders. In fact, research has shown that modernization and individual modernity do not predict elder status in the same way. Using an individual's occupational status as an index of exposure to "modernity," Bengston and colleagues found that cultivators, urban nonindustrial workers, and urban factory workers across six societies, which varied in degree of modernization, *all* held roughly the same level of favorable attitudes toward aging and the value of the aged (Bengston, Dowd, Smith, and Inkeles 1975). Yet using the same attitudinal measures, the degree of society-wide modernization was significantly associated with lower status of elders: the position of the aged was rated more favorable in the less modernized societies (Bangladesh, India, Nigeria) than in the more modernized societies (Argentina, Chile, Israel). Cowgill and his colleagues also found the same disjunction between modernization and modernity when they noted that Ireland, Israel, and the Soviet Union, all societies considered high in modernization, accorded a higher status to the elderly than they would have predicted (Cowgill and Holmes 1972). They concluded that "historical peculiarities," such as maintenance of traditional values and the persistence of traditional family structure, were offsetting processes that operate in the context of modernization. That is, ethnic identification is a source of subcultural variation and cultural conservatism even in postindustrial societies.

Given this lack of clarity in basic concepts, it is difficult to know what indicators to choose when assessing a society's degree of modernization. Palmore and Manton (1974) did perhaps as well as one can by using increased economic productivity, occupational shifts away from agriculture, and increased educational levels as indicators of modernization. Increased economic productivity can be assessed in terms of gross national product (GNP) per capita and points to the increased capacity of young and middle-aged adults to surpass the aged in accumulating wealth. Occupational shifts away from agriculture can be assessed by the annual percentage change in the proportion of the labor pool engaged in agriculture. The shift away from agricultural production is likely to indicate a lesser significance for control over land, a major source of elder authority. It also indicates migration away from the countryside to cities, removing young people from the command of elders. Finally, increased education, as indicated by the percentage of the population that is literate, points to decline in oral traditions and a reduction in the value of elders as sources of community knowledge. These indicators do not cover all the facets of modernization outlined by Cowgill (e.g., individualism), but they do more tightly define the content of some of the central features of the process.

The sampling problems in research on modernization are also significant. Silverman (1987) points out that the sample of fourteen "societies" used by Cowgill and Holmes (1972) in their study of modernization in fact represents a variety of social units: the "preliterate societies" (i.e., Sidamo, Igbo, Bantu) are actually tribal groups within African nation-states that have by and large accepted the task of becoming modern; the "transitional societies" are represented by aboriginal Indian communities in Mexico (Zapotec) and the United States (Pima) but also by nation-states (Samoa, Thailand); and the "modern societies" range from highly agrarian Ireland to such industrial giants as the United States. "These very different examples of societies," Silverman (1987a) points out, "exist contemporaneously but are arranged on a scale so that the preliterate are equated with the preindustrial versions of the modern societies."

It is important to note that with all the faults of the theory, from basic concepts to measurement issues to sampling, virtually every cross-cultural study of the position of the elderly has confirmed Cowgill's overall prediction. Qualifications on the claim and refinements in measures and sampling have of course emerged as well, but the fundamental association between resource control and elder status appears well established, along with the effect of modernization in altering elder control over such resources. Thus, whatever the criticism of Cowgill's theory, it is nonetheless an impressive contribution to cross-cultural research on aging. Major revisions in the theory, however, have helped clarify what it is about modernization that affects elder status and have also situated the theory within a more general and more adequate theoretical framework.

What, then, is it about the set of changes associated with modernization that most radically threatens the traditional authority of the aged? Insight on this question comes from Palmore and Manton's analysis (1974). They looked separately at the effect of a number of different indicators of modernization to see how each affected the relative socioeconomic position of the elderly across thirty-one different societies, which, however, only represented societies limited to modern nation-states that varied according to their primarily agrarian or industrial orientation. The indicators of modernization, as described above, included GNP per capita, percentage change in the proportion of the labor force engaged in agriculture, and three measures of educational attainment (adult literacy rate, percentage of school-age youths attending school, and percentage of population in higher education). Relative socioeconomic position of the elderly was assessed according to the degree to which the aged (those aged 65+) and those likely to displace them in status (those aged 25–64) equally participated in employment opportunities and education, as assessed in a set of "equality indices." Palmore and Manton then regressed the equality indices on the indicators of modernization to test whether modernization was indeed associated with lower elder status across the thirty-one societies.

Given this operationalization, if the Cowgill theory of modernization were accurate, the regression line in each case should have a negative slope, representing the inverse relationship between elder status (degree of equality between the age groups) and modernization. In fact, Palmore and Manton (1974) found something else entirely. Introduction of a quadratic term in the regression equations improved their predictive power. Thus, rather than a linear (left-to-right) negative slope, many of the regression lines showed a curvilinear shape, or a j-shaped curve, in which high elder status was associated with societies both very low *and* very high on the modernization indices. Figure 8–1, taken from Palmore and Manton's (1974) research, illustrates this relationship for the case of equality of employment for young and old as predicted by GNP per capita.

The least modernized societies (i.e., those with lowest GNP per capita: Iraq, Iran, El Salvador, and the Philippines) show the greatest degree of equality in employment between young and old. Societies that show somewhat higher modernization according to the GNP measure (e.g., Norway, the Netherlands, and Puerto Rico) show the expected decline in equality between old and young, and thus poorer socioeconomic status for elders. Yet societies highest in this measure of modernization (e.g., Canada and the United States) show an upturn in equality between elders and juniors on employment. Thus, modernization theory's assertion of an inverse relationship between economic complexity and elder status may apply only to societies within a certain range of modernization. Societies at the upper end of development evidently experience an improvement in elder status.

Other indicators of modernization, however, do support Cowgill's prediction. Figure 8–2, again taken from Palmore and Manton (1974), shows the expected negatively sloped line for the regression of equality of employment on percentage of the population engaged in agriculture. Here societies with the greatest percentage of labor in agriculture have elders with the highest socioeconomic status, as indexed by equality of employment (i.e., whether they are economically active or not). Such societies include Iraq, Iran, the Philippines, Ghana, Honduras, and El Salvador. Societies with the lowest percentage of the labor force in agriculture show the least equality of employment between young and old. Such societies include Sweden, Canada, the United States, New Zealand, and the Netherlands. In the latter societies, people aged 65+ have retired and left the work force, a hallmark of societies whose work force has by and large abandoned agriculture.

Thus, some facets of modernization have the predicted effect on elder status, while others bear a more complicated relationship to such status. Inclusion of societies with the greatest amount of moderniza-

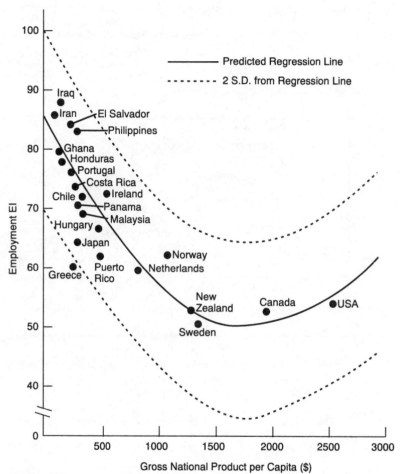

Figure 8–1 Gross National Product per Capita and Employment Equality Index ($r^2 = .79$)

Reprinted with permission, from E. B. Palmore and K. Manton, "Modernization and Status of the Aged: International Correlations," *Journal of Gerontology,* Vol. 29, p. 209, Fig. 1, 1974. Copyright © The Gerontological Society of America.

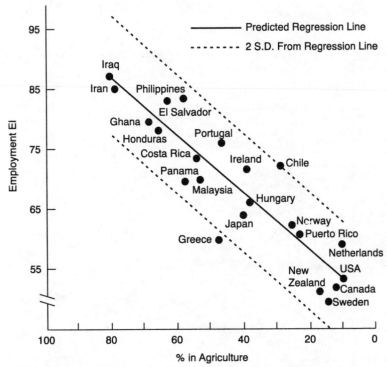

Figure 8–2 Percentage in Agriculture and Employment Equality Index
($r^2 = .83$)

Reprinted, with permission, from E. B. Palmore and K. Manton, "Modernization and
Status of the Aged: International Correlations," *Journal of Gerontology*, Vol. 29, p. 209,
Fig. 4, 1974. Copyright © The Gerontological Society of America.

tion, the so-called postindustrial societies, shows that the position of
the elderly may actually begin to improve at the highest levels of modernization. Cowgill and Holmes (1972), on the other hand, had restricted their inquiry to societies at the low and middle end of modernization and thus would not have been able to detect the curvilinear
trend in elder status.

In fact, the Cowgill sample was also artificially truncated at the lower
end of modernization because the sample excludes hunter-gatherer

populations and societies practicing nonintensive horticulture, as pointed out by Fry (1985). Once such societies are included in an analysis of the effects of modernization, the Cowgill theory must again be modified. Lee and Kezis (1980–81) have shown that modernization is associated with an *increase* in the status of elders if we restrict the range of such societies to those lowest in modernization. That is, among hunter-gatherers, seminomadic groups, and nonintensive horticulturalists, all societies low on indicators of modernization, elder status is rather low. Among the more "modernized" societies at this low end of modernization, such as populations practicing sedentary intensive agriculture, elder status is high. Thus, in the Lee and Kezis study, increasing literacy (a sign of modernization) was associated with an increase in elder status. Taking modernization across the widest range of human societies, then, it would appear that elder status is not unimodal, as Cowgill hypothesized, but rather bimodal (Silverman 1987a); that is, higher in sedentary agricultural populations and in postindustrial societies, and lower in the least modernized societies and also in societies still early in the process of modernization.

To summarize, the different components of modernization affect the position of the aged in variable and perhaps offsetting ways. A shift away from agriculture makes elders less economically active and reduces their control of resources, leading to loss of status; the aged in such cases no longer contribute to production and their claim to centrality and to support in infirmity may be challenged on this ground. Yet increases in education and economic productivity, other features of modernization, improve the status of the aged, which is visible when we compare hunter-gatherer populations with sedentary agricultural populations, or newly industrialized nations with postindustrial nations. What should we make of these qualifications to the theory? The lack of an adequate theoretical framework for examining modernization rears its head again, for it was never really clear in Cowgill's original formulations what the central components of modernization or elder status were.

A series of cross-cultural investigations by Maxwell and Silverman have taken up this concern and led to a more adequate appraisal of the modernization question. An important early paper (Maxwell and Silverman 1970) independently approached the modernization problem by stressing the connection between aging, possession of "utile" cultural knowledge or information, levels of social participation, and elder status. They begin their analysis by examining the relationship between age and cultural expertise. The two should be positively associated, so that those who live longest should have the greatest command over cultural knowledge. If such knowledge is useful, the aged would thus be brought into social spheres and accordingly be rewarded with high status. The cultural expertise at issue would include, for example, ritual knowledge, technical knowledge in tool-making, knowledge of land boundaries, skill in arbitrating disputes, knowledge of the best sites for hunting, and so forth. Since the commodity at issue is knowledge, one might also imagine that even with physical decline, elders would still be valuable to a community and accordingly receive high respect.

Maxwell and Silverman (1970) then go on to introduce two offsetting processes that are likely to alter this relationship between aging, useful knowledge, and esteem. First, in societies with a precarious subsistence base, informational prowess is unlikely to compensate for lack of physical vitality in old age. The demands of daily subsistence are too great; accordingly, the functionally impaired elder is likely to be devalued despite impressive cultural expertise. In societies in which some measure of subsistence security has been achieved, on the other hand, the increased command of useful knowledge that accompanies aging is likely to compensate for loss of physical vitality.

Second, in societies undergoing rapid social change, what is recognized as useful knowledge is likely to change quite rapidly. For example, new technologies and activities, dissolution of land tenure systems, and disaffection from traditional religion as a result of missionary activity all render portions of the cultural information pool "inutile": such information is no longer useful or relevant. The cultural expertise that comes with aging, then, is less valuable to a society, and so elders are also less valuable to a society. The result is decreased participation in social life and lower esteem. In societies insulated from such change, on the other hand, cultural knowledge remains "utile" for longer periods (or becomes "inutile" at a slower rate); accordingly, the process of aging allows for greater accumulation of useful knowledge, with greater social participation and esteem for the aged as a consequence.

This approach to the sources of elder status is valuable for a number of reasons. It accounts for the low status of the aged in societies least affected by modernization: in these subsistence-poor societies, cultural expertise cannot compensate for loss of physical vitality. The approach also explains why modernization is likely to result in lower status for elders in societies moving from agricultural subsistence to industrialization: the social changes bound up with modernization increase the rate at which a society's information pool becomes inutile.Accordingly, the knowledge that elders accumulate across the lifespan in such conditions is likely to be obsolete and less valuable to a society. In this way, elders are displaced from social life and devalued in status.

The stress on the utility of cultural knowledge and the conditions under which such information is likely to be more or less valued goes a long way toward putting the modernization debate on an adequate theoretical footing. That is, *modernization breaks the relationship between aging and the accumulation of cultural expertise.* However, two questions remain. First, does information utility bear the expected relation to elder status? And, second, is information, or cultural expertise, truly the most important resource for predicting elder status? How important are the other resources mentioned earlier in this chapter, such as control over material resources?

Maxwell and Silverman (1970) assessed the first question using a holocultural approach, that is, they drew on the Human Relations Area Files (HRAF), a collection of ethnographic materials on 186 societies, and selected thirty societies that had complete codes for informational control and elder status. At the same time, they examined the ecological conditions of these societies and their rates of social change. The thirty societies were selected so that no two cases shared the same sampling province (Murdock and White 1969). Thus, each society could be considered an independent case, an important consideration given the potential autocorrelation between measures for societies that are geographically proximate and likely to have influenced one another. One virtue of this sample is that it was not restricted to any particular range of societies with respect to modernization, a fault inherent in many of the studies described above; also, it included societies from all the major ethnographic regions of the world. Informational control was coded along six dimensions: participating in community events, consulting, making decisions, entertaining, arbitrating, and teaching. Status of the aged was defined according to the presence or absence of twenty-four items marking deference or alternatively contempt and exclusion. A status score was derived by subtracting the number of negative items from positive items and dividing by the total number of items for which there was information.

The results from this analysis are interesting in two regards. First, the six information control types formed a unidimensional scale of what might be called the informational centrality of the elderly. That is, the six items formed a satisfactory Guttman scale, so that societies in which elders had a teaching role were also likely to have elders involved in each of the other information domains. Table 8.1, taken from Maxwell and Silverman (1970), shows the scalogram with respect to the information domains.

It is clear that elder informational control is organized hierarchically. The presence of control in the information domains (marked by a "1" in the table) clusters to the left of the diagonal, showing that informational control by elders across the domains is not random but is rather gained or lost in gradations. Knowing that elders teach (1) or arbitrate (2) in a society allows one to predict with high confidence that elders will also entertain (3), help make decisions (4), consult (5), and participate (6). Participation, the lowest level of information control, is common across virtually all the societies.

Given the hypothesis of association between control of information and high status, one would expect that societies in the upper portion of Table 8.1 would accord the elders highest status. In fact, this is what the authors found. The correlation (*gamma*) between information control and elder status was .69, a highly significant finding, "thus giving relatively strong support for the hypothesis that the control of informational processes among the aged will predict the degree of esteem they enjoy within a particular society" (Maxwell and Silverman 1970, 387). The authors also point out that nomadic populations predominate in the lower portion of the table, while sedentary agricultural populations predominate in the upper portion.

A later study carried the investigation further by examining the centrality of informational control relative to other kinds of access to resources (Silverman and Maxwell 1983). Using a sample of ninety-five societies drawn from the HRAF, the authors tested the relationship between four types of elder control over resources and an expanded "deference index" as an indicator of elder status. Control over information was compared to control over material resources (land, wealth), control over social resources (rights to adoption of children or choice of

Table 8.1 Scalogram of Informational Control Among the Aged

		1	2	3	4	5	6
I.	Bali	1	1	1	1	1	1
	Bushman	1	1	1	1	1	1
	Monguor	1	1	1	1	1	1
	Ainu	1	1	1	1	1	1
	China	1	1	1	A	1	1
	Rural Irish	1	1	1	1	A	1
	Navaho	1	1	A	1	A	1
II.	Korea	1	1	1	1	1	0
	Tiv	1	1	1	1	1	0
	Kikuyu	1	1	1	A	1	0
III.	Chukchee	1	1	1	1	0	0
	Gond	1	1	A	1	0	0
	Mandan	1	1	A	1	0	0
	Ifugao	1	1	A	1	0	0
IV.	Tallensi	1	1	1	0	0	0
	Serbs	1	1	1	0	0	0
	Lapps	1	1	1	0	0	0
	Ojibwa	1	1	1	0	0	0
	Micmac	1	1	1	0	0	0
	Inca	1	1	1	0	0	B
V.	Gilyak	1	1	0	0	0	0
	Siriono	A	1	0	0	0	0
VI.	Rewala	1	0	0	0	0	0
	Nahane (Kaska)	1	0	0	0	0	0
	Western Tibet	1	0	0	0	B	0
	Aleut	1	0	0	0	0	B

Total N = 26; Coefficient of Scalability = .74

From R. G.. Maxwell and P. Silverman, Information and esteem: Cultural considerations. *Internationational Journal of Aging & Human Development* VI (4):383. Used by permission.

spouse), and control over supernatural resources (special powers with respect to curing, divination, and witchcraft) as predictors of elder status. Using multivariate analyses, the authors were able to show that informational control retained its association with elder status, even after partialing out the effects of the other resource control measures. That is, the relationship between informational control and elder status is independent of the other types of resource control. In fact, control over information is a better predictor of elder status than any of the other resource control measures. Silverman (1987a) points out that within the information control measure three components appear to be most significant: a role for elders as decision makers in group efforts; a consultative role in which elders serve as sources of information requested by others; and a "reinforcement" role in which elders are expected to compliment or admonish people according to their behavior.

Returning to the question of modernization, we are now in a position to specify more precisely when social conditions will promote higher status for elders. Because control of information is the central determinant of elder status, modernization processes will affect elder status most negatively when they democratize information, when the flow of information is opened up to the point that expertise is no longer linked to age, but rather depends on a wide variety of occupational statuses and formal training. This is not just another way of saying that elder knowledge becomes "inutile," as first suggested by Maxwell and Silverman (1970). Rather, modernization carries with it a more extensive alteration of the information economy in societies.

Silverman (1987a) reports on one test of the association between such a general level of information flow and elder status. Using "social rigidity" as a proxy for the kind of restricted information flow that might predict high elder status, the authors again consulted the HRAF for indicators of such rigidity. Four items appeared to index social rigidity: endogamy (restrictions on the flow of spouses between communities), the presence of formal associations that do not cut across communities, the presence of gender-based groups or activities, and restrictions on the movement or behavior of women. Silverman (1987a) reports that social rigidity defined in this way does predict informational centrality for elders and high status. Since such social rigidity may persist even in the face of modernization, it may be an additional variable attenuating the effect of modernization on elder status.

In short, if modernization affects the position of elders, it would appear that it does so through a radical alteration of the organization of information in society, removing the accumulation of valued information from the aging process, and hence eliminating a valued role for elders in social life. To the extent that the different components of modernization do not break the link between information control and age, modernization will not radically demote the elderly as sources of authority in society. A shift away from agriculture evidently does decrease the value of information controlled by elders and does result in a decline of status for them. On the other hand, a rising GNP evidently is associated with informational centrality for elders, because their status begins to improve again in the final phases of modernization. Between modernization and changes in elder status stands a variety of countervailing factors, such as the degree of social rigidity and persistence of ethnic traditions, each of which may maintain the link between access to valued information and age.

Generational Equity in Cross-Cultural Perspective

We have seen that the inequality between young and old in less developed societies is based on differential control over resources, and, in particular, on manipulation of the mechanisms by which elders transfer rights to such resources. The latter is critical to the ability of elders to maintain a position of authority when impairment begins to make them dependent on the young. Modernization tips this inequality in favor of the young, altering at the same time the relationship between the accumulation of cultural expertise and aging. Possession of such cultural expertise appears to be the best predictor of elder status and confers high status on elders even when they no longer command other types of resources.

Foner (1984) concludes that intergenerational conflict based on such generational inequity is modal, a cross-cultural universal that is "a systematic product of the way rewards and roles are allocated in each society." Yet throughout her treatment of "the inequality between young and old," Foner hints at the many domains in which seniors and juniors share a common interest. For example, juniors benefit from their apprenticeship to seniors to the point that many defer to seniors even when they need not. Provision of support for the aged is also modal even when elders no longer have power over juniors. This would not be likely if elders were simply lifelong oppressors of their adult children. While there are clearly societies in which elders exploit their juniors, such as the East African age-set systems in which elders monopolize younger women as wives, these represent exceptional cases of intergenerational competition. The more usual case, one suspects, is competition within the framework of general cooperation, with recognition by both seniors and juniors of the common stake they share in the welfare of a household or descent group.

The same can be said of the "generational equity" debate that has emerged in recent years in the more developed nations. In analyzing income data for the United States, Preston (1984) stressed the "inequity" between generations when he argued that the economic well-being of the elderly has improved in the past decades, while that of children has deteriorated. He pointed out that government expenditures on the elderly had increased during this period, while such expenditures for children had declined. The implication was that an elderly political lobby had unduly skewed public expenditures in favor of the aged and that "greedy geezers" were living well at the expense of poor children. Preston's analysis unleashed a storm of criticism, not the least being a book-length response stressing "The Interdependence of Generations" (Kingson, Hirshorn, and Cornman 1986).

Here, too, an initial bias regarding rivalry or interdependence will influence how one views such issues. As Kingson and colleagues point out, many elderly are in fact quite poor, and the economic well-being of the elderly need not come at the expense of children (after all, the government could spend more on both groups and less on something else). In any case, we have seen in this chapter that government transfers play only a minor role in the income mix of the elderly. We know from chapter 6 also that wealth flows between the generations, with many elders supporting family members junior to them.

More critically, Kingson and his colleagues point out that a perspective stressing "inequity" and conflict ignores a necessary lifespan developmental perspective in thinking about intergenerational transfers. It freezes the position of children and elders at opposite ends of the lifespan, forgetting that children become elders, that elders were once children, and that income transfers between the two are a constant across the lifespan. In fact, at any given moment there are usually three generations in such mutual dependence and support. Parents invest heavily in children, while in the later part of the lifespan, parents receive transfers from children, who are now themselves adults investing in their own children. We have seen in earlier chapters how the flow of intergenerational transfers demonstrates continuity far more than conflict.

Are elders, then, "too powerful" and "receiving too much," as the generational equity argument asserts? Our survey of the status of the elderly across cultures shows that the question cannot be stated so baldly. The diversity of the elderly population and the interdependence of generations make such a simple opposition between young and old inaccurate. The severely impaired elder is probably receiving too little, and a great many elders are helping support adult children who are unable to provide for their own children. Our survey shows that the "generational equity" argument has its basis in one component of intergenerational relationships: the competition over access to resources associated with succession. But our survey has also shown another side to intergenerational relationships: a mutual investment of resources between successive generations. The former is set within the latter, which constrains how far such competition may go. We may conclude, then, with Kingson (1986), that using "generational equity" as a basis for policy is shortsighted.

Part III

Health Decline and Death

We have spoken often of senescence in this book, the process by which bodily systems are inevitably compromised with increasing age. Organ systems lose their reserve capacity, so that diseases gain an increasingly lethal character. Likewise, performance is impaired. Physical function is restricted, and cognitive processing is slowed in a number of domains. The progression of senescent processes can be roughly expressed in terms of "biologic age," and a variety of biomarkers, reviewed in chapter 1, can be used to estimate the extent of such senescence.

A consequence of senescence is the strong association of age and mortality, even when we eliminate mortality related to trauma and acute disease. It is possible to die of old age, and the last years of life are typically marked by impairments related to the presence of chronic diseases. These impairments represent one dimension of disease *morbidity* in late life, and it appears that such chronic disease morbidity may be an inescapable feature of old age; thus, in the developed societies, increasing life expectancy has so far also meant an increase in the time spent in such a disabled state, rather than an extension of "active life expectancy" (Olshansky, Carnes, and Cassel 1990). We have also seen that at least part of the morbidity or "frailty" typical of late life appears to be distinct from identifiable disease conditions and independently predicts mortality (Ford, Folmar, Salmon, et al. 1988).

Late life, then, means increased risk of impairment in function and cognition, and increased likelihood of death. The universality of this feature of aging bears repeating, however, because it is often slighted in cross-cultural research. A look at some of the standard collections of ethnographic studies of the aged (Fry 1981; Fry and Keith 1986; Amoss and Harrell 1981; Sokolovsky 1990) shows that health decline and death do not figure prominently. Even in ethnographies of nursing homes, places where death is inescapably present, treatment of death appears to be muted (see chapter 10). The emphasis, instead, is on the resources of the elderly, the ways elders manage to retain a purchase on social life despite impairment and dependency. This is natural because the focus of most ethnographic research is to demonstrate the extent of cultural variation in the presence of a common biologic inheritance. And the ethnographic record does indeed show great variation in responses to impairment and death, both by elders and by their kinsmen. In some societies, dependency linked to impairment is reviled; younger people go so far as to say that death is preferable to certain chronic conditions (Sackett and Torrance 1978). In other societies, impairment is accepted, perhaps grudgingly, but accepted nonetheless. In one society, impairment quickly marginalizes an elder; in another, efforts are made to bring an elder into social life despite fairly great impairment. In one society, severe impairment is literally a death warrant, as close kinsmen kill a person who is now seen as an unacceptable burden. In another society, such death-hastening is unthinkable, or at least must be conducted surreptitiously and can only be partially acknowledged.

Another source of the relative neglect of an immediate focus on health decline and death may be our own discomfort in raising the topic. We would rather talk about successful adaptation to health decline. Related to this discomfort is the sheer difficulty of inquiring about death, one's own anticipated death or the death of a parent. Each, understandably, is a source of great emotion.

Yet the more direct focus on health decline and death is appropriate and has been adopted here for the final two chapters of this volume. We stress health decline in chapter 9 and death in chapter 10. The direct focus on impairment is useful because it forces us to raise questions about the transcultural definition of functional or cognitive impairment. We will see that even quite basic measures of locomotion or neurologic function may be affected by cross-cultural variation. For example, assessment of impairment is difficult across cultures because functional capacity is indexed by the ability to perform certain roles, yet performance of these roles varies across cultures. Similarly, overall prevalence estimates of *severe* dementia are roughly similar across cultures (Yu, Liu, Levy, et al. 1989; Weissman, Myers, Tischler, et al. 1985; Blay, De Jesus Mari, Ramos, et al. 1991; Park, Park, and Ko 1991); yet cross-cultural variation in the prevalence of less severe forms of dementia is quite marked, suggesting variation in the sensitivity of measures across cultures and sociocultural bias (Gurland, Wilder, Cross, et al. 1992). Such bias is most significant in the still unclear relationship between literacy and performance on neuropsychologic testing. Thus, even when prevalence rates are similar across cultures, we find that elder women are over-represented among dementia cases in China, which presumably reflects their restricted access to schooling (Yu, Liu, Levy, et al. 1989).

The direct focus on impairment is also useful for making clear variation in the degree to which elder participation in social life is compulsory or voluntary. Elders in the more developed societies have the option to select the types of social activity to which they wish to apply their potentially limited physical resources. Elders in village-based societies are less likely to have this option; as Draper and Harpending (1990) put it, here elders are "compulsorily active."

Finally, in chapter 10 we turn to death-hastening behavior, one area in which cross-cultural investigation is well-established (see the recent reviews by Maxwell and Silverman [1989] and Glascock [1990]). Yet cross-cultural investigation has slighted what would seem to be the more important source of variation in treatment of death, that is, the dying process and last year of life for the severely decrepit elder. The daily life of the dying elder is unlikely to attract the attention given to gerontocide, yet it is perhaps the better marker of cross-cultural variation in the condition of the most severely impaired elder.

9

Aging, Health, and Dependency

In this chapter, we return to issues first raised in the earliest chapters of this volume. In chapters 1 and 2 we asked whether aging has a different demographic profile across societies varying in scale and technological capacity. The central question raised there was whether people die at the same ages, and in the same proportions relative to age, in different societies. We saw that differences in life expectancy affect the timing of such vital events as marriage and the transition to parenthood or grandparenthood, giving a different significance to each year of life. More generally, we noted a trend toward increasing control over "accidental mortality" in developed countries, defined as a broad-based reduction in deaths across the lifespan as a whole, which is visible in the increased "rectangularization" of survival curves.

In our early treatment of these issues, we restricted ourselves to mortality as an indicator of population differences. We even went so far as to examine aging in terms of mortality, that is, as the rate in which people are removed from a population, since age in all societies remains the best predictor of mortality. However, it is clear that a focus on mortality is only half the story. The result of greater control over mortality in human populations is not simply longer life and older populations (evident in population aging), but also increased expression of senescent processes, especially functional decline. If the earlier chapters focused on mortality, here we must take up age-related *morbidity*, the disease conditions and functional limitation that are bound up with late life, and which play so important a role in an elder's sense of well-being and ability to participate in social life.

Morbidity is far more difficult to examine. Mortality, for the most part, is obvious and dichotomous. One is dead or alive, and one's status as a person and position in a community clearly changes with death. Morbidity, on the other hand, represents a continuum of health impact and accordingly involves gradations in one's ability to participate in social life. It is also difficult to measure because it bears a variable relation to disease states. For example, we saw in earlier chapters that *frailty*, a generalized morbid state linked to functional limitation and perhaps nutritional insufficiency (Braun, Wykle, and Cowling 1988), appears to be partly distinct from disease states and is an independent predictor of mortality. Finally, morbidity is subject to social influence. For example, an impairment that leads to disability or handicap, such as cataracts that prevent one from driving, may render an elder severely dependent in the United States, where driving is necessary for a whole host of self-maintenance activities and may even form the basis of social definition as a competent adult. But in a village-based society, in which subsistence gardening is the major source of provisioning, and where elders are charged to stay home and care for young children to allow parents to do garden work, the same impairment does not carry a similar social cost. Thus, morbidity is difficult to assess for a number of reasons: it is a continuous state, with many gradations; it represents the additive effect of different diseases (i.e., disease co-morbidities); and it has different social consequences depending on the significance of a particular impairment for performance of roles that vary from culture to culture.

Having made this strong distinction between morbidity and mortality, it should also be mentioned that mortality may not always be so clear cut; the life-sustaining technology of the intensive care unit has made the distinction less clear. Ethnographic research also shows that the clarity of mortality decisions varies across the lifespan. Thus, deaths of infants before the age of 1 often go unremarked, and unreported, in health regimes characterized by high fertility and high mortality. Such children often go unnamed until they survive this period of greatest vulnerability. Nations (1986) reports that illegitimate children in northeast Brazil are called "little angels" and are not considered to be of this earth; consequently, if they die (usually from diarrheal disease and nutritional insufficiency), they are not registered as having died but are rather considered to have returned to heaven, their appropriate place. In developed countries, where vital registration systems are more extensive, we do not find such scope for cultural determination of the presence or absence of a death. The cultural determination appears instead in describing the *cause* of the death, what the person died from. The accuracy of death certificates in this regard is highly variable and subject to a wide range of nonmedical factors (Hahn, Mulinare, and Teutsch 1992), which points to the difficulty of linking multiple disease conditions and morbid states to death.

If even mortality shows such variation across cultures, then variation in the measurement, recognition, and consequences of morbidity will certainly be greater. We propose to examine aging and morbidity along these three axes. We turn first to measurement issues, asking how well assessment instruments used in developed countries perform in societies that differ radically in ecology and culture. We are concerned with measures of functional health, instruments to assess cognitive capacity, and self-rated health. We then turn to the relationship between aging and disability, drawing together the results of the few cross-cultural surveys and ethnographic studies available that have addressed the issue. Finally, we take up the relationship between disability and the personal autonomy of the elderly.

This last is perhaps the most challenging to survey because the active life, while a universally desired goal, has a different significance across cultures. Listening to American elders (or at least the affluent elderly), one would think that an active life, despite disability, and the control over events that this implies, is a universal feature of successful aging. In fact, we must follow Draper and Harpending (1990) and distinguish between compulsory and voluntary activity in late life. In the developed countries, impaired elderly have the option of variably disengaging from activity, and of optimally selecting what sorts of social activity they wish to participate in, as a means of most efficiently investing what may be a diminished physical and emotional capacity (Fredrickson and Carstensen 1990). Elderly in developing countries who lack physical capacity (as well as less affluent elderly in developed nations) may be "involuntarily active," forced to participate in social activity beyond what they might willingly choose, given a certain range of impairment. Successful aging in the developed countries involves

maintainii[...]es as possible, but one must recognize that a[...]for example, have the option of not
participatii[...]o it, a luxury often not available to
the less aff[...]loping countries.

A simila[...]d for "independence." Independence is an[...]society in which only the psycho-
logically un[...]tch, do not depend on others in
every impor[...]such societies, elders expect to
depend on o[...]hing laudable about being on the
receiving en[...]critical is the capacity to participate in the h[...]joint social activities such as village meeting[...]events. In such societies, independence is
not the desired state we take it to be, but rather a sign of removal from
a community and hence a predictor, perhaps, of death.

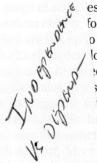

Comparative Study of Aging and Morbidity

The paucity of data on morbidity in elderly outside the developed countries is striking. Lamentations about missing or poor-quality data on
features of aging outside the developed countries are a common refrain
in this book, and here, as elsewhere, we are forced to consult a variety
of sources. These include World Health Organization surveys; United
Nations disability statistics; a variety of single country studies, such as
the Shanghai dementia study (Yu, Liu, Levy, et al. 1989); and the rare
two-country cross-national comparison. An unexpected but excellent
source is the U.S. National Medical Expenditures Survey, which includes an extensive study of health and aging among U.S. Native
Americans and Alaskan Inuit. Every effort has been undertaken to
identify relevant cross-cultural material on aging and morbidity, but the
yield is smaller than the authors would have wished.

Aside from the late recognition that developing countries are aging
(see chapter 3), one additional reason for the lack of comparative information on aging and morbidity is the difficulty of measuring functional
and cognitive decline. This leads to the question: Why is it so difficult
to measure decrements in mental and physical functioning in different
elderly populations? After all, there are pancultural requirements of
daily living such as the ability to feed oneself or to maintain an ade-

quate orientation to one's environment, and these, it would seem, should be easy to survey. Yet it is important to proceed with caution here. While there are clear sociobiologic capacities required for daily living, which are lost or compromised with disease, survey items meant to assess these capacities often tap more general features of daily living that do vary across cultures. Developing valid cross-cultural assessment instruments (and transcultural definitions of impairment) is a great challenge and an interesting lesson in cross-cultural research.

Measuring Functional Capacity in Other Cultures

The original intent of the Activities of Daily Living (ADL) scale, the most widely used measure of functional capacity in the aged, was to assess "primary socio-biological functions" (Katz, Ford, Moskowitz, et al. 1963; Katz and Akpom 1976), which are presumably outside cultural influence. For example, ADL scale items ask about dependence in transferring from bed to an upright position, about continence, and about the ability to feed oneself, which are all meant to assess what would seem to be the most primitive locomotory and neurologic components of functioning. Katz and his colleagues considered these the most primitive because they were learned first and retained longest after the onset of dementing disease. Other ADL items, such as the ability to use the toilet and dress and bathe oneself, were somewhat less basic in that they were learned, conceivably subject to cultural influence, and lost earlier on in dementing disease. Thus, the ADL scale is a semi-Guttman scale, in which dependence in the more basic activities (e.g., feeding) implies dependence in the less basic ones (e.g., bathing). Likewise, in recovery from chronic disease (such as stroke or heart attack) ADL competence is gained incrementally; patients first regain the capacity to transfer, feed, and control their bowels, and only later regain the capacity to bathe, dress, and use the toilet. A number of studies have confirmed the hierarchical relationship between ADL items, although some controversy still exists in regard to which activity of daily living is lost last (Spector 1991; Travis and McAuley 1990). With disease, elders become dependent (i.e., lose the ability to perform ADL tasks, in the following order: bathing, dressing, toileting, transferring from bed, continence, and feeding). Travis and McAuley (1990) found that the hierarchical order of ADL function in a community population was different from that in a nursing home population; in the community population, feeding ability was lost before continence.

Given the evidence that ADL tasks are linked to primary sociobiologic function in this sense, we would expect the hierarchical relationship between the items to exist in every society. What little research there is on functional capacity of elders in the developing countries supports this view, although we have been unable to identify studies that explicitly scaled ADL items for elders in these populations. Thus, in the WHO study of aging in the Western Pacific, a study of the elderly in Fiji, Malaysia, the Philippines, and the Republic of Korea (with a probability sample of about 3,600: see Andrews, Esterman, Braunack-Mayer, and Rungie 1986), age and decrements in ADL functioning are strongly associated, so that elders between ages 60–64 perform a mean of roughly 85 percent of the ADL tasks unassisted, while elders aged 80+ perform a mean of only 60 percent unassisted. Similar results were found in a survey of eleven countries in Europe and a number of surrounding nations (including Kuwait, the former USSR, and the Balkan states) (Heikkinen, Waters, and Brzezinski 1983). Similar percentages are reported for the United States. While this association between age and ADL capacity does not explicitly confirm the predicted hierarchical loss of function, it shows that ADL capacity behaves the same way in a wide variety of societies, and points to the ability of the scale to tap pancultural components of age-related morbidity.

Is ADL function, then, independent of cultural influence? Or, in what amounts to the same thing, do the scale items tap the same latent construct, functional capacity, in every society? Here we must speculate because the research that would definitively settle the question has not yet been done. Ikels (1991) cautions against a culture-neutral interpretation of ADL items because functional capacity has a psychological component, and this psychological component may vary with culture. For example, the ability to feed oneself requires not merely the requisite motor and sensory capacity, but also motivation to do so. An elder with such ADL capacity may still refuse to feed himself (and be scored as ADL-incompetent on the item) because of cultural considerations. An extreme case relevant here is the death-hastening behavior reported in North Arnhem among Australian aborigines (see chapter 10). In cases of death-hastening, chronically ill elders who have been abandoned by their community may refuse food and drink and in some cases not take steps to obtain nourishment, even when they are able to do so (Eastwell 1982; Glascock 1983).

However rare this case, it does point to a disjunction between capacity ("can do") and performance ("does do"), which may be confounded in ADL measures. As described above, an elder man may be able to feed himself, but severe depression may interfere with motivation to eat; consequently, he may be fed by a relative or health aide and be classified as ADL-dependent, even though the capacity is in fact intact. In principle, asking whether an elder "can do" an ADL task independently, as opposed to whether the elder "does do" the task, should eliminate this confound. But in administering the ADL items, one can never be sure that respondents make the same distinction. The result is subtle cultural influence at the level of motivation to perform the task and corresponding measurement error.

Once we attempt to assess more complex functional capacity, measurement error is bound to increase because cultural variability is given far greater scope in people's responses to functional health items. For example, scale items of the Instrumental Activities of Daily Living (IADL) scale developed by Lawton and Brody (1969) attempt to assess the functional capacities required for independence in daily life beyond the primary sociobiologic focus of the ADL items. IADL items assess how dependent an elder is with respect to light housework, preparation of meals, grocery shopping, laundry, getting to places beyond walking distance, using the telephone, managing money, and taking medications. Here Ikels's doubts about the cross-cultural validity of functional assessment items certainly carry force. As she points out in a study of function and disability among Chinese elders, "it is not immediately obvious what are relevant IADL in different settings. Certain items may be totally irrelevant, while others may be specific to a particular age or gender such that the inability to perform certain activities is socially meaningless" (1991, 653). Clearly, using the telephone is irrelevant in places where there are no telephones, just as the ability to manage money is a poor indicator if an elder woman never performed this task even when she was capable of doing so. In fact, use of IADL items is fraught with difficulty even in the United States, where quite often an elder male (or a caregiving proxy for the elder) will claim lack of capacity in preparing meals because the elder has never performed the task (e.g., "He can't because he doesn't know how"). Here too the confusion of capacity and performance is evident, but in this case it is much worse because so many of the IADL tasks are bound up with social roles and more general ways of life, both of which vary across cultures. This variability appears as measurement error in instruments that tap IADL functioning. For example, IADL measures show more variability across countries than ADL measures (Andrews, Esterman, Braunack-Mayer, and Rungie 1986).

Ikels (1991) provides an amusing illustration of the difficulty in assessing functional capacity when so much of that capacity is attached to performance of particular roles, which in turn reflect more general cultural ideas regarding independence. Here the focus was not a specific IADL item, but rather a more general summary measure of independence. When she asked Hong Kong Chinese elders whether they were able to live alone she received a multitude of answers: "no," because they would not like it; "don't know," because they never tried it; "no," because it would be too expensive; and so on. None of these answers has anything to do with physical capacity; hence the question is clearly invalid. Thus, if one is interested in functional capacity, the more the question is linked to specific functional competencies, the better.

When we use measures of function that are even broader in scope, such as the ability to walk up stairs or carry groceries (as in the 1984 Supplement on Aging to the U.S. National Health Interview Survey), the conflation of social roles and physical capacity is more extensive and likely to be even harder to disentangle when the functional health items are administered in other cultures.

What can we conclude from this brief survey of attempts to measure the functional capacity of elderly across different societies? First, we find that such research has not been done very often. Second, we note that when such measurement is attempted, it is often difficult to separate physical capacity from expected role performance. This conflation is most striking in the instrumental tasks of daily living, and less so in the activities of daily living. ADL items do seem to tap an invariant sociobiologic relationship between functional competence and basic locomotory and neurologic functioning. We saw, however, that even among the ADL items, some bear a closer relationship to primary sociobiologic function than others. This brief discussion of the ways culture and functional capacity may be conflated should be kept in mind when we turn later to the results of surveys of elder function across different societies.

Measuring Cognitive Impairment in Other Cultures

Cognitive function, which subsumes such basic processes as orientation to environment, word-finding ability, short-term memory, attention, and pattern recognition, is severely affected by cardiovascular (e.g., stroke and multi-infarct disease) and neurologic disease (especially Alzheimer's disease). Because the incidence of these diseases increases with age, cognitive capacity is routinely assessed in the elderly with a wide variety of instruments designed to measure cognitive function. For example, the prevalence of Alzheimer's disease in the 85+ population has been estimated to be more than 45 percent; and the prevalence in U.S. nursing homes is higher.

Here too one would not expect cultural variation to affect the measurement process to any significant degree. Many of the items that assess cognitive function in the Mini-Mental State Examination (MMSE) (Folstein, Folstein, and McHugh 1975), or the Blessed Roth Information-Memory-Concentration Test (Blessed, Tomlinson, and Roth 1968), both popular assessment tools, seem quite remote from cultural influence. For example, the scales ask respondents their name, the name of the current season, the date of World War II, what they ate for their last meal, where they live, and the current date. Other items ask respondents to count backwards from 20 (or to subtract consecutive 7s from 100), to name the months of the year, and to repeat a difficult sentence. Still other items, which are perhaps more culture-bound, ask respondents to give the name of the current president or to copy a figure (see D'Andrade 1973 for an experiment on cultural variation in pattern recognition). The intent of these items is to assess basic cognitive operations that are essential for day-to-day function. Note that the items do not attempt to assess mental health or affective functioning, which is clearly more bound up with cultural variability. For example, if one wishes to assess psychoses by asking if someone has "heard voices," or depression by asking someone about thoughts of suicide, one immediately faces cultural variation in the comfort with which people will admit to such behavior, variability in how proscribed such behavior is, and notable variation in the ways psychiatric distress is typically expressed.

How well do these scale items assess cognitive function in the elderly outside the developed nations? While there undoubtedly is some primary domain of cognitive function, it is less clear that these items assess it in culture-neutral ways. The primary confound in assessing cognitive function is *literacy*, which varies across cultures and varies widely within cultures across income groups and genders. Thus, even instruments that have been altered to make items more realistic (e.g., dropping the pattern-copying item in societies without access to paper and pencil, eliminating the "last president" question in favor of village leader, dropping serial recitation of the months in societies less anchored to calendar-based time reckoning), and which have been appropriately back-translated, are still likely to reflect the effects of literacy differentials and thus do not provide a direct measure of cognitive capacity.

Yet evidence from cross-cultural research suggests that these measures of cognitive function are relatively stable across societies, which supports their validity as cross-cultural research tools. For example, administration of the Chinese Mini-Mental State Examination shows rates of severe cognitive impairment in the elderly nearly identical to those reported in the United States (roughly 7 percent for elders aged 65+) (Yu, Liu, Levy, et al. 1989). The problem is rather the inability of the measures to control for the effect of literacy within different societies. Because women and lower income groups have less access to education and hence are more likely to be illiterate, rates of cognitive impairment in these groups are more than likely inflated. Thus, while the overall prevalence of severe impairment is similar in the United States (New Haven) and the People's Republic of China (Shanghai), the male–female contribution to the overall prevalence rate differs markedly between the two countries. The rate of severe cognitive impairment among Shanghai women is 10.3 percent, which is three times that of New Haven women. Yu and colleagues conclude that "such a large excess in rates due to gender differences is unusual and calls attention to the presence of sociocultural factors that may have accounted for a lower performance on the cognitive impairment test by older Chinese women" (Yu, Yiu, Levy, et al. 1989, 102).

The Shanghai data show that rates of severe cognitive impairment decrease dramatically as one's educational level increases: for those aged 75+, the prevalence of severe impairment is 25.8 percent among those with no schooling, 12.5 percent among those receiving education from tutors or mobile teachers, 8.8 percent among those having attended elementary school, and 3.5 percent among those attending high school or college. The same trend is visible for U.S. elderly (Weissman, Myers, Tischler, et al. 1985), and for three of the four countries surveyed in the WHO Western Pacific study (Fiji, Malaysia, and the Republic of Korea, but not the Philippines) (Andrews, Esterman, Braunack-Mayer, and Rungie 1986). Older Chinese women, however, perform more poorly than men on measures of cognitive impairment even when differences in educational levels are controlled, a finding still to be adequately explained.

Why should literacy, acquired relatively early in the lifespan, affect late-life test performance with respect to the basic components of cognitive functioning? The answer is uncertain. It may be an effect of educational training on cognitive capacity; or long-term refinement of intellectual skills made possible by education; or, more likely, a side effect of literacy training, such as simple familiarity with test-taking; or, finally, some more general interpersonal effect of education. Explaining the effect of education here, as elsewhere, is difficult. For example, literacy is also associated with lower infant mortality across the world. Even a few years of elementary-level education for women is associated with a significant reduction in infant mortality in developing countries (Edmonston 1990; Lindenbaum 1990); yet the reasons for this reduction remain unclear. The effects of education or literacy are diffuse.

Returning to male–female differences in late-life cognitive testing, it should also be recognized that the tests assess particular types of knowledge. If male–female differences persist when variation in educational level is controlled, it may result from the degree to which certain test items draw on domains of "male knowledge" (e.g., politics, history, numerical manipulation), a bias that might be corrected, for example, by asking about quantities used in cooking. Whatever the mechanism by which lifelong learning affects test performance, we can conclude with Yu and her colleagues that the similar prevalence rates found in diverse cultures "point up a universal constancy in the way the MMSE [Mini-Mental State Examination], with appropriate modifications, behaves across cultures, and highlights the significant difference that basic educational deficits make in human cognitive functioning" (Yu, Liu, Levy, et al. 1989).

Self-Rated Health in Cross-Cultural Perspective

A final measurement issue involves older adults' self-rated health, that is, assessments of one's health as poor, fair, good, or excellent, and the correlates of such self-assessments. Among U.S. elders, a number of regularities have been established for self-reports. Elderly report their health as being good or excellent at higher rates than younger age groups, despite poorer functional health and a greater number of medical conditions (Ferraro 1980; Liang, Bennett, Whitelaw, and Maeda 1991). Elderly women are likely to report poorer health and more symptoms than elderly men, even when physicians rate their health status as similar (Fillenbaum 1979). It should also be mentioned that older Americans are likely to rate the quality of their lives more positively than young people (Bradburn 1969). Finally, self-reports about health appear to be fairly accurate for a range of prospective health outcomes, such as mortality risk and likelihood of hospitalization. Thus, older adults who rate their health as poor are at great risk for poor health outcomes even when their level of physical health (as assessed by medical examination) is controlled for. In other words, self-ratings carry an independent predictive effect for health outcomes (LaRue, Bank, Jarvik, and Hetland 1979; Mossey and Shapiro 1982; Fillenbaum 1984; Idler and Angel 1990). The mechanism linking self-rating to outcome, however, is unclear.

Does this same set of relationships obtain in cultures other than our own? Here too our inquiry is frustrated by lack of comparative data. This absence of data is especially irksome because self-ratings are easy to obtain and are likely to be sensitive indicators of cultural ideas about the relationship between physical health and more general well-being in late life. Some questions that must be raised include: Do older people in other societies also rate their health more positively than younger people? Does functional impairment affect well-being the same way across different societies? Is the association between aging and functional decline equally salient in different societies? Does a self-rating of poor health have equal prognostic significance in developing countries?

The little data available show significant variability with respect to self-rated health and its correlates. This lends support to Liang's caution regarding interpretation of cross-cultural investigation of health and illness: "Cross-cultural differences in health and illness reflect not only genuine variation in the incidence and prevalence of morbidity, disability, and mortality, but also the social processes by which these data are generated. These processes may be far removed from the biological reality" (Liang, Bennett, Whitelaw, and Maeda 1991). Thus, in interpreting the comparative material, we must keep in mind that both the experience of aging (i.e., risk for impairment, access to supports that mitigate the effect of impairment) and the standards by which poor or good health is assessed vary across cultures.

Comparing elderly in the four Western Pacific nations surveyed in the WHO study, we find that a majority of elderly in all four countries consider themselves "quite healthy," but that women do not consistently rate their health as being poorer than men. Age and self-ratings appear to be virtually uncorrelated: in Fiji, Korea, and the Philippines equal numbers of elderly in different age brackets considered their health good; only in Malaysia is a poorer self-rating associated with age, and this appears only for those aged 80+ (Andrews, Esterman, Braunack- Mayer, and Rungie 1986). Published results from the survey are limited to information on the percentages in each country who view themselves as "quite healthy," but the authors also report that other self-assessments of health (e.g., 5-point scale ratings and comparisons of one's health to other people of the same age) closely follow suit.

The European comparative health survey of the elderly in eleven countries, on the other hand, shows quite substantial variations in health perceptions (Heikkinen, Waters, and Brzezinski 1983). Comparing the percentages of elderly who claimed their health was "bad or fairly bad" is instructive. Data on these self-ratings cross-classified by age, site, and gender are shown in Tables 9.1 and 9.2, which we have derived from that survey (Heikkinen et al. 1983, Table 19). Table 9.1 gives the complete cross-classification, using the fifteen sites of the survey and the six age brackets surveyed. Table entries represent the percentages of elderly men and women in each age bracket and site who assessed their health as "bad or fairly bad." In this table, as in Table 9.2, we have dropped the Bialystok, Poland, site because data are missing for the oldest age stratum. It may be helpful to point out the location of

Table 9.1 Percentages of Elders Who View Health as "Bad" or "Very Bad" by Age, Site, and Gender

	Site	60–64	65–69	70–74	75–79	80–84	85–89
Male	Brussels	30	13	17	19	29	4
	Leuven	14	6	7	15	7	6
	Berlin	17	12	12	26	18	24
	Tampere	26	28	26	32	23	27
	Midi	16	18	20	20	16	20
	Normandy	9	17	13	13	23	0
	Greece	15	17	16	25	44	48
	Florence	6	13	17	10	8	12
	Ombrone	22	15	17	27	15	25
	Amiata	14	12	9	20	16	15
	Kuwait	4	8	9	8	16	26
	Bucharest	6	13	20	26	17	11
	Kiev	18	26	35	35	37	33
	Belgrade	18	23	25	32	31	34
	Zagreb	17	20	29	35	40	30
Female	Brussels	34	0	28	31	12	15
	Leuven	21	17	21	6	0	4
	Berlin	14	16	16	25	26	26
	Tampere	19	30	23	29	29	25
	Midi	17	24	23	24	21	19
	Normandy	14	14	27	21	25	43
	Greece	18	32	35	40	43	55
	Florence	16	14	15	18	21	18
	Ombrone	27	20	27	29	30	32
	Amiata	15	15	18	25	17	22
	Kuwait	13	10	23	20	24	22
	Bucharest	19	21	29	25	29	26
	Kiev	33	38	44	41	55	48
	Belgrade	29	34	35	37	44	40
	Zagreb	29	36	38	38	39	32

After Heikkinen, Waters, and Brzezinski 1983, table 19

the less familiar sites: Leuven is in Belgium, Tampere in Finland, Midi in France, and Lower Ombrone and Amiata in Italy. The fifteen sites represent eleven countries for a full sample of close to 17,000 respondents.

Table 9.2 is a marginal subtable of Table 9.1, summing across sites to produce a perhaps more accessible cross-classification of age by gender for respondents' self-assessments of poor health. Each cell in this table represents the mean percentage of respondents reporting bad or fairly bad health in each age by gender group. It should be noted for both tables that the percentages reported mask considerable variation in sample size. Therefore, analysis of these tables must be considered suggestive only.

Beginning with Table 9.2 because of its summary character, we note two clear trends: a greater percentage of women rate their health more poorly than men at every age, and the relationship between poorer self-assessments and increasing age holds only for women. However, this age by gender interaction in self-ratings is a trend only; the chi-square test of association is not significant (X^2 = 5.462, 5 df, p < .37). Turning now to the full set of data in Table 9.1, we find that the site variable, the location of the fifteen sets of respondents and our proxy for cultural variation, is critical for understanding these health self-assessments. Using log-linear methods, we find that there are main effects for age, site, and gender: each exerts an independent influence in the levels of poor health reported. Variation in the table is best accounted for with

Table 9.2 Mean Percentage of Health Rated "Bad" or "Very Bad": Cross-Classification of Age by Gender for 15 Sites

Age	Gender	
	Male	Female
60–64	15.5	21.2
65–69	16.0	21.4
70–74	18.0	26.8
75–79	22.9	27.3
80–84	22.7	27.7
85–89	21.0	28.5

After Heikkinen, Waters, and Brzezinski 1983, table 19.

two interaction terms: an age by site effect (p .01), and a site by gender effect (p < .01). The age by gender interaction term is insignificant (as in Table 9.2). Thus, site (e.g., Florence as opposed to Belgrade) evidently alters the self-assessment one would expect simply from examining the effects of age and gender.

Incidentally, examining mean percentages of poorly rated health by site (not shown) does not show a very clear pattern. The clearly rural sites (Midi, rural Greece, and Amiata) are not associated with uniformly high or low self-ratings relative to the other sites. Nor are the most urban sites associated with uniformly better or worse ratings. About the only consistent trend is west-to-east variation: as one moves from western Europe to eastern Europe and the Balkans, elderly rate their health increasingly more poorly. This may reflect greater economic pressures and poorer access to health services or it may represent a response style, a tendency for elderly in the eastern region to speak about their health more negatively independently of economic conditions. We cannot be sure because the type of analysis that would clarify these issues (i.e., a multivariate procedure controlling for the effect of income, education, and related covariates) has not been conducted.

What are the determinants of an elder's poorer self-assessment of health? Research by Liang, Bennett, Whitelaw, and Maeda (1991) represents the only study we have identified that explicitly compares the determinants of self-rated health in a cross-cultural framework. Using a subsample of respondents drawn from the 1984 U.S. Supplement on Aging to the National Health Interview Survey (n=4,042) and a national probability sample of Japanese elderly (n=2,200), Liang was able to assess whether a set of sociodemographic and health variables functioned the same way in American and Japanese elders' assessments of their health.

Their results are worth describing in some detail, for Liang's research is one of the few that has gone beyond "semantic" equivalence in cross-cultural research, that is, ensuring the equivalence of research instruments across cultures through, say, back-translation, to "metric" and "structural" equivalence (Liang, Bennett, Whitelaw, and Maeda 1991). Metric equivalence refers to the relationship between observable indicators and latent variables in different cultures: "observable indicators [must] have the same relationships with the theoretical construct in different cultures." In other words, items that assess functional capacity such as the activities of daily living scale (ADL) mentioned above, must tap this unobservable construct in the same way. This, in practice, can be assessed with psychometric methods to assure that items have roughly equal means and variances, that they form similarly reliable scales, and that they bear the same relationship to external criterion measures. Finally, by structural equivalence, Liang is concerned that "causal linkages between a given variable and its causes and consequences are invariant across cultures." Here the test is whether a causal model derived in one culture (e.g., through structural equation modeling) obtains equally well in another culture.

Applying these methods to the American and Japanese samples, Liang and his colleagues were able to assess the three types of equivalence in cross-cultural research. Most interesting from the perspective of this inquiry are the variations they discovered in the determinants of elder self-rated health in the two cultures. For both Japanese and American elders, self-rated health was significantly related to age, chronic illness, and functional status. Greater age was associated with a more positive self-rating of health, while a greater number of chronic health conditions and poorer functional health were associated with poorer self-assessments. For American elders but not the Japanese, education was significantly associated with health self-assessments: American elders with higher educational achivement are likely to rate their health better. For Japanese elders, education does not bear a significant relationship to self-ratings. It should be noted that in this analysis, these predictive relationships hold independently of all the other variables in the model; the effects of these other variables are partialed out in the structural equation procedure.

Thus, the process by which self-assessments of health emerge clearly differs between American and Japanese elders: for Americans, education predicts self-ratings; for Japanese it does not. Given what we know from chapter 5 on differences in living arrangement between the countries, could it be that U.S. elders use education to compensate for less intense family support (by purchasing services and maintaining independent living), while education for Japanese elders does not play this role (because they rely on the family support typical of shared households)? Liang's comparative research suggests such hypotheses and represents an important advance in cross-cultural gerontology.

Aging and the Disablement Process

Having surveyed some of the conceptual issues relevant to measuring morbidity cross-culturally, we turn to comparative studies of the health of the elderly. We have targeted for inquiry aging and the *disablement process*, a phrase coined by the World Health Organization (1980) to provide a framework for analyzing the consequences of disease in a cross- cultural framework. Manton, Dowd, and Woodbury (1986) point out the utility of this approach. First, viewing disablement as a process gives proper scope to the ways disease, in the form of morbidity, affects individual characteristics and behaviors over time. Second, it high-lights the variability characteristic of morbid processes, where the ex-pression of functional impairment *as disability* is affected by social, eco-nomic, and cultural factors. The role of cultural factors in the disablement process is likely to be greater in old age because older people are unlikely to be working, and therefore the definition of dis-ability as the inability to remain economically active may no longer apply; greater scope for cultural determination is therefore likely (Manton, Dowd, and Woodbury 1986).

The WHO framework for understanding disablement involves a dis-tinction between impairment, disability, and handicap. "Impairment" refers to loss or abnormality of *function*; "disability" to loss or restric-tion of *activity* because of such impairment; and "handicap" to loss or limitation in *role performance* as a result of disability (Chamie 1989; World Health Organization 1991). It is important to distinguish among the three components of disablement. While impairment involves clear physical properties, its expression as disability and handicap depends on cultural factors. For example, social roles vary according to culture, as we have pointed out; thus, disabilities need not lead to the same handicap in all societies. Also, disabilities may be more or less recog-nized in societies: in some societies, a disability may be significant only insofar as it hinders fulfillment of a role; in others, disabilities may be labeled, acknowledged, and made the basis of self-definition even when they do not impair role performance. The latter, it should be pointed out, is the basis for discrimination against the disabled.

The distinction between impairment and disability is also critical from the perspective of measuring the impact of elder morbidity.

Chamie (1989), surveying the International Disability Statistics Data Base (DISTAT), points out that very different results emerge depending on whether one's focus is impairment or disability. Population estimates of the impact of disease morbidities are much lower if screening stresses impairments, and higher when the focus is disability, because disability is more inclusive. While impairment is defined by specific functional losses (e.g., vision loss, paralysis), disability involves limitations in activity; and such limitations imply greater range in the severity of impairment. For example, moderate arthritis may prevent an elder from walking far or result in a need for help in such personal care activities as bathing. Such an elder must certainly be counted as disabled, yet using an impairment criterion alone might result in an undercount of this type of morbidity.

The measurement implications of focusing on impairment as opposed to disability are extremely important because the developing countries of Asia and Africa, as Chamie points out, generally use impairment-specific measures and thus identify only the most severe and visible cases of disablement. Developed countries, on the other hand, are more likely to use broad-ranging disability measures. Thus, developing country surveys count as morbidity the more severe conditions such as blindness, deafness, paralysis, and amputated limbs; developed country surveys pick up a greater range of morbidity because the surveys include hearing loss, the inability to walk several blocks, the inability to read small print, and other activity limitations as reportable morbidities (Chamie 1989). The results obtained by these two different approaches to the disablement process show notable differences. Impairment-based screening results in lower crude disability rates and higher sex ratios for the percentage disabled (i.e., more men than women are disabled by this method). Disability-based screening results in higher crude disability rates and sex ratios closer to 1.0, or, if anything, greater disability in women. This greater disability in older women in developed countries may be the result of a mortality selection effect: men with more severe disabilities are likely to die at earlier ages.

Examples of this variation in crude disability rates are evident in United Nations disability statistics (DISTAT). In Egypt, in adults aged 60+, the crude disability rate due to chronic disease is 3,826 per 100,000, or roughly 0.4 percent (Egyptian National Health and Medical

Survey 1979–1981). In Uruguay, in adults aged 65+, the crude disability rate due to chronic disease is about five times higher (12,121 per 100,000 for males, and 17,801 for females), or roughly 1.5 percent (Uruguay, Survey of the Chronically Ill 1984). Contrast these figures with disability prevalence estimates reported for the United States, which are based strictly on limitations of activity. Using inability to perform one ADL or IADL task, about 5 percent of American elders aged 65+ are disabled (Hing and Bloom 1990).

Given this variation in definitions, and the consequently high variation in prevalence rates for disability across cultures (ranging from 0.2 percent to 20.9 percent for twenty countries in the United Nations data base), it is striking, however, that regularities still appear in the relationship between disablement and other features of social experience. Disability rates are higher in the fifty-five countries listed in the DISTAT archive among the more poorly educated and lower income groups, among the elderly, in rural areas, and in the less developed countries (Chamie 1989; World Health Organization 1991). The fifty-five–country survey data also reveal that the causes of late-life morbidity are similar. Vascular disease (stroke, heart disease) and cancers are major causes of disablement in late life. There is, however, some evidence for variation in the *composition* of dementia types across cultures. In a study of extremely elderly Palauans (those aged 90+ in a Pacific island population), Jensen and Polloi (1988) found that while the prevalence of dementia was similar to that reported for U.S. elderly, the contribution of vascular disease to dementia cases (as in multi-infarct dementia) was much lower.

Other significant variation in the causes of late-life morbidity is evident in epidemiologic research conducted as part of the U.S. National Medical Expenditures Survey conducted in 1987. One component of this research was the Survey of American Indians and Alaska Natives, or SAIAN, a special study designed to examine the health conditions and personal health practices of Native Americans who reside on or near reservations and who are eligible to receive services from the U.S. Indian Health Service. While the five most prevalent chronic diseases in the U.S. population as a whole and in the SAIAN population were the same (hypertension, arthritis, diabetes, cardiovascular disease, and gall bladder disease, in that order), the SAIAN population has a higher prevalence of diabetes (Type II, or noninsulin dependent diabetes mellitus) for both sexes and at every age. The total prevalence of diabetes for SAIAN elders aged 65+ is 27.4 percent, while for the U.S. population aged 65+ it is only 14.2 percent (Johnson and Taylor 1991). For women aged 65+, differences in the prevalence of diabetes are even more striking: 31.8 percent of SAIAN elderly women are affected, while only 13.5 percent of elderly U.S. women are affected. SAIAN elders are also more affected by gallbladder disease. U.S. elders, on the other hand, have a higher prevalence of cancer.

The increased prevalence of Type II diabetes and gallbladder disease among U.S. Native Americans and Inuit is worth an additional comment. Weiss (1990) and Szathmary (1990) have shown that the prevalence of the two diseases is uniformly higher in Amerindian, or "new world," populations than in "old world" populations. This is true of U.S. Native Americans, Mayan Indians in the Yucatan Peninsula of Mexico, and South American indigenous populations. It is also true of populations that have intermarried with indigenous populations, such as Mexican-Americans in the southwest United States. The high prevalence is relatively recent (since the 1950s) and appears to involve shifts in diet, increasing obesity in late life, and genetic factors. In other words, this "new world syndrome" may be a consequence of modernization in which a genetic trait useful in the hunter-gatherer past of the Amerindian peoples (and hence selected for) has now become a source of disease in changed environmental conditions (Neel 1962, 1982). Among the Pima Indians of the U.S. southwest, diabetes and gallbladder disease clearly reach epidemic proportions in late life (Knowler, Pettitt, Bennett, and Williams 1983).

This brief summary of variation in morbidity rates and the sources of such variation is not exhaustive and points out some of the difficulties in establishing valid cross-cultural estimates of the prevalence of disability among the aged. In summary, Figure 9–1, taken from Manton and Soldo (1985), shows the relationship between morbidity, disability, and mortality expressed as three hypothetical survival curves (see chapter 2). The vertical axis displays the percentage of the population that survives to a given age free of morbidity, disability, or death. The horizontal axis summarizes the age dimension. The figure shows that at about age 20 the population begins to experience each of the three health events, with morbidity most common. The area under the morbidity curve (A) represents person-years lived free of disease. Note that

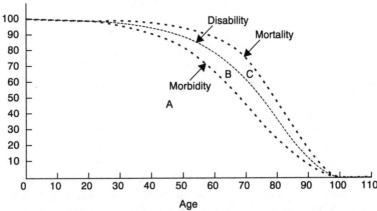

Figure 9–1 The mortality (observed), morbidity (hypothetical), and disability (hypothetical) survival curves for U.S. females in 1980.

Reprinted, with permission, from K. C. Manton and B. J. Soldo, "Dynamics of Health Changes in the Oldest-Old," *The Milbank Quarterly,* Vol. 63, no. 2, p. 34 (Spring 1985). Copyright © The Milbank Memorial Foundation.

morbidity and disability are characterized by different curves: not all morbidity results in disability. Thus, the area between the disability curve (B) and the morbidity curve (A) represents the person-years characteristic of this population in which morbidity, such as a chronic health condition, does not translate into disability. The width of this band narrows in late life. The area between the mortality curve (C) and disability curve (B), on the other hand, represents the number of disabled person-years characteristic of the population.

This life-table treatment of the relationship between morbidity and disability shows the value of distinguishing between morbidity and disability. We have seen that the relationship between the two is apt to vary according to culture. Aside from true differences in the incidence of disabling diseases, cultures also differ in the ways disability is expressed, especially in late life. Thus, a life-table analysis of morbidity and disability curves in different cultures is likely to show variation in the position of the disability curve (curve B in Figure 9–1) relative to the morbidity (A) and mortality (C) curves. Different cultures are thus likely to show varying widths in the area between the morbidity and disability curves, and between the disability and mortality curves, depending on the activities elders must perform. However, the overall shape of the curves is likely to be similar. We have also seen that on top of such variation in the expression of disability, disability in late life can also be measured in vastly different ways depending on whether the focus is specific impairments or limitations in activity due to impairment.

It is best to conclude this discussion with a summary of the research that has been most successful in overcoming these obstacles. Two studies are worth mentioning in this regard, Manton's research on aging and the disablement process in Indonesia (Manton, Dowd, and Woodbury 1986), and his re-analysis of the WHO study of aging in the Western Pacific (Manton, Myers, and Andrews 1987).

Data for the Indonesian study were collected in 1976–1977 by the Indonesian government in collaboration with WHO technical staff. The final sample consisted of 4,604 households, 22,468 people of all ages, drawn from fourteen provinces across Sumatra, Java, and Bali. In this research, disability was defined broadly, so chronic disease impairments, functional disabilities, and handicaps in daily living all led to designations of disability. The prevalence of disability in this sense for Indonesians of all ages was 10.4 percent, for those aged 45+ (the cutpoint for old age in this research) 25.5 percent. The authors used a grade-of-membership statistical technique to establish discrete impairment–disability profiles and to see how membership in each profile or type differed according to sociodemographic features, subjective health ratings, and measures of physical disability and impairment.

Four such profiles emerged in their analysis for the aged 45+ sample: "rural males," "urban males," "middle age females," and "elderly females." Thus, among Indonesian older adults age is more salient for women than for men in discriminating between types of disability, while for men the rural-urban distinction appears most important. The female groups are on the whole less educated and less likely to be heads of households. The rural male and elderly female groups are similar in that they resort to traditional healers most frequently and in that they are predominantly engaged in agricultural activities. The rural males differ from the other three groups in that they receive relatively little support from family and relatives for their daily care. The four groups differ as well in their subjective health assessments, physical disabilities, and social impairments. The rural males suffer most from pulmonary complaints, the urban males from arthritic problems and internal organ symptoms.

Most interesting from a comparative perspective is the differential impact of these health complaints on handicaps, or role performance. For the elderly female group, disabilities are far more likely to translate into handicaps when it comes to participation in community meetings, religious ceremonies, and ritual meals. This distinctive disability profile suggests a particular interaction between age and gender in producing handicaps among these Indonesian elders. In other words, elderly disabled women are more likely to be considered handicapped, that is, unable to perform these communal roles. More generally, the grade of membership analysis shows that female adolescents and elderly women show a similar pattern of social handicaps, which again suggests a general social or cultural disadvantage for women that is accentuated in late life. Widowhood would appear to affect women more severely than men, at least in terms of community roles, an important hypothesis suggested by the grade-of-membership analysis.

A similar analysis of the WHO survey of aging in the four Western Pacific countries (Fiji, Malaysia, the Philippines, and the Republic of Korea) reveals additional variation in the experience of disability and aging. Five profiles of disablement emerged in the analysis: type 1, a generally healthy group of aged, primarily women, impaired only in vision; type 2, a second generally healthy group, primarily male, with select acute medical problems; type 3, a group with chronic medical conditions and high rates of hospitalization, but few limitations in the activities of daily living (ADL) or instrumental activities of daily living (IADL); type 4, a primarily female group with chronic conditions and IADL limitations only; and type 5, a group with a wide range of both ADL and IADL problems and dementing disease (Manton, Myers, and Andrews 1987). Elders aged 75+ are over-represented in the fourth and fifth groups, as one might expect. The third group is an acutely ill population, primarily male, that is able to remain in the community because of extensive family support and its own economic resources. The fourth group is old, primarily female, and dependent on families for instrumental support. The fifth group represents the oldest and most frail group of elders and the only group in the Western Pacific countries likely to utilize formal nursing home care.

Turning now to the social interaction correlates of membership in each of the particular groups in the WHO survey, we find that the two healthy groups participate far more in religious activity and community affairs, as one would expect, and that they see less of their relatives than individuals in the more impaired groups. This follows from the greater needs of elderly in the more impaired categories, which are satisfied primarily through family support. We note also that primary caregiving support for the more impaired elders comes from adult children, while primary support for elders in the more healthy categories is provided by spouses. This, too, is suggested by the age differences between the groups.

Finally, and most important from the standpoint of comparative analysis, the distribution of the five types is quite different across the four countries surveyed (Manton, Myers, and Andrews 1987). Types 1 and 4, the healthy group and group primarily in need of instrumental support, predominate in Malaysia; thus, here the elderly population is primarily female, with limited medical problems. This is the same pattern found in Indonesia (Manton, Dowd, and Woodbury 1986) and may be typical of developing countries. Elder males are simply more scarce in these populations, as are elders with severe chronic diseases. Types 1 and 3, the healthy group and a relatively younger-aged group with acute medical conditions, predominates in the Philippines. Manton and his colleagues suggest that this pattern reflects lower life expectancy and a high proportion of older *urban* dwellers, who are able to make use of modern medical facilities. Types 2 and 5, a healthy male group and a severely frail elderly group, predominate in the Republic of Korea, showing that males appear more frequently among the elderly as well as among the extremely frail. It should be noted that Korea is the most affluent of the four countries. Thus, the Korean case may illustrate a potential consequence of late-stage modernization on the demographic profile of the aged. Finally, in Fiji types 2, 3, and 4 predominate; the extremes of health and ability in old age are not as strongly represented.

The grade-of-membership analysis is an extremely valuable technique for establishing broad differences across populations in the disablement process. The differences between the four countries in the experience of aging and disablement suggest a number of hypotheses about the impact of modernization and increasing affluence in developing countries. Will such modernization lead to an increase of elderly *males*, as in Korea? Will urbanization and the access to advanced medical care it implies result in a new chronically ill population of elders? Additional questions emerge that can only be answered with more detailed field studies. Why, for example, do the extremes of health, both the most healthy and most infirm, appear less prominent in Fiji? The grade-of-membership analysis of the Western Pacific survey draws attention to the potential impact of sociocultural variation in leading to different outcomes for the four countries.

Cross-Cultural Variation in the Impact of Disability

Disability clearly threatens one's capacity to perform activities, whatever one's age. And, as we have seen, some kind of limitation in activity is inescapably bound up with the meaning of disability. Yet the impact of disability will vary depending on the range of activities one is expected to perform. Since this range of expected activities for the elderly varies across cultures, disability is likely to mean different things in different places. For example, cataract conditions are typical of the elderly in Melanesian populations, but this debility is not made the basis of disability because it does not interfere with daily activity to any great degree. These elders are able to perform gardening tasks, help in the construction of village houses, participate in cash cropping, and attend communal events such as mortuary ritual and village court hearings (Albert 1987). Because the elders do not typically read, drive, or perform work requiring acute vision, cataracts are an impairment, to use the distinction drawn above, but not a disability. For American elders, on the other hand, cataracts are clearly a disability because the condition interferes with activities that would otherwise be performed daily and that are considered to be of great value.

An additional source of variability in the impact of disability for the aged involves attitudes toward functional limitation. Someone unable to perform daily activities necessary for subsistence or self-maintenance is *dependent* on others for these tasks; yet the meaning of such dependency varies dramatically across cultures. Dependency can be seen as a moral failing, as in American culture, or as an acknowledged, acceptable stage in the lifecourse, when one is bitter perhaps at the loss of function but not unhappy with receiving support from children and other kin. In American society, dependency of any sort is inadmissible, even when one's needs are clear, beyond one's control, and modal for advanced age. In the sample of San Francisco elders studied by Clark (1973) and Clark and Anderson (1967), for example, the rejection of dependency went far beyond the loss of prestige or status so important to social exchange theory (see chapter 6). Clark reports for this sample a "morbid fear, assuming almost phobic proportions, of any sort of dependency." Receiving help was simply illegitimate: "We observed in this sample a host of secondary defences against dependency—a denial of need; hostility toward potential helpers, even in the face of disabilities and limitations that required assistance from others; a contempt for the real or imagined weaknesses of others; and, in some cases, a grandiosely inflated self-image" (Clark 1973, 82). Contrast this attitude toward dependency with that of the Igbo of eastern Nigeria. Shelton (1972) describes Igbo late life in these terms: "Becoming an elder, in a real sense, is analogous to one's becoming a member of a leisure class of persons who are given goods and services because of their merits related to their accomplishments and their having attained old age."

One suspects that both descriptions of dependency are exaggerated: Clark's American informants, it appears, were for the most part those at greatest risk of losing functional capacity and had not yet experienced the sort of dependency they condemned; likewise, Shelton's Igbo elders, one suspects, were also mostly fully functional and able to exercise their claims to privileged status. In fact, there is a great dearth of information, even for American elders, on what it means to be dependent and receiving care from others. Does the truly dependent American elder still have the same fear of dependency? Or does some process of individual adaptation alter one's adherence to such community norms? Does the Igbo elder who is no longer able to enforce his claims to leisure and provisioning still receive the deference and support he has coming to him? One problem with research on dependency in late life has been inattention to the range of disability typical of late life, and the context-specificity of attitudes toward dependency both among those receiving support and those providing it.

Thus, there are at least three independent sources of variation one must recognize in assessing the impact of disability on the elderly: variation in the incidence of morbidity leading to disability, variation in the demands of everyday life that may be affected by such disability, and variation in attitudes regarding dependency in the ability to fulfill the demands of everyday life. While recognition of these sources of variability is hardly profound, it bears repeating, for much of the debate about the wish of elders to "disengage" from social participation, and more generally, about the effects of "modernization" on the status of the elderly, ignores this heterogeneity in the contexts in which aging occurs. For example, in the extensive set of studies collected in *Aging and Modernization* (Cowgill and Holmes 1972), it is striking how few health statistics are presented; yet disability in the aged must clearly affect their status even in a society that accords great privileges to the elderly. In these largely ethnographic studies, it is impossible to know what percentage of the elderly show disabilities and the extent to which these disabilities affect the ability of the elderly to work and enforce their claim to the support that should normatively come their way. This criticism should not be construed as an attack on the search for cross-cultural regularities in the aging experience, but rather as a plea for more careful measurement of clearly significant covariates that must be controlled for in predicting the status of the elderly in different cultures.

Recent studies are more satisfying in this regard. They show that roughly 5 percent of the elderly in populations of vastly different size and scope is extremely frail (i.e., unable to perform the activities and roles critical for personal care and social participation) and that the position of these elderly is clearly different from that of healthier, more functional elderly who continue to perform economically significant roles, and who can accordingly enforce claims to deference, authority, and provisioning.

For example, Barker (1989), using a probability sample of Pacific Islander elders in Niue, reports that fully half of her respondents had some kind of disability that interfered with their ability to work. Twenty percent of these disabled elders had been restricted in their work activities for more than five years. The major restriction in this case was an inability to perform work in gardens that lay some distance from villages. On the other hand, of this disabled group, most were still able to perform domestic tasks such as taking care of children, cleaning, and preparing food; and none needed help with personal care tasks. A small group of elders, roughly 7 percent of the sample, however, were frail by Niue standards: they were no longer able to get food or cook for themselves, and no longer were able to attend church, a rough proxy for being housebound. Thus, in Niue there is a range of dependency, including severe disability. Most elders suffering disease morbidities do not require personal or skilled nursing care, and virtually all perform services that maintain their place in the household economy. The inability of elders to work in gardens is partly compensated for by their ability to perform domestic tasks and free up the labor of younger adults, a pattern reported for many cultures. It is likely that the experience of the severely impaired and more functional Niue elder differs markedly. Barker does not report on the subjective sense of dependency in these elders, but one can imagine that this would vary between the two groups of elderly, and perhaps by the ability of households to provide for elders.

Draper and Harpending (1990) provide a rare amount of detail on the functional health of elders in two related, but different populations, the !Kung and Herero of Botswana, Africa. This research is particularly valuable because it shows that even in societies in which elderly are highly respected and accorded generous support when disabled, the dependencies associated with aging can still be considered undesirable. This is so because elderly in these populations are forced to remain active even when they are limited by disabilities. They are "involuntarily active," unable to withdraw from social affairs and a range of demanding responsibilities even when they want to, because a scarcity of labor means they have to fend for themselves and because village members in the course of daily affairs make demands on them. As Draper puts it in summarizing the experience of these African elders, "They led full and complex lives because people and circumstances did not leave them alone" (Draper and Harpending 1990).

In the midst of such activity, the !Kung and Herero elders spoke quite negatively about aging and the dependency associated with disability, despite their active lives and despite a great mobilization of family and village support on their behalf. The common refrain was, "When you are old, all of your strength is gone; you can't do anything for yourself." Similarly, elder !Kung and Herero rated the quality of their lives relatively poorly compared with the lives of younger people, a reversal of the pattern in developed nations. In fact, the Herero elders rated their satisfaction with life poorest in a seven-site comparison, including sites in the United States, Ireland, and Hong Kong, in addition to Botswana (Draper and Harpending 1990).

We conclude that local conditions strongly influence the impact disability will have on the experience of aging. One cannot assert universally that activity, even with disability, is good for the elderly because it leads to higher satisfaction with life (as asserted by Palmore and Maeda 1985 in a Japan–United States comparison). This claim neglects the involuntary social participation typical of the aged in small-scale societies and the nonaffluent in developed nations. Nor does it appear that the provision of elder support, and the respect accorded to elders, is uniform in the face of varying degrees of disability, for such disability may affect an elder's ability to enforce a claim to provisioning and care. The changes typical of modernization are likely to affect elderly differently depending on the type and degree of disability they face. Finally, the !Kung and Herero data show that concern for independence is not limited to developed countries or American elders. Even in societies characterized by communal ideologies and an extreme degree of personal interdependence in everyday transactions, loss of functional capacity, and hence a dependence on others, can be sorely felt.

10

Death, Death-Hastening, and Decrepitude

We are often tempted to think that the debate over euthanasia and concerns about the quality of life in old age are restricted to the more developed countries. For example, in the United States the chronically ill can request "Do Not Resuscitate" (DNR) orders; and physicians, families, and patients must often decide whether life-sustaining technologies should be applied or withdrawn. The problem has become more difficult with the discovery that technologies used for temporary acute care, such as mechanical ventilation and parenteral nutrition, can also be used to keep people alive who have suffered massive and multiple organ system failure. A new branch of law has developed to allow patients to ensure that their wishes with respect to such medical treatment will be honored. Also, elders anticipating future decrepitude and mental incompetence are advised to secure living wills, in which they specify their wishes for life-sustaining procedures.

Adjacent to this formal system of preparation for death is an informal, more hidden or subterranean system of planning regarding death. Such an informal system is available to family caregivers and to the aged themselves as death becomes increasingly likely. It includes knowledge of which physicians at which hospitals will respect a DNR or remove a ventilator in the absence of clear evidence of elder preference; networks for securing information that will enable suicide; and the complex process by which families prepare for a death at home, which in some cases may involve removing an elder from a hospital or nursing home in anticipation of the death. While it is impossible to gauge how active a role families and medical staff take in arranging the context of death for decrepit elders, it is clear that "arranged death" is part of the landscape of extreme late life. Thus, Glascock concludes that "the elderly are definitely killed by various direct and indirect means in American society" (Glascock 1990).

But while the legal complexities involved in preparing for death may be specific to the more developed nations, concern for the quality of life in the case of such elders and recourse to euthanasia certainly are not. "Death-hastening" behavior is reported across a wide spectrum of societies; some societies clearly practice gerontocide, that is, active killing of severely impaired elders. It is sobering to read accounts of such assisted death, even when we imagine that death would be preferable to certain conditions of extremely poor health. Thus, C. W. Hart reports the following among the Tiwi, an Australian aboriginal population that he studied in 1928:

> It was Tiwi custom, when an old woman became too feeble to look after herself, to "cover her up." . . . The method was to dig a hole in the ground in some lonely place, put the old woman in the hole, and fill it with earth until only her head was showing. Everybody went away for a day or two and then went back to the hole to discover to their surprise, that the old woman was dead, having been too feeble to raise her arms from the earth. Nobody had "killed" her, her death in Tiwi eyes was a natural one. (Cited in Sokolovsky 1990, 4–5)

Hart's report, unlike many other ethnographic compilations, is significant because it is not merely a report of a "custom" (which may or may not ever take place). In fact, Hart witnessed such a "covering up" and was consulted about its propriety because he stood as a classificatory "son" of the blind old woman who was put to death. He reports that only sons and brothers could undertake such death-hastening; and all had to agree about its propriety beforehand, "since once it was done they did not want any dissension among the brothers or clansmen, as that might lead to a feud." Thus, all close kin took part in the act and all took responsibility for it. Significantly, in this case the woman was tolerated for quite some time despite severe impairment ("Toothless, almost blind, withered and stumbling around, she was physically quite revolting and mentally rather senile.") The "covering up" took place only when she had become completely blind and was constantly falling over logs and into fires. Hart was able to excuse himself from the death-hastening but took part in the mortuary ritual that followed the death.

The Tiwi case represents the more extreme pole in death-hastening, an active alteration of conditions that is designed to kill an elder. In other nonindustrial societies we find more passive strategies to hasten death, such as leaving an impaired elder behind, perhaps even with a supply of food, when a forager group breaks camp and moves on. The film, *The Ballad of Narayama*, is a poignant fictional portrayal of death-hastening in preindustrial Japan, in which sons are enjoined to carry elders on their backs to a remote mountain peak reserved for such assisted dying. Thus, the ethical debates about active and passive involvement in death-hastening apply equally to societies at both ends of the scale of technological development. Similarly, we can assume that the tension between one's attachment to a decrepit parent and the inescapable recognition that the elder has become a burden is not confined to technologically advanced societies.

Also, we should recognize that the process by which the decrepit elder is killed or allowed to die often involves the participation, to one degree or another, of the elderly themselves. Elders may resist or may resign themselves to death. *The Ballad of Narayama* is particularly poignant because it shows how elders in some cases must also play a part in such ritualized killing, actively ceding their autonomy as competent individuals and accepting the role of decrepit elder. We can thus generalize Glascock's comment, quoted above, and say that the elderly are killed by various direct and indirect means in a variety of cultural settings, and that elders also play some role in this process. Yet we know very little of the elder's role in such assisted dying. We return to this point below.

Gerontocide (gericide, senilicide) is often surveyed in studies of the aged. However, it is surprising to note how few studies report on what would seem to be the natural complement of such assisted death, that is, the dying process or last year of life for the severely decrepit elder. Variation in the last year of life for such elderly is likely to reveal much about different societies. While a focus on the daily life of the cachectic elder does not have the lurid appeal of death- hastening activity, it is probably a better marker of the condition of elders across different societies. Unfortunately, there are few studies of the last year of life of the dying elder, even in the United States. Even the nursing home, where death is a weekly occurrence, and people entering know they will die, has not been studied from the perspective of death and dying, despite books in which *death* or its analogues appear in the title (Shields 1988; Gubrium 1975; M. Moss personal communication).

We report on two studies of the dying elder, in addition to death-hastening, with the understanding that it is studies like these, rather than studies of gerontocide, that are likely to be most informative on cultural variation in the treatment of death and the dying elder.

Death-Hastening in Comparative Perspective

How prevalent is death-hastening activity across the globe? And what sorts of conditions, social, material, or ecological, are associated with the killing of decrepit elders? Before proceeding with an examination of these issues, it is necessary to specify what we mean by *death-hastening*. Maxwell and Silverman (1989) define gerontocide as "the killing or abandonment of old people, including their exposure to the natural elements." Glascock (1990) adopts a more expansive definition, including in death-hastening or death-accelerating all "nonsupportive treatment that leads directly to the death of aged individuals." Using Glascock's definition, killing, abandoning, and exposure to natural elements represent only a subset of death-hastening behaviors, as he would include euthanasia and elder abuse as additional examples of death-hastening, and perhaps even suicide (in that elders may feel pressure to remove themselves from being a burden on their children). Thus, gerontocide represents a subset of death-hastening behaviors, a difference that should be kept in mind when we report findings from different cross-cultural surveys of such practices.

Beginning with the more restricted definition of elder killing, we turn first to Maxwell and Silverman's (1989) survey of gerontocide. They drew a systematic sample of ninety-five societies from Murdock and White's HRAF Standard Cross-Cultural Sample (Murdock and

White 1969). The investigators then read the ethnographic accounts of the societies and scored them on indicators of gerontocide. Gerontocide was present in twenty of the societies and absent in seventy-five, yielding a prevalence rate of 21 percent in a worldwide sample of human societies. In seventeen of the seventy-five societies that did not practice gerontocide, the practice was explicitly disallowed or condemned. Virtually every region of the world was represented among the practitioners of gerontocide.

Maxwell and Silverman (1989) went on to examine correlates of the practice. Surprisingly, difficult environments (in which food is scarce) and nomadic subsistence patterns (in which the elderly must continually change settlements), two ecological factors that are typically thought to be strongly associated with gerontocide (e.g., Simmons 1945), were *not* significantly correlated with gerontocide in the sample of ninety-five societies. In fact, Maxwell and Silverman found that an *irregular* food supply was associated with a slightly *lower* likelihood of gerontocide, perhaps because in such cases elders' cultural expertise in finding food or producing such food is especially valuable. Similarly, Maxwell and Silverman point out that *seminomadic* peoples are more likely to practice gerontocide than fully nomadic peoples. Seminomadic transhumance, in which populations occupy different settlements during different seasons of the year, is associated with an increased likelihood of gerontocide because goods are accumulated in such societies; thus, moving the elderly is more cumbersome than in fully nomadic foraging populations (Maxwell and Silverman 1989). Thus, the two most popular explanations for gerontocide do not stand up to statistical scrutiny.

What features of social organization, then, best predict gerontocidal practices? A third ecological factor to be considered, also identified by Simmons (1945) in his early investigation of the problem, is the degree of sedentary cultivation. Simmons hypothesized that hunting, herding, and fishing populations would be more likely to practice gerontocide than sedentary agricultural populations. Maxwell and Silverman were able to confirm the significance of this ecological factor: 38 percent of the forager-fisher-pastoralist societies practiced gerontocide, while only 12 percent of the cultivating populations did so, a highly significant finding (p = .01).

This ecological factor is correlated with a number of social structural variables, all of which bear an allied predictive relationship to gerontocide. Thus, Maxwell and Silverman found that societies with greater social stratification, which is a feature of sedentary agricultural populations, are less likely to practice gerontocide. They also found that societies characterized by lower scores on a "social rigidity" measure (societies in which subgroup solidarity is not strong: see chapter 8), were also likely to practice gerontocide. Maxwell and Silverman explain this association in terms of an individual's identification with a community. In socially rigid societies, a community is unlikely to turn on one of its own. Where such group identity is less strong, killing an elder member is less like killing one of your own.

A lower degree of stratification is a feature of less complex societies, but high social rigidity is also a feature of such societies. While the former is associated with the presence of gerontocide, the latter is not. Thus, it is wrong to link gerontocide to level of social complexity or technological development in any simple way (see Maxwell and Silverman [1989] for an alternative view). Cutting across level of social complexity is a more fundamental cultural variable that we may best sum up as the degree to which elders are incorporated into social groups. When such identification of an elder with a group is high, we would expect gerontocide to be less likely.

Unilineal descent groups represent the paradigmatic example of such identification of elders with social groups; after all, it is in these societies that elders are apical founders, ancestors who may even be merged with mythical figures and whose name may come to designate an entire lineage (see chapter 8). We would thus expect gerontocide to be less prevalent in societies characterized by the presence of such corporate descent groups. In fact, Maxwell and Silverman (1989) found just this association. Comparing societies with unilineal descent (a proxy for the presence of corporate descent groups) to those with bilateral descent, they found that only 9 percent of the societies with unilineal descent practiced gerontocide, while 39 percent of those with bilateral descent did so. In their set of bivariate cross-tabulations, rule of descent turned out to be the strongest predictor of gerontocide (p = .001).

Glascock (1990) used a sample of sixty societies included in Naroll's HRAF Probability Sample File (Naroll, Michik, and Naroll 1976). He coded forty-one of these societies for a more detailed breakdown of death-hastening behaviors, including killing, abandoning, denying food, and denying all support, as well as countervailing supportive behavior and behavior that is nonsupportive but also nonthreatening. Using this definition, twenty-one of the forty-one societies, or just over half, practice death-hastening, and killing appears to be the most frequent form of death-hastening: fourteen of the twenty-one societies practicing death-hastening, or two-thirds, kill elders. The prevalence of death-hastening and killing, in particular, is striking. In addition, Glascock (1990) points out that when killing occurs, the elderly are most often killed violently: "beaten to death (three societies), buried alive (three societies), stabbed (two societies), or strangled (one society)." Despite the violence, such killing is a family affair, largely planned and carried out by sons; and there does not appear to be any asymmetry in the gender of elders killed in these societies, for men and women are equally likely to be killed.

Glascock also found that the presence of such behaviors was perfectly compatible with nonthreatening, even supportive, behavior toward elders. In other words, death-hastening is selective within the societies that practice it; some elders receive support, while others are killed. In fact, gerontocidal or death-hastening behavior is reserved for the decrepit elder. Glascock (1990) points out that killing is more likely in societies that make a sharp distinction between the decrepit elder and the intact elder. If the source of such extreme treatment of the decrepit is the burden these elders pose to a family or community, it is worth noting that decrepitude in many societies is conceived as a kind of death, and that death-hastening may then be viewed less as a way of removing an elder from life than as the completion of a process already begun by the elder. Thus, in a variety of societies the same word is used both for *death* and for *seriously ill, feeble,* or *decrepit* (Glascock 1990; Counts and Counts 1984–85). The border between life and death in such cases is not sharp. Glascock found that a third of the societies in the HRAF Probability Sample File made a strong distinction between decrepit and intact elders.

Finally, an important point made by Glascock and others (Eastwell 1982) is that the label of "decrepit" is largely linked to the presence of chronic disease that interferes with a person's ability to perform expected social roles. Eastwell (1982), in a study of the Murngin (an aboriginal Australian population), has shown that elders labeled decrepit may play a role in their own death, as they begin to refuse food and water. But he also makes clear the way these aboriginal communities encourage such behavior among elders. Younger people may actively deny an elder water, leading to death by dehydration. They also begin mortuary rituals for the elder before the death and in the presence of the elder.

We have surveyed gerontocide and death-hastening in a variety of non-Western societies, and earlier we indicated that death-hastening in the more developed societies does occur, but is most often an affair within families or between a family and a doctor. Recent research shows that the elderly themselves, along with family caregivers, play a large role in medical decisions regarding their care (Diemling, Smerglia, and Barresi 1990); but little information is available about the role of elders in decisions regarding termination of medical treatment or care. This information is obviously difficult to obtain but would clearly be very valuable in understanding how elders accept or do not accept the "decrepit" label in more developed societies.

An important additional domain for cross-cultural investigation of death-hastening behavior involves hospital or nursing home care for elders who wish to refuse food and water. Davidson and her colleagues (1990), in a survey of 169 nurses in seven countries, found marked cross-cultural variation among nurses with regard to the degree to which they would respect an elderly patient's wish not to be fed. Nurses in the United States, Australia, Sweden, and Finland were more likely to respect the autonomy of elderly patients and not force them to eat or drink. Nurses in the People's Republic of China, by contrast, universally thought it best to override the patients' autonomy in the interest of keeping the elder alive. In Israel, nurses were evenly split on the issue. Thus, in some cultures the "autonomy principle" held sway, while in others the "beneficence principle" was dominant. Davidson and her colleagues (1990) point out that the issue is further complicated by a variety of other factors, including nurses' judgments about the patient's quality of life and perceptions of how much the patient is suffering. Even when accepting the patient's wishes may be best for a patient (as compared with force feeding or insertion of a nasogastric tube), the significance of an offer of food and water as a symbol of compassion and concern makes the position of the nurse as an unwitting death-hastener extremely difficult. A great deal more research on these issues is required if we are to understand elder death-hastening in the more developed societies.

Comparative Research on the Last Year of Life

We have already indicated that death-hastening behavior may not be the best indicator of cross-cultural variation in the dying process among elders. More to the point is the quality of the last year of life among elders, which offers a direct window on variation in the social experience of decline and ultimately death. A focus on the last year of life allows one to explore cultural variation in the impact of death for elders, their families, and their communities. Of course, the time unit of one year as defining the last period of life is arbitrary, but it is valuable for drawing attention to the need to analyze time-linked variation in the experience of decline and the alterations in social relationships bound up with such decline. In fact, Lawton, Moss, and Glicksman (1990) found substantial variation in family members' reports of when an elder "first really began to go downhill." In this research, the median period of such family-identified decline in elders was fourteen months.

Lawton's study of the quality of the last year of life for American elders (Lawton, Moss, and Glicksman 1990) is an extremely important study because it offers a yardstick for assessing the experience of dying in a cross-cultural framework. However, the application of this yardstick in comparative research remains to be carried out, and so we are restricted here to a report of Lawton's findings for an American sample of urban elderly.

Lawton and his colleagues began with a random sample drawn from the death certificates of a major urban center in a twelve-month period. They then narrowed this pool of recently deceased people further by excluding all those under age 65, all those who died in nursing homes (roughly 25 percent of American elder deaths nationwide), all those who spent more than three of their final twelve months in acute hospital care, and all those without a named informant on the death certificate. In this way, they identified a sample of elders who had died in the community, and who had family members or friends who could report on the experience of death and decline in the elder. With this procedure, they successfully interviewed 200 survivors who could report on the death of the community-resident elder. While men, whites, and spouses of the deceased were less likely to grant an interview (suggesting some bias in generalizing from this sample to the population of community-resident elders as a whole), the sample still represents one of the few that centers on survivors of the recently deceased. Lawton and his colleagues than identified a comparable group of community-dwelling elders who had not died in the same time period, matching these to the deceased by age, sex, and geographic residence. They did this by beginning at the household of the deceased and interviewing people in adjacent residences until they found a living elder who matched the deceased in these features. The two groups of elders differed only in the relationship of the informant to the targeted elder. Informants for elders who had died in the last year were more likely to be adult children; informants for living elders were more likely to be spouses or family members other than adult children. This difference is consistent with what we have seen earlier (chapter 6): adult children are likely to be caregivers to older, more infirm parents whose spouse is likely to have already died. Thus, the Lawton sample represents a first opportunity to compare the experience of the last year of life with that of an ordinary year of life for a matched sample of elders.

As one might expect, the trajectory of decline was accelerated for the last year of life group; this group declined over the year far more rapidly than the control group in functional health and cognitive competence. The last year of life group also showed more rapid decline in psychological well-being (more depression, less interest in the world), satisfaction with time use, and opportunities to make visits to the homes of relatives and friends than the control group. On the other hand, the last year of life group showed an increase in the number of times relatives came to visit the elder, and no decline in the number of visits from friends over the year. Thus, comparing the last year of life to an ordinary year, we find that physical decline and its effects on psychological well-being are clearly greater in the former group; in fact, they accelerate noticeably in the final three months of life. However, social isolation of the dying elder is *not* evident. In fact, the last year of life group receives an increased number of visits from relatives, and no decline in visits from friends, despite the physical decline these elders undergo.

Lawton's analysis is even more revealing in regard to measures of the quality of the last year of life. Lawton and his colleagues found that the popular conception of the final months of life as unremittingly painful, with mental faculties clouded, increased depression, and social withdrawal, is not supported by the data. Even at the point of death, 45 percent of the elders experienced only minor pain, 60 percent had complete mental clarity, 45 percent were "never" or only "seldom" depressed, and 29 percent had relatives visiting three or more times each week. More striking, perhaps, is the persistence of "high-quality" months for the dying elder even to the month of death. Examining nine domains of life (pain, degree of mental acuity, functional health, social participation, time use, null behavior, depression, interest in the world, and the feeling that life is worth living), Lawton and colleagues found that high-quality months declined over the year most precipitously in only two of the domains, pain and functional health. They conclude: "By the 4th month before death, one-half exhibited negative QOL [quality of life] in the pain domain, while in the ADL [activities of daily living] domain that point was reached 2 months before death. Otherwise, even down to the final month the majority of subjects were in the positive range" (Lawton, Moss, and Glicksman 1990, 23). Combining the nine domains into a single quality of life index, 84.7 percent of the elders began their last year with high quality of life; and even in the final month of life, 64.9 percent of the elders had positive quality of life in five or more of the domains.

The last year of life study offers rare insight on the quality of life and social experience of the dying, community-resident elder. It also offers a way to assess the social experience of the dying elder and provides a convenient yardstick for comparative research on the quality of life at the end of life. A surprising finding from the American research is the persistence of high-quality months in many domains even until the end of life. Thus, the dying elder remains the focus, or becomes an increased focus, of family attention in the last year of life. Likewise, 45.5 percent of the informants for these deceased elders reported that the elder felt there was "a great deal to live for," even in the final month of life. The inescapable conclusion is that "the end of life has a substantial component of life as it always was," as Lawton puts it, an important conclusion that is less obvious than it might seem.

Equally significant is that physical decline leads to less of a general decline in quality of life than one might have expected. For example, family contact increases, and contact with friends remains at its prior levels, leading to high quality in the domain of social participation. Also, a substantial portion of the dying elderly evidently still feel that life is worth living.

Would we find the same relationship between physical decline and quality of life if we applied the Lawton domains and quality of life index to dying elderly in other societies? This research has not yet been undertaken, so we are forced to speculate. One hypothesis worth investigating involves the quality of life of the dying elder in societies that differ in the degree to which they distinguish between the "old" and the "decrepit." Given the research summarized earlier in this chapter, we hypothesize that the quality of life for declining elders in societies that strongly distinguish between old and decrepit is likely to be poorer. In such societies, for example, the decrepit label carries with it social isolation, even expulsion from a community, where in the American case continued social contact is one source of good quality of life despite decline. Thus, we would expect to find poorer quality of life for the dying elder in societies that label certain elders "decrepit," and, by extension, in societies that practice gerontocide or the more extreme forms of death-hastening.

On the other hand, the study cited above is restricted to elders who have declined and died in the community; nursing home deaths and deaths preceded by long hospitalizations were excluded in the Lawton sample. The quality of the last year of life may be poorer for this population of elders, perhaps because they are partly removed from family and friends. Indeed, many survivors of elders who have died at home choose to keep a parent or spouse home for just this reason (Sankar 1991). Thus, it is important to consider variability in the social context of decline among American elders. Such variability, most easily indexed in the location of the elder at death, may affect the quality of the last year of life. We might expect such variability to be less salient in societies without access to long-term care institutions, and thus to have a more uniform quality of life in the last year before death. But this, too, is a hypothesis in need of well-designed research.

Finally, we can expect to see cross-cultural variation in the response of a community to elder decrepitude. One might imagine a continuum of response from a pole of extreme exclusion of such an elder from social life to an opposite pole of maximum inclusion. Such an inclusive response probably depends on access to a prosthetic environment, in which an elder would be able (and encouraged) to exercise whatever capacities are still intact. For example, even demented elders show certain benefits (e.g., reduction in psychiatric behaviors) when environments are altered to stimulate and shelter the Alzheimer's patient selectively (Lawton, Fulcomer, and Kleban 1984).

Viewing responses to decrepitude in terms of such a continuum, how do less developed and more developed societies compare? Our initial inclination, perhaps, is to expect the small-scale, village-based society to show the more inclusive response; after all, here elders have higher status and, if they do not, at least extended family units are present to provide for the elder. Yet this intuition is not borne out in the ethnographic accounts available. Take, for example, the Kaliai of New Britain (Papua New Guinea), the population mentioned at the very beginning of this book. This population of shifting horticulturalists makes very little use of formal medical care, and thus has little access to the prosthetic devices (e.g., wheelchairs, eyeglasses) that would extend the functional capacity of declining elders. By all accounts elders are respected, consulted, and deferred to; yet with the onset of dependency linked to cognitive and physical decline, Kaliai elders fare poorly on the question of inclusion in community life. They are excluded from social life even as younger people provide them with firewood, water, and food (Counts and Counts 1984–85).

The Kaliai, it might even be said, push the elder into decrepitude and death by beginning the mortuary cycle before an elder's death. Counts and Counts report that an old man was decidedly ambivalent about being pushed out of the community of the living: "On the one hand, he cooperated in the mortuary ritual and danced with the masked ancestor figures who had come to honor him. But he also bitterly protested his exclusion from the planning of his grandson's initiation, and he continued to try to direct the proceedings even though younger kin ignored his advice and gently led him away" (1984–85, 234). This elder, by any account, clearly had the capacity to participate in social life, at least to some extent, but found himself forcibly and publicly excluded.

Of course, from the one example we cannot generalize to other societies with similar social organization, let alone to the entire range of societies that we have been calling "developing" or "less developed."

Yet reports of such cases lead us to hypothesize that the status of *decrepit* elders may be better in societies that have access to the prosthetic technology that allows impaired elders to be included in social life. Thus, in speaking about the status of elders across cultures, we must distinguish between the status of well elderly and the status of severely impaired elderly. High status in the one may not imply high status in the other, both across societies and within the same society. This question, too, could profit from careful research.

Elder Abuse in Comparative Perspective

Elder abuse is not restricted to the declining or decrepit elder; likewise, a subset of elder abuse cases involve lifelong dysfunctional relationships between adult children and parents, or between spouses. Also, it is clear that an additional subset of elder abuse cases in the more developed societies is perpetrated by formal sector health aides. Yet because one risk factor for elder abuse is impairment in an elder (and related caregiver stress), and because outcomes of such abuse include neglect and even death of the elder, we include the topic in this chapter.

Definitions of elder abuse vary. Similarly, estimates of its prevalence are wildly discrepant, partly because it is now known that reported cases represent only a fraction of the true prevalence. Little is known about elder abuse outside the developed countries. Indeed, even in the developed countries, and despite recognition of its widespread occurrence, until recently very little was known about the extent of elder abuse. The reliability of state reporting systems in collecting statistics on elder abuse is also unclear, with many states lacking mandatory reporting of such cases. The first attempt to compile statistics on elder abuse from state reporting systems in the United States did not appear until 1990 (Tatara 1990).

This compilation, derived from a national survey of state adult protective service and aging agencies, is perhaps the best source on the nature and extent of the problem in a developed society. Limiting elder abuse to the domestic arena (that is, excluding cases of mistreatment in long-term care institutions), state agencies reported a total of 140,000 cases of elder abuse in 1988, the most recent year for which data are available. Extrapolating this prevalence to the universe of all reportable cases in 1988 yields an estimate of two million incidents in the United

States (Tatara 1990). This figure represents cases of "abuse, neglect, and exploitation" as state agencies themselves define them. The closest approximation to a prevalence figure in the United States is 3.77 *reports* per 1,000 elders in urban states, and 2.60 per 1,000 in rural states. Since these figures represent reports, rather than individual cases, they cannot be taken as population estimates. Across the twenty-four states for which data are most reliable, "neglect" is the most common form of abuse, followed by "physical abuse" and "financial/material exploitation." The most frequent perpetrators are adult children, who account for 30 percent of the incidents, other relatives (17.8 percent), and spouses (14.8 percent). The most frequent victim is an elderly woman.

The first question, then, from a comparative perspective is variation in the prevalence of elder abuse. Unfortunately, even in the United States, where reporting systems for collecting data are present, the prevalence of elder abuse is unclear. It is easy to see why. If an elder husband mistreats a frail wife, for example, even to the point that social service agencies or police intervene, the case may be considered spouse abuse rather than elder abuse and never be reported to state reporting agencies. There is a preference to keep and resolve such affairs within families in any case. Similarly, the border between abuse and crime is often poorly defined. If a home health aide steals from an elder, it is hard to know whether this should be considered criminal theft or elder financial abuse. Likewise, the components of abuse are in some cases difficult to delimit. Thus, "neglect" is a slippery concept, let alone "emotional abuse." There are those who feel that institutionalizing a family member is a form of "neglect."

If establishing the presence of elder abuse in the United States is difficult, it is probably even more difficult in societies that lack such a reporting apparatus. We have not been able to identify studies that report prevalence figures outside the developed countries, although in earlier chapters we reported on cases of neglect that could plausibly fall into the category of "abuse." These include the nutritional bias against elderly women in Java and aboriginal Australia (see chapter 2) and the poor economic position of Nepalese elders even when they co-reside with elder sons (see chapter 5).

While we cannot report on variation in the prevalence of elder abuse, a recent study on elder abuse in Native American communities offers a second axis for comparison, which is somewhat more amenable to cross-cultural investigation. This axis involves variation in the conceptualization of elder abuse, specifically the degree to which it is viewed as a family or community problem. Evidence from a study of two Native American reservations suggests that Native Americans view elder abuse as a function of general community health, not simply as a problem in family relationships (Maxwell and Maxwell 1992). This is in contrast to mainstream American attitudes and the perspective of clinicians, who view it as deviant behavior within a family. The contrast is clearest in the different remedies elder abuse is seen to require: in the American case, family therapy and perhaps legal protection; in the Native American case, a community meeting and healing ceremonies.

In fact, the conceptualization of elder abuse as a community problem in the Native American setting is perhaps more appropriate than the family deviance model because elder abuse in Native American communities has much to do with alcohol abuse by young adults, who neglect elderly as a result, and go so far as to steal elders' social security money in pursuit of the habit (Maxwell and Maxwell 1992). Better economic conditions, visible in increased opportunity for productive labor, seem to decrease the risk of elder abuse; thus, the reservation with better economic opportunity showed a lower prevalence of elder abuse and less severe types of elder abuse among reported cases. In this sense the Native American conceptualization of elder abuse as a community problem is accurate.

The Native American data are important from another perspective as well. Pillemer (1985) has presented data showing that severe elder abuse, violent physical abuse, is most likely to involve an abuser who is *dependent* on the elder, both emotionally and materially. When elders are dependent on caregiving children, by contrast, elder abuse rarely involves physical violence but rather takes the form of neglect. Maxwell and Maxwell (1992) found just this contrast between the two reservations they studied. The more economically distressed community saw greater rates of physical abuse, largely centering on access to elders' social security checks. The less distressed community had virtually none of this more disturbing elder abuse.

Thus, despite the lack of data on elder abuse in cross-cultural research, it is apparent that variation is likely. In addition, as we see with the Native American data, the cross-cultural perspective is helpful in qualifying hypotheses drawn from research on the elderly conducted in the United States.

11

What Next? Hypotheses for Cross-Cultural Investigation

We have presented the experience of being old from a number of perspectives. Section I explicitly examines aging from biologic, biodemographic, and cultural standpoints. We noted that "old age" is not easily defined, that aging has biologic, chronologic, and social components that only partly overlap. Nor is old age a single kind of social experience. Section II demonstrates striking cross-cultural and cross-national differences among elders in living arrangements, intergenerational experiences, social relationships, and progression through the lifecourse. Finally, section III makes clear that variations in experiences persist even into extreme old age because the effects of impairments brought on by senescence differ across cultures. Even death is experienced differently from one culture to another.

A number of broad conclusions can be drawn from this survey. First, we note that cross-cultural data on old age are uneven: minimal in some domains, substantial in others. Where the ethnographic record is strong and cross-national survey results are available, we have discussed topics in depth, as in the case of cultural variation in the transcultural definition of impairment. Where cross-cultural data are weak, we have had to rely on data primarily or only from developed nations. For example, variation in the intragenerational relationships of the elderly has not been a field of research for developing nations. Similarly, little is known about cross-cultural variation in elders' last year of life. Throughout our inquiry, we have tried to draw attention to these and other under-researched areas of elder experience in the hope of spurring investigators to undertake the relevant research.

A second conclusion involves the need for a demographic perspective in assessing cultural variation. Aging is a population process as well as an individual experience. Aging in older populations (those with high proportions of people age 60+ or 65+) differs in major ways from aging in younger populations. Because population aging is inextricably linked to declines in fertility (see chapter 3), the demographer will point to differences in life expectancy and other life-table functions, as well as to the different fertility regimes and population structures that distinguish young and old populations. Yet population aging also has enormous cultural significance that affects individual experiences of aging. We have seen that declining fertility and fewer children per family mean fewer potential caregivers in late life, shifts in intergenerational wealth flows, new concerns about generational equity, and much else.

Demography is equally critical for determining when a difference in some dependent measure of interest is truly a matter of cultural variation. An example can be seen in our discussion of living arrangements in chapter 5. An increase in the proportion of nuclear households in a society would seem to imply a decrease in shared living arrangements between elders and their children. It might be taken as a sign of modernization and a decline in the status of elders. We are thus tempted to view the proportion of nuclear households in societies as a proxy for such cultural measures as social integration of elders in families or care of frail elders. Yet we have seen that the proportion of nuclear households reflects a host of demographic processes with no clear connection to elder status. For example, household composition fluctuates across the lifecourse. Nuclear households emerge after the death of an elder, and shared households form as parents and adult children age. Without knowledge of this base rate of household variation (which may differ across cultures), it is impossible to know whether a difference in the proportion of nuclear households is an artifact of measurement or a real cultural difference.

Similarly, decreases in infant mortality without corresponding decreases in overall fertility will eventually lead to an increase in the proportion of nuclear households, even when the rate at which elders co-reside with adult children remains constant. In such a case, we might be tempted to look for a decline in the strength of elder–adult children ties, when in fact the same proportion of elders is sharing households with adult children. There are more nuclear households simply because each adult child sharing a residence with an elder has more surviving siblings (Martin 1990).

On the other hand, demography without cultural analysis is also likely to lead us astray. For example, using sharing living arrangement as a proxy for elder well-being is inadequate, as seen in Nepal and China. In these countries, elders share residences with married sons (the normative arrangement) at nearly traditional levels. Yet these elders, especially in urban areas, are clearly worse off than were their own parents at similar ages. With adult sons now working in wage labor, a father's control of land no longer binds a son to him, and hence no longer assures provisioning of the elder. In Nepal, about half the co-residing elders receive no support from sons. No longer beholden to the father for rights to land, sons feel free to neglect parents in favor of material goods, their own conjugal ties, and the schooling of children (Goldstein, Schuler, and Ross 1983).

What is true of demography is true as well for elder health status. It is impossible to speak of the condition of "the elderly" in a society without minimally distinguishing between healthy and frail elders. We have been struck by the paucity of health data in ethnographic studies of the elderly, for it is clear that a society that accords high status to an elder able to enforce his claim to seniority may not accord high status to an elder who is frail or mentally incompetent. In this book, we have stressed the cross-cultural assessment of elder functional capacity because the position of older people is so intimately linked to health decline. Recognizing this connection alerts us to the significance of the vast range of compensating processes available to elders across the globe, from manipulations of reciprocity in social relationships to use of the strategic bequest in resource transfer.

Beyond these broad comparative points, our survey of aging from a cross-cultural and cross-national perspective is valuable for identifying specific hypotheses for future investigation. Enough data are now available to pose many researchable hypotheses, listed here to demonstrate how they knit together the various strands of our inquiry.

Hypotheses are organized by topic, chosen carefully to present only highly focused hypotheses in which outcome measures and predictors can be specified.

Living Arrangements: Aging Parents and Adult Children

Cultural beliefs and practices strongly influence living arrangements of the elderly. In many of the world's societies, co-residence of elderly parents with adult children is both the norm (or ideal) and the actual modal pattern. In other societies, such as those of the United States and Europe (Heikkinen et al. 1983), separate households are both the norm and the modal pattern.

While culture is a strong determinant of elders' living arrangements, other factors are also important in the formation of parent–adult child households. These factors vary cross-culturally. In the United States, a parent's increasing frailty and need for personal care, associated with increasing age, affect the decision of where the parent will live. Parental dependency is not a factor among Israeli Arabs (Weihl 1983) and Japanese (Palmore and Maeda 1985), for whom co-residence is the modal pattern regardless of parents' age or state of health. Older persons' marital status and gender may be powerful predictors of co-residence, as in Latin America and the Caribbean (De Vos 1990) and in Mexico, where shared residence of older men follows a bimodal pattern related to their participation in family-run businesses and their marital status (Christenson and Hermalin 1991).

Hypothesis 1.   In societies where co-residence is not the modal pattern, co-residence of aging parents with children is positively associated with the parent's increasing dependency (or with age).

Hypothesis 2.   In societies where co-residence is the modal pattern, marital status and gender (not age or physical dependency) are the best predictors of shared living arrangements.

Modernization may change living patterns directly, as with the geographical dispersion of the extended family in sub-Saharan Africa and the substitution of remittances and visits for shared living; or very little, if at all, as in Japan, a highly modernized nation, where co-residence remains the common practice. Or the effects of modernization on elders' living arrangements may be indirect, for example, in Nepal, where an elder may need the traditional red box of heritable goods, even if the box is empty, to encourage co-residence by a hopeful inheritor (Goldstein, Schuler, and Ross 1983).

Economic considerations also play a part in elders' living arrangements. These may take the form of parents' economic contributions, as in Newfoundland (Canada) and Russia where pension checks make elders, female and male, valuable additions to households (McCay 1987; McKain 1972). In India (Vatuk 1982) and Java (Evans 1990) gender is important, as older women are less likely than older men to co-reside because men have greater control of resources. In the United States, it may be not the parents' but the adult children's economic needs that influence the formation of shared households.

Hypothesis 3.   Elders' economic contributions to a household (goods, labor, money) are correlated with shared living arrangements.

Hypothesis 4.   Adult children's economic or other needs can predict co-residence with parents.

Family Relationships: Reciprocity

Family relationships throughout the world are characterized by reciprocity and material and nonmaterial exchanges.

Intergenerational reciprocity may be broadly conceived, for example, as nonmaterial rewards (affection, approval or blessing, permission) from the parent in return for instrumental support from children, often within a lifetime framework, for example, as "net lifetime intergenerational exchange" (Caldwell 1982) in a "life-term social arena" (Moore 1978). In Japan a mother's affection is seen as equivalent in exchange value to her daughter's caregiving (Akiyama, Antonucci, and Campbell 1990). In agrarian societies (much of the developing world), reciprocity between parents and children is conceived in terms of life-time obligations, with adult children "owing" parents throughout the children's lives (LeVine and LeVine 1985).

On the other hand, intergenerational reciprocity may be more narrowly conceived in terms of immediate equivalence of exchanges in the more restricted time frame of the immediate present. In the United States, for example, an exchange obligation is discharged only when a strict equivalent is returned. Elders' impairments are more likely to translate into exchange deficits, accompanied by interpersonal strain, lower self-esteem, and lower satisfaction with their present quality of life. Nevertheless, implementation of the lifetime reciprocity model in the United States and Europe might possibly refine our understandings both of family reciprocity patterns in general and of family caregiving to dependent elders—as suggested by Climo's (1992) study of long-distance caregiving in the United States and Kendig's (1986) study of Australian family caregiving.

Hypothesis 5. Intergenerational transfers will favor the elderly when exchange obligations are broadly conceived.

Hypothesis 6. Older persons' status is higher when exchange obligations are broadly conceived.

Hypothesis 7. Older persons' self-esteem is higher when exchange obligations are broadly conceived.

Hypothesis 8. Older persons' satisfaction with their present lives is higher when exchange obligations are broadly conceived.

Family Relationships: Caregiving

While spouses (especially wives) are important caregivers in all societies, research emphasis has been on adult children in this capacity. Throughout the world children and their surrogates (often daughters-in-law and grandchildren) are the primary caregivers of aging parents. The ethic of filial care is a strong influence in children's acceptance of this responsibility regardless of the nature of their relationship with the parent (Horowitz 1985).

Hypothesis 9. Children's willingness to care for aging parents is not dependent on affection. However, the nature of the parent–child relationship is likely to influence the quality of care frail elders receive.

Hypothesis 10. Lack of affection for a parent may have negative effects on the quality of caregiving and lower the threshold for death-hastening behavior (neglecting, abusing, or killing the elder).

Demographic patterns and trends such as fertility declines, population aging, and labor migration affect the availability of appropriate or preferred caregivers and caregiver selection.

In the United States, caregiver selection is driven by the demographic imperatives of sex of caregiver, proximity to elder, and status as an only or unmarried child—with selection invariant across subcultures (Ikels 1983). Outside the United States, a wider variety of kin may fulfill the caregiving role, as can be seen in the African ethnographic record in regard to elders who are childless (or, in particular, sonless) and hence lack the most appropriate caregivers. This problem may be met, as it has been in many African societies, by various strategies that expand the range of caregiver choice, including child fostering (Bledsoe and Isiugo-Abanihe 1989; Sangree 1987) and care by daughters and even granddaughters instead of sons and daughters-in-law (Peil, Bamisaiye, and Ekpenyong 1989).

As fertility declines in more and more nations, the problem of caregiver scarcity will undoubtedly become much more widespread. In this situation, old age support considerations may affect wider spheres of family behavior such as marriage patterns and norms of caregiver selection. For example, elderly Taiwanese without a son are now encouraging their daughters to marry a man with an older brother who is co-residing with their parents, freeing the "second son" to live with his parents-in-law (Hermalin et al. 1990).

Hypothesis 11. Demographic imperatives influence availability of caregivers and caregiver selection in culturally appropriate ways. Individuals may utilize existing strategies to achieve old age security or changes may occur in the norms of caregiver selection, traditional marriage patterns, or other social spheres in response to caregiver scarcity.

Modernization and Succession to Seniority

This domain is perhaps the most thoroughly investigated in cross-cultural research, particularly concerning elders' control of valued resources. Generalizing on conclusions developed in previous research (see chapter 8 and Maxwell and Silverman 1970, 1989; Silverman and Maxwell 1978, 1983), we suggest that modernization affects the status of the elderly primarily by breaking the link between aging and the accumulation of cultural expertise, that is, elders' control of information. This is not a novel formulation, but it stresses the feature of modernization that may matter most for elder status. As such, it is useful for understanding why modernization does not always lead to a decline in elders' condition. Cross-cultural studies of aging and cultural expertise (the measurement of which is far advanced; see Romney, Weller, and Batchelder 1986) would add greatly to our understanding of elder status.

Hypothesis 12. Modernization affects the status of the elderly primarily by breaking the link between aging and the accumulation of cultural expertise.

Health Decline, Death, and Death-Hastening

Distinctions between "intact" and "decrepit" elders vary cross-culturally, including variation in the degree to which elders are recognized as having crossed from healthy to infirm. The clarity of the distinction between intact and decrepit may have definite effects on the quality of life, particularly in the last year of life, and to death-hastening practices that include neglect and abuse as well as outright killing. In general, the more precisely the decrepit state is distinguished from the intact state, the more the decrepit elder is likely to be removed from active participation in social life.

Hypothesis 13. Where the distinction between intact and decrepit elders is clear, the likelihood of death-hastening will be greater.

Hypothesis 14. Where the distinction between intact and decrepit elders is clear, the quality of the last year of life will be poorer.

Hypothesis 15. Where the distinction between intact and decrepit elders is clear, the likelihood of the elders' removal from social life is greater.

Definitions of disability among the elderly vary both cross-culturally and intraculturally. Disability is clearest when it interferes with occupational performance (Manton et al. 1986) and less clear for retirees from the labor force in developed countries who may devote themselves primarily to the pursuit of personal pleasure. In agrarian societies, older persons may continue working but with reduced energy inputs (Halperin 1987) or change their "occupations" (socially productive roles) to those that require little physical strength, for example, advice-giving, ritual performance, and even "singing for their supper" (Teitelbaum 1988). In any of these situations, the criteria for disability may be unclear, ambiguous, or irrelevant.

Elders' desire to avoid being "overbenefited" (receiving more than they give) varies cross-culturally, but seems universally to be linked with disability. American elders' negative attitudes toward and avoidance of being overbenefited stem from the cultural ideal of personal independence (Clark 1972; Clark and Anderson 1967; Johnson 1987). Japanese and African elders' positive attitudes toward and desire for overbenefiting are related to cultural ideals of children's lifetime obligations to parents and cultural acceptance of dependency as appropriate in old age. But regardless of cultural perceptions, disabled elders who require personal care are likely to find their situation personally distasteful (Cattell 1989a; Counts and Counts 1985). They may use compensating mechanisms (such as being underbenefited in some domains) or other means to avoid the "decrepit" label or to enhance the quality of their life.

For example, health decline and impairment in late life are likely to be associated with an"oppositional" or aggressive interpersonal style. Studies in senior centers (Myerhoff 1978), nursing homes (Savishinsky 1991; Shields 1988), and in community settings in the United States and abroad (Foner 1984; Rosenberg 1990) all point to the adaptive value of griping and complaining. This oppositional relationship style allows impaired elders to exert competencies they still have and to maintain power over others while also keeping distant from their impaired peers.

Hypothesis 16. Variability or ambiguity in the definition of disability is greater among elderly than among younger adults.

Hypothesis 17. Disabled persons of any age, including the elderly, seek to compensate for unbalanced exchanges related to personal care by being underbenefited in other domains of life.

Hypothesis 18. Older persons, especially as they experience impairments and disabilities, develop an oppositional, aggressive, and complaining interpersonal style.

Determinants of self-rated health among older adults vary crossculturally, and the predictive value of self-rated health for health outcomes and the occurrence of death may be limited to a few countries such as the United States (Mossey and Shapiro 1982). Education is a significant predictor of self-rated health among American elders but not among Japanese elders (Liang et al. 1991). The WHO survey of the elderly in eleven European countries found great variation in self-rated health, with a general decline in ratings from western to eastern Europe (Heikkinen, Waters, and Brzezinski 1983). In two African populations that accord privileges to elders, the elders gave themselves surprisingly low health ratings (Draper and Harpending 1990)—though one might expect lower health ratings among people of all ages in developing countries, given the nutritional and health-care advantages of persons living in developed countries.

Hypothesis 19. The determinants of self-rated health vary crossculturally.

Hypothesis 20. The predictive value of self-rated health for health outcomes varies cross-culturally.

The health advantages of persons living in developed nations may become increasingly significant with advancing age and its concomitant health decline. Quality of life in the final year(s) often depends on access to a prosthetic environment that allows an elder to participate in social life to some degree despite severe impairment. Wheelchairs, nutritional supplements, lasers for cataract surgery, and post–stroke rehabilitation therapy—to name but a few—make impairment and the end of life less isolating for frail elders and more satisfying for family caregivers.

Hypothesis 21. The quality of the last year of life for frail elders will be better in developed nations than in developing countries because of access to medical and prosthetic technologies.

Health and Social Participation

Social engagement or activity has often been put forth as a universal feature of successful aging and elders' positive morale or psychological well-being (but see Carstensen [1987] and Fredrickson and Carstensen [1990] for a dissent). However, the relationship between social engagement and morale should be qualified according to whether such engagement is voluntary or compulsory. We suggest that this relationship will be positive only in societies that allow elders to choose to be involved in social activity or to withdraw from it.

The distinction between voluntary and compulsory activity in late life is an important one, especially in regard to elderly whose health and functionality are impaired. The !Kung or Herero elder in Botswana who is forced to participate in social life in spite of impairments is likely to have low morale (Draper and Harpending 1990). American elders have greater latitude in deciding whether to be socially involved, and their freedom to withdraw from social activity may be a positive factor in their psychological well-being.

Hypothesis 22. Psychological well-being (morale) will be higher among impaired elders when activity is voluntary, lower when activity is compulsory.

Another aspect of social participation in late life is that the elderly are likely to focus on existing friendships rather than on making new friends (Matthews 1986). Given the imminence of death as "social closure" (Fredrickson and Carstensen 1990), elders are likely to invest their limited resources in long-term friendships that are linked to positive emotions. We would expect this "selectivity theory" to apply cross-culturally to late-life friendships.

Hypothesis 23. The very old form few new friendships, instead investing their energies and resources in long-term friendships.

Each of these hypotheses merits monographic treatment in itself. Each also requires sustained field and survey investigation to collect the data for relevant measurement and testing. Some of the hypotheses are more specific than others; some already have relevant bodies of literature; others are informed guesses, based on research conducted in allied areas. The next step is to plan cross-cultural research that explicitly addresses these hypotheses. It is our hope that this book will spur such efforts.

References

Akiyama, H., T. C. Antonucci, and R. Campbell (1990). Exchange and reciprocity among two generations of Japanese and American women. In J. Sokolovsky (Ed.), *The cultural context of aging: Worldwide perspectives* (pp. 127–138). New York: Bergin and Garvey.

Albert, S. M. (1986). The iconography of New Ireland malagan. *Journal of the Polynesian Society 95*:239–252.

—— (1987). The work of marriage and of death: Ritual and political process among the Lak. Unpublished dissertation, The University of Chicago.

—— (1988). How big are Melanesian big men? In B. Isaac (Ed.), *Research in economic anthropology* (vol. 10, pp. 159–200). Greenwich, CT: JAI Press.

—— (1990a). Caregiving as a cultural system: Conceptions of filial obligation and parental dependency in urban America. *American Anthropologist 92*(2):319–331.

—— (1990b). The dependent elderly, home health care, and strategies of household adaptation. In J. Gubrium and A. Sankar (Eds.), *The home care experience: Ethnography and policy* (pp. 19–36). Newbury Park, CA: Sage.

—— (1992a). Psychometric investigation of a belief system: Caregiving to the chronically ill parent. *Social Science and Medicine 35*:699–709.

—— (1992b). Ethnic variation in caregiving selection. Oral presentation, Gerontological Society of America, Washington, DC.

Albert, S. M., S. J. Litvin, E. M. Brody, and M. H. Kleban (1991). Caregiving daughters' perceptions fo their own and their mothers' personalities. *The Gerontologist 31*(4):476–482.

Albert, S. M., and M. Moss (1990). Consensus and the domain of personal relations among older adults. *Journal of Social and Personal Relationships 7*:353–369.

Alexander, R. D. (1987). *The biology of moral systems.* New York: Aldine.

Almagor, U. (1978). The ethos of equality among age-peers. In P. T. W. Baxter and Uri Almagor (Eds.), *Age, generation and time: Some features of East African age organisations* (pp. 69–93). New York: St. Martin's.

Amoss, P., and S. Harrell (1981). Introduction: An anthropological perspective on aging. In P. T. Amoss and S. Harrell (Eds.), *Other ways of growing old* (pp. 1–24). Stanford, CA: Stanford University Press.

Andrews, G. R., A. J. Esterman, A. J. Braunack-Mayer, and C. M. Rungie (1986). *Aging in the Western Pacific: A four-country study.* Manila: World Health Organization.

Antonucci, T. C. (1985). Personal characteristics, social support, and social behavior. In R. H. Binstock and E. Shanas (Eds.), *Handbook of aging and the social sciences*, 2d. ed. (pp. 94–128). New York: Van Nostrand.

Aquilino, W. S. (1990). The likelihood of parent-child coresidence: Effects of family structure and parental characteristics. *Journal of Marriage and the Family 52*:405–419.

Archbold, P. (1983). Impact of parent-caring on women. *Family Relations 32*:39–45.

Argyle, M. (1986). Rules for social relationships in four cultures. *Australian Journal of Psychology 38*:309–318.

Argyle, M., and M. Henderson (1984). The rules of friendship. *Journal of Social and Personal Relationships 1*:211–237.

Aries, P. (1961). *Centuries of childhood.* New York: Random House.

Baltes, P. B., and M. M. Baltes (1990). *Successful aging: Perspectives from behavioral science.* Cambridge: Cambridge University Press.

Bannister, J. (1988). *Implications of the aging of China's population.* Center for International Research, Staff paper no. 4. U.S. Bureau of the Census. Washington, DC: U.S. Government Printing Office.

Barker, J. (1989). Health and functional status of the elderly in a Polynesian population. *Journal of Cross-Cultural Gerontology 4*:163–194.

Baxter, P., and U. Almagor (Eds.) (1978). *Age, generation, and time: Some features of East African age organizations.* London: Hurst.

Beall, C. M. (1983). Ages at menopause and menarche in a high altitude Himalayan population. *Annals of Human Biology 10*:365–370.

Beall, C. M., and C. A. Weitz (1989). The human population biology of aging. In M. A. Little and J. D. Hass (Eds.), *Human population biology: A transdisciplinary science* (pp. 189–200). Oxford: Oxford University Press.

Beard, B. B. (1991). *Centenarians: The new generation.* Ed. N. K. Wilson and A. J. Wilson. Westport, CT: Greenwood Press.

Beaubier, J. (1976). *High life expectancy on the Island of Paros, Greece.* New York: Philosophical Library.

Becerra, R. M. (1983). The Mexican American: Aging in a changing culture. In R. L. McNeeley and J. L. Colen (Eds.), *Aging minority groups* (pp. 108–118). Beverly Hills, CA: Sage.

Benet, S. (1974). *Abkhasians: The long-living people of the Caucasus.* New York: Holt, Rinehart.

Bengston, V., J. J. Dowd, D. H. Smith, and A. Inkeles (1975). Modernization, modernity, and perceptions of aging: A cross-cultural study. *Journal of Gerontology 30*(6):688–695.

Bengston, V., and J. A. Kuypers (1971). Generational difference and the "developmental stake." *Aging and Human Development 2*(1):249–260.

Bengtson, V. L., and J. F. Robertson (Eds.) (1986). *Grandparenthood.* Beverly Hills, CA: Sage.

Bengston, V., C. Rosenthal, and L. Burton (1990). Families and aging: Diversity and heterogeneity. In R. H. Binstock and L. K. George (Eds.), *Handbook of aging and the social sciences* (pp. 263–287). New York: Academic.

Bentley, M. E. (1988). The household management of childhood diarrhea in rural North India. *Social Science and Medicine 27*:75–85.

Berg, R. L., and J. S. Cassells (Eds.) (1990). *The second fifty years: Pro-*

moting health and preventing disability. Washington, DC: National Academy Press.

Bernardi, B. (1952). The age-system of the Nilo-Hamitic peoples. *Africa* 22:316–332.

Bernheim, B., A. Shleifer, and H. Summers (1985). The strategic bequest motive. *Journal of Political Economy 93*(6):1045–1076.

Binstock, R. H., and S. G. Post (Eds.) (1991). *Too old for health care? Controversies in medicine, law, economics, and ethics.* Baltimore: Johns Hopkins University Press.

Biswas, S. K. (1985). Dependency and family care of the aged in village India: A case study. *Journal of the Indian Anthropological Society 20*:238–257.

Blay, S. L., J. de Jesus Mari, L. R. Ramos, et al. (1991). Validity of a Brazilian version of the mental status questionnaire as a screening test. *International Journal of Geriatric Psychiatry 6*:779–785.

Bledsoe, C., and U. C. Isiugo-Abanihe (1989). Strategies of child fosterage among Mende grannies in Sierra Leone. In R. Lesthaeghe (Ed.), *African reproduction and social organization in sub-Saharan Africa* (pp. 442–474). Berkeley: University of California Press.

Blessed, G., B. E. Tomlinson, and M. Roth (1968). The association between quantitative measures of dementia and of senile change in the cerebral grey matter of elderly subjects. *British Journal of Psychiatry 114*:797–811.

Borgatti, S. (1990). ANTHROPAC 3.2. Software and provisional documentation. Unpublished manuscript.

Bott, E. (1957). *Family and social network: Roles, norms, and external relationships in ordinary urban families.* 2d. ed. New York: Free Press.

Bould, S. B., B. Sanborn, and L. Reif (1989). *Eighty-five plus: The oldest old.* Belmont, CA: Wadsworth.

Bradburn (1969). *The structure of psychological well-being.* Chicago: Aldine.

Braun, J. V., M. H. Wykle, and W. R. Cowling (1988). Failure to thrive in older patients: A concept derived. *The Gerontologist 28*:809–812.

Brock, D. B., J. M. Guralnik, and J. A. Brody (1990). Demography and epidemiology of aging in the United States. In E. L. Schneider and

J. W. Rowe (Eds.), *Handbook of the biology of aging* (pp. 3–23). New York: Academic.

Brody, E. M. (1985). Parent care as a normative family stress. *The Gerontologist 25*:19–29.

——— (1990). *Women in the middle.* New York: Springer.

Brody, E. M., P. Johnsen, M. Fulcomer, and A. Lang (1983). Women's changing roles and help to the elderly: attitudes of three generations of women. *Journal of Gerontology 38*:597–607.

Butler, R. N. (1975). *Why survive? Being old in America.* New York: Harper & Row.

Cain, L. D. (1964). Life course and social structure. In R. E. L. Faris (Ed.), *Handbook of modern sociology* (pp. 272–309). Chicago: Rand McNally.

——— (1976). Aging and the law. In R. H. Binstock and E. Shanas (Eds.), *Handbook of aging and the social sciences* (pp. 342–368). New York: Van Nostrand.

——— (1986). The consequences of reproductive failure: Dependence, mobility, and mortality among the elderly of rural South Asia. *Population Studies 40*:375–388.

Caldwell, J. C. (1981). *The theory of fertility decline.* London: Academic.

Callahan, D. (1987). *Setting limits: Medical goals in an aging society.* New York: Simon & Schuster.

Campbell, D. T., and J. C. Stanley (1963). *Experimental and quasi-experimental designs for research.* Chicago: Rand-McNally.

Carstensen, L. L. (1987). Age-related changes in social activity. In L. L. Carstensen (Ed.), *Handbook of clinical gerontology* (pp. 222–237). New York: Pergamon.

Carucci, L. M. (1985). Conceptions of maturing and dying in the 'middle of heaven.' In D. A. Counts and D. R. Counts (Eds.), *Aging and its transformations: Moving toward death in Pacific societies* (pp. 107–129). Lanham, MD: University Press of America.

Cattell, M. G. (1982). Anthropological approaches to age: Implications for anthropological research of a comparison of age groups and age-mates in Africa and Melanesia. Master's thesis, Bryn Mawr College.

——— (1988). *Family support for the aged in rural Kenya: Intergenerational exchange and old age security.* El Paso, TX: Society for Cross-Cultural Research.

———— (1989a). Old age in rural Kenya: Gender, the life course and social change. Ph. D. dissertation, Bryn Mawr College.

———— (1989b). Knowledge and social change in Samia, Kenya. *Journal of Cross-Cultural Gerontology* 4:225–244.

———— (1990). Models of old age among the Samia of Kenya: Family support of the elderly. *Journal of Cross-Cultural Gerontology* 5:375–394.

———— (1991). Aging-in-place: Older persons' assessment of urban neighborhood resources. Unpublished final report to The Retirement Research Foundation, Park Ridge, IL.

———— (1992a). *Aging and social change: Rural Kenya and urban America.* Santa Fe: Society for Cross-Cultural Research.

———— (1992b). Old people and the language of complaint: Examples from Kenya and Philadelphia. Paper presented at Language and Aging Pre-session, Georgetown University Roundtable on Languages and Linguistics, Washington, DC.

———— (1992c). Praise the Lord and say no to men: Older Samia women empowering themselves. *Journal of Cross-Cultural Gerontology* 7:307–330.

———— n.d. Between the generations: Intergenerational contracts and care of the elderly in Samia, Kenya. In T. S. Weisner, C. Bradley, and P. L. Kilbride (Eds.), *Troubled families: Intergenerational relationships and ecology in contemporary western Kenya* (in preparation).

Chamie, M. (1989). Survey design strategies for the study of disability. *World Health Statistics Quarterly* 42(3):122–146.

Cheal, D. (1988). *The gift economy.* Cambridge: Cambridge University Press.

Cherlin, A. J., and F. F. Furstenberg (1986). *The new American grandparent.* New York: Basic Books.

Chow, N. W. S. (1988). *Caregiving in developing east and Southeast Asian countries.* Tampa: International Exchange Center on Gerontology, University of South Florida.

Christenson, B. A., and A. I. Hermalin (1991). A demographic decomposition of elderly living arrangements with a Mexican example. *Journal of Cross-Cultural Gerontology* 6:331–348.

Clark, M. (1973). Cultural values and dependency in later life. In D. O.

Cowgill and L. D. Holmes (Eds.), *Aging and modernization* (pp. 263–274). New York: Appleton-Century-Crofts.

Clark, M., and B. Anderson (1967). *Culture and aging.* Springfield, IL: Charles C. Thomas.

Climo, J. (1992). *Distant parents.* New Brunswick, NJ: Rutgers University Press.

Coale, A., and P. Demeny (1966). *Regional model life tables and stable populations.* Princeton: Princeton University Press.

Cohen, C., and J. Sokolovsky (1989). *Old men of the bowery: Strategies for survival among the homeless.* New York: Guilford.

Cohler, B. J. (1981). Personal narrative and life course. In A. B. Baltes and O. G. Brim, Jr. (Eds.), *Life-span development and behavior* (vol. 4, pp. 205–241). New York: Academic.

Counts, D. A., and D. R. Counts (1984–85). The cultural construction of aging and dying in a Melanesian community. *International Journal of Aging and Human Development 20*:229–240.

———— (1985). I'm not dead yet! Aging and death: Process and experience in Kaliai. In D. A. Counts and D. R. Counts (Eds.), *Aging and its transformations: Moving toward death in Pacific societies* (pp. 131–155). Lanham, MD: University Press of America.

Cowgill, D. O. (1974). Aging and modernization: A revision of the theory. In J. Gubrium (Ed.), *Late life: Communities and environmental policy.* Springfield, IL: Charles C. Thomas.

———— (1986). *Aging around the world.* Belmont, CA: Wadsworth.

Cowgill, D. O., and L. Holmes (Eds.) (1971). *Aging and modernization.* New York: Appleton-Century-Crofts.

Coyne, J. C., and A. Delongis (1986). Going beyond social support. *Journal of Consulting and Clinical Psychology 54*:454–460.

Crews, D. E. (1990). Anthropological issues in biological gerontology. In R. Rubinstein (Ed.), *Anthropology and aging: Comprehensive reviews* (pp. 11–38). Dordrecht: Kulwer Academic Publishers.

Crews, D. E., and J. R. Bindon (1989). Age, glucose, and fat patterning in an obese population. *The Gerontologist 29* (Special Issue):225A.

Crimmins, E. M., and D. G. Ingeneri (1990). Interaction and living arrangements of older parents and their children. *Research on Aging 12*:3–35.

Crystal, S., and D. Shea (1990). Cumulative advantage, cumulative disadvantage, and inequality among elderly people. *The Gerontologist 30*(4):437–443.

Cumming, E., and W. H. Henry (1961). *Growing old: The process of disengagement.* New York: Basic Books.

Cutler, R. G. (1975). Evolution of human longevity and the genetic complexity governing aging rate. *Proceedings of the National Academy of Science 72*:4664–4668.

Cutrona, C. E., and D. W. Russell (1987). The provisions of social relationships and adaptation to stress. *Advances in Personal Relations 1*:37–68.

D'Andrade, R. G. (1973). Cultural constructions of reality. In L. Nader and T. W. Maretzki (Eds.), *Cultural illness and health* (pp. 115–127). Washington, DC: American Anthropological Association.

Davidson, B., R. V. Laan, A. Davis, et al. (1990). Ethical reasoning associated with the feeding of terminally ill elderly cancer patients: An international perspective. *Cancer Nursing 13*:286–292.

De Vos, S. (1990). Extended family living among older people in six Latin American countries. *Journal of Gerontology, Social Sciences 45*:87–94.

Diemling, G. T., V. L. Smerglia, and C. M. Barresi (1990). Health care professionals and family involvement in care-related decisions concerning older patients. *Journal of Aging and Health 2*:310–325.

Donner, W. (1987). Compassion, kinship, and fosterage: Contexts for the care of the childless elderly in a Polynesian community. *Journal of Cross-Cultural Gerontology 2*:43–60.

Dorjahn, V. R. (1989). Where do the old folks live? The residence of the elderly among the Temne of Sierra Leone. *Journal of Cross-Cultural Gerontology 4*:257–278.

Doty, P. (1986). Family care of the elderly: The role of public policy. *Millbank Quarterly 64*:34–75.

Dowd, J. P. (1975). Aging as exchange: A preface to theory. *Journal of Gerontology 30*:584–94.

Dowd, J. J. (1986). The old person as stranger. In V. W. Marshall (Ed.), *Later life: The social psychology of aging* (pp. 147–190). Beverly Hills, CA: Sage.

Draper, P., and H. Harpending (1990). Work and aging in two African societies: !Kung and Herero. In B. R. Bonder (Ed.), *Occupational performance in the elderly* (in press).

Draper, T., and A. C. Marcos (Eds.) (1989). *Family variables: Conceptualization, measurement and use.* Newbury Park, CA: Sage.

Duijn, C. M. van, D. Clayton, V. Chandra, et al. (1991). Familial aggregation of Alzheimer's disease and related disorders: A collaborative re-analysis of case-control studies. *International Journal of Epidemiology 20* (supplement):13–20.

Early, J. D., and J. F. Peters (1990). *The population dynamics of the Mucajai Yanomama.* New York: Academic.

Eastwell, H. D. (1981). Voodoo death and the mechanism for dispatch of the dying in East Arnhem, Australia. *American Anthropologist 84*:5–18.

Eckert, J. K. (1980). *The unseen elderly: A study of marginally subsistent hotel dwellers.* San Diego: Campanile Press.

Edmonston, B. (1990). Agricultural resources, community development, and early childhood mortality in Bangladesh. In A. C. Swedlund and G. J. Armelagos (Eds.), *Disease in populations in transition: Anthropological and epidemiological perspectives* (pp. 333–352). Westport, CT: Bergin and Garvey.

Eisenstadt, S. N. (1954). African age groups: A comparative study. *Africa 24*:100–113.

Elder, G. H., Jr. (1974). *Children of the Great Depression.* Chicago: University of Chicago Press.

——— (1975). Age differentiation and the life course. *Annual Review of Sociology 1*:165–190.

——— (1982a). Family history and the life course. In T. K. Hareven (Ed.), *Transitions: The family and the life course in historical perspective* (pp. 17–64). New York: Academic.

——— (1982b). Hard times in women's lives: Historical influences across 40 years. *American Journal of Sociology 88*:241–269.

——— (1985). Perspectives on the life course. In G. H. Elder, Jr. (Ed.), *Life course dynamics: Trajectories and transitions, 1968–1980* (pp. 23–49). Ithaca, NY: Cornell University Press.

Elder, G. H., Jr., and E. C. Clipp (1988). War experience and social ties: Influences across 40 years in men's lives. In M. W. Riley, B. J. Huber, and B. B. Hess (Eds.), *Social structures and human lives: Social change and the life course* (vol. 1, pp. 306–327). Newbury Park, CA: Sage.

Evans, J. (1990). The economic status of older men and women in the

Javanese household and the influence of this upon their nutritional level. *Journal of Cross-Cultural Gerontology 5*:217–242.

Evers, S. E., J. W. Orchard, and R. G. Haddad (1985). Bone density in postmenopausal North American Indian females and Caucasian females. *Human Biology 57*:719–726.

Ferraro, K. (1980). Self-ratings of health among the old and old-old. *Journal of Health and Social Behavior 21*:377–383.

Ferrucci, L., J. M. Guralnik, A. Baroni, et al. (1991). Value of combined assessment of physical health and functional status in community-dwelling elderly: A prospective study in Florence, Italy. *Journal of Gerontology, Medical Sciences 46*(2):52–56.

Field, D., and M. Minkler (1988). Continuity and change in social support between young-old, old-old, and very old adults. *Journal of Gerontology, Psychological Sciences 43*:100–106.

Fillenbaum, G. G. (1979). Social context and self-assessments of health among the elderly. *Journal of Health and Social Behavior 20*:45–51.

Fillenbaum, G. G. (1984). *The wellbeing of the elderly: Approach to multidimensional assessment.* Geneva: World Health Organization.

Fiore, J., J. Becker, and D. B. Coppel (1983). Social network interactions: a buffer or a stress? *American Journal of Community Psychology 11*:423–439.

Folstein, M. F., S. E. Folstein, and P. R. McHugh (1975). Mini-mental state: A practical method for grading the cognitive state of patients for clinicians. *Journal of Psychiatric Research 12*:189–198.

Foner, A. (1981). Perspectives on changing age systems. In M. W. Riley, R. P. Abeles, and M. S. Teitelbaum (Eds.), *Aging from birth to death. Vol. 2: Sociotemporal perspectives* (pp. 217–228). Boulder: Westview Press.

Foner, A, and D. I. Kertzer (1978). Transitions over the life course: Lessons from age-set societies. *American Journal of Sociology 83*:1081–1104.

——— (1979). Intrinsic and extrinsic sources of change in life-course transitions. In M. W. Riley (Ed.), *Aging from birth to death. Vol. 1: Interdisciplinary perspectives* (pp. 121–136). Boulder: Westview Press.

Foner, N. (1984). *Ages in conflict: A cross-cultural perspective on inequality between old and young.* New York: Columbia University Press.

Ford, A. B., S. J. Folmar, R. B. Salmon, et al. (1988). Health and function in the old and very old. *Journal of the American Geriatrics Society 36*:187–197.

Fortes, M. (1940). The political system of the Tallensi of the Northern Territories of the Gold Coast. In M. Fortes and E. E. Evans-Pritchard (Eds.), *African political systems* (pp. 239–271). London: Oxford University Press.

———— (1949). *The web of kinship among the Tallensi.* London: Oxford University Press.

———— (1984). Age, generation, and social structure. In D. I. Kertzer and J. Keith (Eds.), *Age and anthropological theory* (pp. 99–122). Ithaca, NY: Cornell University Press.

Frank, G., and R. M. Vanderburgh (1986). Cross-cultural use of life history methods in gerontology. In C. L. Fry and J. Keith (Eds.), *New methods for old age research: Strategies for studying diversity* (pp. 185–212). South Hadley, MA: Bergin and Garvey.

Fredrickson, B. L., and L. L. Carstensen (1990). Choosing social partners: How old age and anticipated endings make people more selective. *Psychology and Aging 5*(3):335–347.

Fries, J. F. (1988). Aging, illness, and health policy: Implications of the compression of morbidity. *Perspectives on Biology and Medicine 31*:407–428.

Fries, J. F., and L. M. Crapo (1981). *Vitality and aging: Implications of the rectangular curve.* San Francisco: W. H. Freeman.

Fry, C. L. (1976). The ages of adulthood: a question of numbers. *Journal of Gerontology 31*:170–177.

———— (1980). Cultural dimensions of age: A multidimensional scaling analysis. In C. L. Fry (Ed.), *Aging in culture and society: Comparative viewpoints and strategies* (pp. 42–64). Brooklyn: J. F. Bergin.

———— (Ed.) (1981). *Dimensions: Aging, culture, and health.* Brooklyn: J. F. Bergin.

———— (1985). Culture, behavior, and aging in comparative perspective. In J. Birren and K. W. Schaie (Eds.), *Handbook of the psychology of aging* (pp. 216–244). New York: Van Nostrand.

———— (1988). Theories of age and culture. In J. E. Birren and V. L. Bengtson (Eds.), *Emergent theories of aging* (pp. 447–481). New York: Springer.

———— (1990). The life course in context: Implications of research. In R. L. Rubinstein (Ed.), *Anthropology and aging: Comprehensive reviews* (pp. 129–149). Norwell, MA: Kluwer.

Fry, C. L., and J. Keith (1981). The life course as a cultural unit. In M. W. Riley, M. Johnson, and A. Foner (Eds.), *Aging and society. Vol. 3: A sociology of age stratification* (pp. 51–70). New York: Russell Sage Foundation.

Fry, C. L., and J. Keith (Eds.) (1986). *New methods for old age research: Strategies for studying diversity.* South Hadley, MA: Bergin and Garvey.

Geertz, C. (1973). *The interpretation of cultures.* New York: Basic Books.

Gergen, K., C. Maslach, P. Ellsworth, and M. Seipel (1975). Obligation, donor resources, and reactions to aid in three cultures. *Journal of Personality and Social Psychology 31*:390–400.

Gibbs, J. L., Jr. (1965). The Kpelle of Liberia. In J. L. Gibbs, Jr. (Ed.), *People of Africa* (pp. 199–240). New York: Holt, Rinehart.

Glascock, A. P. (1983). Decrepitude and death hastening: The nature of old age in Third World societies. In J. Sokolovsky (Ed.), *Aging and the aged in the Third World: Part 1* (pp. 43–66). Studies in Third World Societies, pub. no. 22. Williamsburg, VA: College of William and Mary.

———— (1986). Resource control among older males in Southern Somalia. *Journal of Cross-Cultural Gerontology 1*:51–72.

———— (1990). By any other name it is still killing: A comparison of the treatment of the elderly in America and other societies. In J. Sokolovsky (Ed.), *The cultural context of aging: World wide perspectives* (pp. 43–56). New York: Bergin and Garvey.

Glascock, A. P., and S. L. Feinman (1981). Social asset or social burden: treatment of the aged in non-industrial societies. In C. L. Fry (Ed.), *Dimensions: Aging, culture, and health* (pp. 13–31). New York: J. F. Bergin.

Glass, J., V. Bengston, and C. C. Dunham (1986). Attitude similarity in three-generation families: Socialization, status inheritance, or reciprocal influence. *American Sociological Review 51*:685–698.

Goodwin, J. S., and P. J. Garry (1988). Lack of correlation between indices of nutritional status and immunological function in elderly humans. *Journal of Gerontology, Medical Sciences 43*:46–49.

Goldstein, M. C., Y. Ku, and C. Ikels (1990). Household composition of the elderly in two rural villages in the People's Republic of China. *Journal of Cross-Cultural Gerontology 5*:119–130.

Goldstein, M. C., S. Schuler, and J. L. Ross (1983). Social and economic forces affecting intergenerational relations in extended families in a Third World country: A cautionary tale from South Asia. *Journal of Gerontology 38*(6):716–724.

Gove, W. R. (1985). The effect of age and gender on deviant behavior: A biopsychosocial perspective. In A. S. Rossi (Ed.), *Gender and the life course* (pp. 115–144). Chicago: Aldine.

Greenhalgh, S. (1990). Toward a political economy of fertility: anthropological contributions. *Population and Development Review 16*(1):85–106.

Gubrium, J. F. (1975). *Living and dying at Murray Manor*. New York: St. Martin's.

Gubrium, J. F., and A. Sankar (1990). Introduction. In J. F. Gubrium and A. Sankar (Eds.), *The home care experience: Ethnography and policy* (pp. 7–15). Newbury Park, CA: Sage.

Gulliver, P. H. (1963). *Social control in an African society. A study of the Arusha: Agricultural Masai of Northern Tanganyika*. Boston: Boston University Press.

Gurland, B. J., D. E. Wilder, P. Cross, et al. (1991). Screening scales for dementia: Toward reconciliation of conflicting cross-cultural findings. *International Journal of Geriatric Psychiatry 7*:105–113.

Gutmann, D. (1977). The cross-cultural perspective: Notes toward a comparative psychology of aging. In J. Birren and K. W. Schaie (Eds.), *Handbook of the psychology of aging* (pp. 302–326). New York: Van Nostrand.

——— (1987). *Reclaimed powers: Toward a new psychology of men and women in later life*. New York: Basic Books.

Gregory, C. (1981). *Gifts and commodities*. Cambridge: Cambridge University Press.

Hagestad, G. O. (1990). Social perspectives on the life course. In R. H. Binstock and L. K. George (Eds.), *Handbook of aging and the social sciences* (3d. ed., pp. 151–168). New York: Academic.

Hagestad, G. O., and L. M. Burton (1985). Grandparenthood, life context, and family development. *American Behavioral Scientist 29*: 471–484.

Hagestad, G. O., and B. L. Neugarten (1985) [1976]. Age and the life course. In R. H. Binstock and E. Shanas (Eds.), *Handbook of aging and the social sciences* (2d. ed., pp. 35–61). New York: Van Nostrand.

Hahn, R. A. (1991). The state of federal health statistics on racial and ethnic groups. *Journal of the American Medical Association 267*:268–271.

Hahn, R. A., J. Mulinare, and S. M. Teutsch (1991). Inconsistencies in coding of race and ethnicity between birth and death in U.S. infants. *Journal of the American Medical Association 267*:259–263.

Halperin, R. H. (1987). Age in cross-cultural perspective: An evolutionary approach. In P. Silverman (Ed.), *The elderly as modern pioneers* (pp. 283–311). Bloomington: Indiana University Press.

Hamilton, W. D. (1964). The genetical evolution of social behaviour. *Journal of Theoretical Biology 7*:1–52.

――― (1966). The moulding of senescence by natural selection. *Journal of Theoretical Biology 12*:12–45.

Hammel, E. A. (1984). Age in the Fortesian coordinates. In D. I. Kertzer and J. Keith (Eds.), *Age and anthropological theory*. Ithaca, NY: Cornell University Press.

――― (1990). A theory of culture for demography. *Population and Development Review 16*(3):455–485.

Hammel, E. A., and N. Howell (1987). Research in population and culture: An evolutionary framework. *Current Anthropology 28*:141–160.

Handel, G., and Hess, B. B. (1972) [1959]. *The psychosocial interior of the family: A sourcebook for the study of whole families.* Chicago: Aldine, Atherton.

Handwerker, W. P. (1990). Demography. In T. M. Johnson and C. F. Sargent (Eds.), *Medical anthropology: Contempory method and theory* (pp. 319–348). Westport, CT: Praeger.

Hareven, T. K. (Ed.) (1978). *Family history and the life course in historical perspective.* New York: Academic.

――― (1981). *Family time and industrial time.* Cambridge: Cambridge University Press.

――― (1982). *Transitions: The family and the life course in historical perspective.* New York: Academic.

Hayflick, L. (1985). Theories of biological aging. *Experimental Gerontology 20*:145–159.

Hayflick, L., and C. E. Finch (1977). *Handbook of the biology of aging.* New York: Van Nostrand.

Heikkinen E., W. E. Waters, and Z. J. Brzezinski (1983). *The elderly in eleven countries: A sociomedical survey.* Copenhagen: World Health Organization.

Hermalin, A. I., Ming-Cheng Chang, Hui-Sheng Lin, et al. (1990). Patterns of support among the elderly in Taiwan and their policy implications. Research report no. 90–4, Population Studies Center, The University of Michigan.

Hess, B. B. (1979). Sex roles, friendship, and the life course. *Research on Aging 1*:494–515.

Hiebert, P. G. (1981). Old age in a South Indian village. In P. Amoss and S. Harrell (Eds.), *Other ways of growing old: Anthropological perspectives* (pp. 211–226). Stanford, CA: Stanford University Press.

Hing, E., and B. Bloom (1990). Long-term care for the functionally dependent elderly. National Center for Health Statsitics. *Vital Health Statistics 13*(104). Washington, DC: U.S. Government Printing Office.

Hirsch, B. J. (1980). Natural support systems and coping with major life changes. *American Journal of Community Psychology 8*:159–172.

Hochschild, R. (1989a). Improving the precision of biological age determinations. Part 1: A new approach to calculating biological age. *Experimental Gerontology 24*:289–300.

——— (1989b). Improving the precision of biological age determinations. Part 2: Automatic human tests, age norms and variability. *Experimental Gerontology 24*:301–316.

Hogan, D. (1981). Subgroup variations in early life transitions. In M. W. Riley, R. P. Abeles, and M. S. Teitelbaum (Eds.), *Aging from birth to death. Vol. 2: Sociotemporal perspectives* (pp. 87–104). Boulder: Westview Press.

Holmes, E. R. (1987). Western Polynesia's first home for the aged: Are concept and culture compatible? *Journal of Cross-Cultural Gerontology 2*:359–376.

Horowitz, A. L. (1985). Family caregiving to the frail elderly. *Annual Review of Gerontology and Geriatrics 5*:194–246.

Howell, N. (1979). *Demography of the Dobe !Kung.* New York: Academic.

——— (1986). Demographic anthropology. *Annual Review of Anthropology 15*:219–246.

Idler, E. L., and R. J. Angel (1990). Self-rated health and mortality in the NHANES-I epidemiologic follow-up study. *American Journal of Public Health 80*(4):446–452.

Ikels, C. (1983). The process of caretaker selection. *Research on Aging 5*(4):491–509.

——— (1990). *The impact of socio-economic status on family care for the elderly.* Chicago: American Anthropological Association.

——— (1991). Aging and disability in China: Cultural issues in measurement and interpretation. *Social Science and Medicine 32*:649–665.

Ikels, C., J. Keith, and C. L. Fry (1988). The use of qualitative methodologies in large-scale cross-cultural research. In S. Reinharz and G. D. Rowles (Eds.), *Qualitative Gerontology* (pp.274–298). New York: Springer.

Ingersoll-Dayton, B., and T. C. Antonucci (1988). Reciprocal and nonreciprocal social support. *Journal of Gerontology, Social Sciences 43*:65–73.

Ingold, T. (1976). *The Skolt Lapps today.* Cambridge: Cambridge University Press.

Jackson, M. (1978). Ambivalence and the last-born: Birth-order position in convention and myth. *Man 13*:341–361.

Jacobs, J. (1974). *Fun city: An ethnographic study of a retirement community.* New York: Holt, Rinehart.

Jensen, G. D., and A. H. Polloi (1988). The very old of Palau: Health and mental state. *Age and Aging 17*:220–226.

Johnson, A., and A. Taylor (1991). *Prevalence of chronic diseases: A summary of data from the survey of American Indians and Alaska Natives* (AHCPR Pub. No. 91–0031). NMES Data Summary 3. Rockville, MD: Public Health Survey.

Johnson, C. L. (1987). Institutional segregation of the elderly. In P. Silverman (Ed.), *The elderly as modern pioneers* (pp. 375–388). Bloomington: University of Indiana Press.

Jones, C. E. (1976). The post-reproductive phase in mammals. *Frontiers of Hormonal Research 3*:1–19.

Kaplan, R. M. (1990). Behavior as the central outcome in health care. *American Psychologist 45*(11):1211–1220.

Katz, S., and A. Akpom (1976). A measure of primary socio-biological functions. *International Journal of Health Services 6*(3):493–508.

Katz, S., A. B. Ford, R. W. Moskowitz, et al. (1963). Studies of illness in the aged: The index of ADL: A measure of primary socio-biologic functioning. *Journal of the American Medical Association 183*(12): 914–919.

Keith-Ross, J. (1977). *Old people, new lives.* Chicago: University of Chicago Press.

Keith, J. (1980). "The best is yet to be": Toward an anthropology of age. *Annual Review of Anthropology 9*:339–364.

————— (1990). Age in social and cultural contexts: Anthropological perspectives. In R. H. Binstock and L. K. George (Eds.), *Handbook of aging and the social sciences* (3d. ed., pp. 91–111). New York: Academic.

Keith, J., C. L. Fry, and C. Ikels (1989). Community as context for successful aging. In J.Sokolovsky (Ed.), *The cultural context of aging: Worldwide perspectives* (pp. 245–261). New York: Bergin and Garvey.

Kemper, P., and C. M. Murtaugh (1991). Lifetime use of nursing home care. *New England Journal of Medicine 324*(9):595–600.

Kendig, H. L. (1986). *Ageing and families: A support networks perspective.* Boston: Allen & Unwin.

Kenny, D. A. (1990). What makes a relationship special? In T. Draper and A. C. Marcos (Eds.), *Family variables: Conceptualization, measurement, and use* (pp. 161–178). Newbury Park, CA: Sage.

Kerns, V. (1983). *Women and the ancestors: Black Carib kinship and ritual.* Urbana: University of Illinois Press.

Kertzer, D. I. (1981). Generation and age in cross-cultural perspective. In M. W. Riley, R. P. Abeles, and M. S. Teitelbaum (Eds.), *Aging from birth to death. Vol. 2: Sociotemporal Perspectives* (pp. 27–50). Washington, DC: American Association for the Advancement of Science.

Kertzer, D. I., and O. B. B. Madison (1981). Women's age-set systems in Africa: The Latuka of Southern Sudan. In C. L. Fry (Ed.), *Dimensions: Aging, culture, and health* (pp. 109–130). New York: Praeger.

Kilbride, P. L., and J. C. Kilbride (1990). *Changing family life in East Africa: Women and children at risk.* University Park: Pennsylvania State University Press.

Kingson, E. R., B. A. Hirshorn, and J. M. Cornman (1986). *Ties that bind: The interdependence of generations.* Washington, DC: Seven Oaks Press.

Kinsella, K. (1988). *Aging in the Third World.* International Population Reports, Series PHHP 95, no. 79. U.S. Bureau of the Census. Washington, DC: U.S. Government Printing Office.

――― (1990). *Living arrangements of the elderly and social policy: A cross-national perspective.* International Population Reports, Staff Paper No. 52. U.S. Bureau of the Census. Washington, DC: U.S. Government Printing Office.

Kirkwood, T. B. L. (1981). Repair and its evolution: Survival versus reproduction. In C. R. Townsend and P. Calow (Eds.), *Physiological ecology* (pp. 165–189). Oxford: Blackwell.

――― (1985). Comparative and evolutionary aspects of longevity. In E. L. Schneider and J. W. Rowe (Eds.), *Handbook of the biology of aging* (pp. 27–44). New York: Van Nostrand.

Kohli, M. (1986). The world we forgot: A historical review of the life course. In V. W. Marshall (Ed.), *Later life: The social psychology of aging* (pp. 271–303). Beverly Hills, CA: Sage.

Knowler, W. C., D. J. Pettitt, P. H. Bennett, and R. C. Williams (1983). Diabetes mellitus in the Pima indians: Genetic and evolutionary considerations. *American Journal of Physical Anthropology 62*: 107–114.

Kunitz, S. J., and J. E. Levy (1991). *Navajo aging.* Tucson: University of Arizona Press.

Kwan, Alex Y. H. (1988). *Caregiving among middle and low income aged in Hong Kong.* Tampa: International Exchange Center on Gerontology, The University of South Florida.

Labouvie-Vief, G. (1985).Intelligence and cognition. In J. E. Birren and K. W. Schaie (Eds.), *Handbook of the psychology of aging* (2d. ed., pp. 500–530). New York: Van Nostrand.

LaFontaine, J. S. (1978). Introduction. In J. S. LaFontaine (Ed.), *Sex and age as principles of social differentiation.* New York: Academic.

Lancaster, J. B., J. Altmann, A. S. Rossi, and L. R. Sherrod (Eds.), (1987). *Parenting across the life span: Biosocial dimensions.* New York: Aldine de Gruyter.

Lancaster, J., and B. King (1985). An evolutionary perspective on the menopause. In J. K. Brown and V. Kerns (Eds.), *In her prime: A new view of middle-aged women* (pp. 7–16). South Hadley, MA: Bergin and Garvey.

LaRue, A., L. Bank, L. Jarvik, et al. (1979). Health in old age: How do physicians' ratings and self-ratings compare? *Journal of Gerontology 34*:687.

Lawton, M. P. (1980). *Environment and aging*. Monterey, CA: Brooks/ Cole.

Lawton, M. P. (1990a). Vulnerability and socioeconomic factors. In Z. Harel, P. Ehrlich, and R. Hubbard (Eds.), *The vulnerable aged: People, services, and policies*. New York: Springer.

—— (1990b). *Housing the elderly: An all-generations issue*. Philadelphia: Philadelphia Geriatric Center. Unpublished manuscript.

Lawton, M. P., and S. M. Albert (1990). *Affective self-management across the lifespan*. Atlanta, GA: American Psychological Association.

Lawton, M. P., E. M. Brody (1969). Assessment of old people: Self-maintaining and instrumental activities of daily living. *The Gerontologist 9*:179–186.

Lawton, M. P., M. Fulcomer, and M. H. Kleban (1984). Architecture for the mentally impaired elderly. *Environment and Behavior 16*: 730–757.

Lawton, M. P., M. Moss, and A. Glicksman (1990). The quality of the last year of life of older persons. *The Milbank Quarterly 68*:1–28.

Leaf, A. (1973). Every day is a gift when you are over 100. *National Geographic 143*:93–199.

Lee, R. B. (1979). The !Kung San: Men, women, and work in a foraging society. Cambridge: Cambridge University Press.

—— (1985). Work, sexuality, and aging among !Kung women. In J. K. Brown and V. Kerns (Eds.), *In her prime: A new view of middle-aged women* (pp. 23–35). South Hadley, MA: Bergin and Garvey.

Lee, G. R., and M. Kezis (1980–81). Societal literacy and the status of the aged. *International Journal of Aging and Human Development 12*(3):221–234.

Legesse, A. (1973). *Gada: Three approaches to the study of African society*. New York: Free Press.

Leith-Ross, S. (1939). *African women: A study of the Ibo of Nigeria*. London: Faber and Faber.

LeVine, R. A. (1978). Comparative notes on the life course. In T. K. Hareven, (Ed.), *Transitions: The family and the life course in historical perspective*. New York: Academic.

Levi-Strauss, C. (1969). *The elementary structures of kinship*. Boston: Beacon Press.

LeVine, S., and R. A. LeVine (1985). Age, gender, and the demographic transition: The life course in agrarian societies. In A. S. Rossi (Ed.), *Gender and the life course* (pp. 29–42). New York: Aldine.

Lewis, O. (1972) [1959]. An anthropological approach to family studies. In G. Handel and B. B. Hess (Eds.), *The psychosocial interior of the family* (pp. 131–140). Chicago: Aldine, Atherton.

Liang, J., C. Chuanyi, and Y. Jihui (1985). *Aging in the People's Republic of China.* Tampa: International Exchange Center on Gerontology, The University of South Florida.

Liang, J., J. Bennett, N. Whitelaw, and D. Maeda (1991). The structure of self-reported health among the aged in the United States and Japan. *Medical Care 29*(12):1161–1180.

Lindenbaum, S. (1990). The education of women and the mortality of children in Bangladesh. In A. C. Swedlund and G. J. Armelagos (Eds.), *Disease in populations in transition: Anthropological and epidemiological perspectives* (pp. 353–370). Westport, CT: Bergin and Garvey.

Linton, R. (1941). Age and sex categories. *American Sociological Review 7*:589–603.

Little, K. L. (1960). The role of the secret society in cultural specialization. In S. Ottenberg and P. Ottenberg (Eds.), *Culture and societies of Africa* (pp. 199–213). New York: Random House.

Lopata, H. Z. (1972). Role changes in widowhood: A world perspective. In D. O. Cowgill and L. D. Holmes (Eds.), *Aging and modernization* (pp. 275–303). New York: Appleton-Century-Crofts.

Luborsky, M. (1987). Analysis of multiple life histories. *Ethos 15*(4): 366–381.

MacCormack, C. (1985). Dying as transformation to ancestorhood: The Sherbro coast of Sierra Leone. *Curare 4*:117–126.

Maddox, G. L. (1963). Activity and morale: A longitudinal study of selected elderly subjects. *Social Forces 42*:195–204.

Mancini, J., and Bliezner R. (1989). Aging parents and adult children: Research themes in intergenerational relations. *Journal of Marriage and the Family 51*:275–290.

Mangen, D. J., V. Bengston, and P. H. Landry (Eds.) (1988). *Measurement of intergenerational relations.* Beverly Hills, CA: Sage.

Manton, K. G., J. E. Dowd, and M. A. Woodbury (1986). Conceptual and measurement issues in assessing disability cross-nationally:

Analysis of a WHO-sponsored survey of the disablement process in Indonesia. *Journal of Cross-Cultural Gerontology 1*:339–362.

Manton, K. G., L. S. Corder, E. Stallard (1993). Estimates of changes in chronic disability and institutional incidence in the U.S. elderly population from the 1982, 1984, and 1989 National Long Term Care Survey. *Journal of Gerontology* (in press).

Manton, K. G., G. C. Myers, G. R. Andrews (1987). Morbidity and disability patterns in four developing nations: Their implications for social and economic integration of the elderly. *Journal of Cross-Cultural Gerontology 2*:115–129.

Manton, K. G., and B. J. Soldo (1985). Dynamics of health changes in the oldest old: New perspectives and evidence. *Milbank Quarterly 63*(2):206–285.

Marshall, V. W. (1985). Conclusions: Aging and dying in Pacific societies: Implications for theory in social gerontology. In D. A. Counts and D. R. Counts (Eds.), *Aging and its transformations: Moving toward death in Pacific societies* (pp. 251–274). Lanham, MD: University Press of America.

—— (1986). Dominant and emerging paradigms in the social psychology of aging. In V. W. Marshall (Ed.), *Later life: The social psychology of aging* (pp. 9–31). Beverly Hills, CA: Sage.

Martin, L. G. (1989). Living arrangements of the elderly in Fiji, Korea, Malaysia, and the Philippines. *Demography 26*(4):627–643.

—— (1990). The status of South Asia's growing elderly population. *Journal of Cross-Cultural Gerontology 5*:93–117.

—— (1991). Population aging policies in East Asia and the United States. *Science 251*:527–531.

Matthews, S. H. (1986). *Friendships through the life course: Oral biographies in old age.* Beverly Hills, CA: Sage.

Mausner, J. S., and S. Kramer (1985). *Epidemiology—An introductory text.* Philadelphia: Saunders.

Mauss, M. (1967) [1925]. *The gift: Forms and functions of exchange in archaic societies.* New York: Norton.

Maxwell, E. K. (1986). Fading out: Resource control and cross-cultural patterns of deference. *Journal of Cross-Cultural Gerontology 1*:73–89.

Maxwell, E. K., and R. J. Maxwell (1992). Insults to the body civil: Mistreatment of elderly in two Plains Indian tribes. *Journal of Cross-Cultural Gerontology 7*:3–23.

Maxwell, R. J. (1970). The changing status of elders in a Polynesian society. *International Journal of Aging and Human Development* *1*:137–146.

Maxwell, R. J., and P. Silverman (1970). Information and esteem: Cultural considerations in the treatment of the aged. *International Journal of Aging and Human Development 1*:361–392.

——— (1989). Gerontocide. In R. Bolton (Ed.), *The content of culture: Constants and constraints. Studies in honor of John M. Roberts* (pp. 511–524). New Haven, CT: HRAF.

Mayer, K. U. (1988). German survivors of World War II: The impact on the life course of the collective experience of birth cohorts. In M. W. Riley, B. J. Huber, and B. B. Hess (Eds.), *Social structures and human lives: Social change and the life course* (vol. 1, pp. 229–246). Newbury Park, CA: Sage.

Mayer, K. U., and W. Muller (1986). The state and the structure of the life course. In A. B. Sorensen, F. E. Weinert, and L. R. Sherrod (Eds.), *Human development and the life course* (pp. 217–224). Hillsdale, NJ: Erlbaum.

Maynard Smith, J. (1976). Group selection. *Quarterly Review of Biology 51*:277–283.

Mazess, R., and S. Forman (1979). Longevity and age exaggeration in Vilcabamba, Ecuador. *Journal of Gerontology 34*(1):94–98.

McCay, B. J. (1987). Old people and social relations in a Newfoundland outport. In H. Strange and M. Teitelbaum (Eds.), *Aging and cultural diversity: New directions and annotated bibliography* (pp. 61–87). South Hadley, MA: Bergin and Garvey.

McKain, W. C. (1972). The aged in the USSR. In D. O. Cowgill and L. D. Holmes (Eds.), *Aging and modernization* (pp. 151–165). New York: Appleton-Century-Crofts.

Mead, M. (1978). *Culture and commitment: A study of the generation gap.* : Columbia University Press.

Medawar, P. B. (1952) [1957]. An unsolved problem in biology. In *The uniqueness of the individual.* London: Methuen.

Medvedev, Z. A. (1974). Caucasus and Altay longevity: A biological or social problem? *The Gerontologist 14*:381–387.

Meyer, J. W. (1988). Levels of analysis: The life course as a cultural construct. In M. W. Riley (Ed.), *Sociological lives: Social change and the life course* (vol. 2, pp. 49–62). Newbury Park, CA: Sage.

Mitchell, W. E. (1978). *Mishpokhe: A study of New York City Jewish family clubs*. The Hague: Mouton.

Moller, V. (1992). Black South African women on excursions: A reflection on the quality of township life for seniors. *Journal of Cross-Cultural Gerontology 7*:399–428.

Moore, S. F. (1978). Old age in a life-term social arena. Some Chagga of Kilimanjaro in 1974. In B. G. Myerhoff and A. Simic (Eds.), *Life's career—aging: Cultural variations on growing old* (pp. 23–76). Beverly Hills, CA: Sage.

Morgan, D., T. Schuster, and E. W. Butler (1991). Role reversals in the exchange of social support. *Journal of Gerontology, Social Sciences 46*(5):278–287.

Mossey, J. M. and E. Shapiro (1982). Self-rated health: A predictor of mortality among the elderly. *American Journal of Public Health 72*:800–808.

Mueller, W. H., M. I. Deutsch, D. A. Malina, et al. (1986). Subcutaneous fat topography: Age changes and relationships to cardiovascular fitness in Canadians. *Human Biology 58*:955–973.

Murdock, G. P., and D. White (1969). Standard cross-cultural sample. *Ethnology 8*:320–369.

Mutran, E. (1985). Intergenerational family support among blacks and whites: A response to culture or to socioeconomic difference? *Journal of Gerontology 40*:382–389.

Myerhoff, B. G. (1978). *Number our days*. New York: Dutton.

Myers, G. C. (1992). Demographic aging and family support for older persons. In H. L. Kendig, A. Hashimoto, L. C. Coppard (Eds.), *Family support for the elderly: The international experience* (pp. 31–68). Oxford: Oxford University Press.

Nag, M., B. N. F. White, and R. C. Peet (1978). An anthropological approach to the study of the economic value of children in Java and Nepal. *Current Anthropology 19*:293–306.

Naroll, R., G. Michik, and F. Naroll (1976). *Worldwide Theory Testing*. New Haven, CT: HRAF.

National Center for Health Statistics (1989). *The 1985 National Nursing Home Survey*. Washington, DC: U.S. Government Printing Office.

National Center for Health Statistics (1991). *Vital Statistics of the United States 1988, Life Tables*. DHS pub. no. 91–1104. Washington, DC: U.S. Government Printing Office.

Nations, M. K. (1986). Epidemiological research on infectious disease: Quantitative rigor or rigormortis? Insights from ethnomedicine. In C. R. Janes, R. Stall, and S. M Gifford (Eds.), *Anthropology and epidemiology* (pp. 97–124). Dordrecht: D. Reidel.

Neel, J. V. (1962). Diabetes mellitus: A "thrifty" genotype rendered detrimental by "progress"? *American Journal of Human Genetics* *14*:353–362.

——— (1982). The "thrifty genotype" revisited. In J. Kobberling and J. Tattersall (Eds.), *The genetics of diabetes mellitus.* New York: Academic.

Needham, R. (1974). Age, category, and descent. In R. Needham (Ed.), *Remarks and inventions* (pp. 72–100). London: Tavistock.

Neel, J. V., and K. M. Weiss (1975). The genetic structure of a tribal population, the Yanomama Indians. XII. Biodemographic studies. *American Journal of Physical Anthropology 42*:25.

Nesse, R. M. (1988). Life table tests of evolutionary theories of senescence. *Experimental Gerontology 23*:445–453.

Neugarten, B. L. (Ed.) (1968). *Middle age and aging: A reader in social psychology.* Chicago: University of Chicago Press.

Neugarten, B. L., and N. Neugarten (1973). Sociological perspectives on the life course. In P. B. Baltes and K. W. Schaie (Eds.), *Life-span developmental psychology: Personality and socialization* (pp. 53–69). New York: Academic.

Norgan, N. G. (1987). Fat patterning in Papua New Guineans: Effects of age, sex, and acculturation. *American Journal of Physical Anthropology 74*:385–392.

Notestein, F. W. (1945). In T. Schultz (Ed.), *Food for the world.* Chicago: University of Chicago Press.

Nugent, J. B. (1990). Old age security and the defense of social norms. *Journal of Cross-Cultural Gerontology 5*:243–254.

Nydegger, C. N. (1981). On being caught up in time. *Human Development 24*:1–12.

——— (1983). Family ties of the aged in cross-cultural perspective. *The Gerontologist 23*(1):26–32.

——— (1986). Age and life-course transitions. In C. Fry and J. Keith (Eds.), *New methods for old age research: Strategies for studying diversity* (pp. 131–162). New York: Bergin and Garvey.

———— (1992). *Issues in American older-family research.* Santa Fe: Society for Cross-Cultural Research.

Okojie, F. A. (1988). Aging in sub-Saharan Africa: Toward a redefinition of needs research and policy direction. *Journal of Cross-Cultural Gerontology 3*:3–20.

Okonjo, K. (1976). The dual-sex political system in operation: Igbo women and community politics in midwestern Nigeria. In N. J. Hafkin and E. G. Bay (Eds.), *Women in Africa* (pp. 56–86). Stanford, CA: Stanford University Press.

Oliver, D. (1955). *A Solomon Islands society.* Cambridge, MA: Harvard University Press.

Olshansky, S. J., B. A. Carnes, and C. Cassel (1990). In search of Methuselah: Estimating the upper limits to human longevity. *Science 250*:634–640.

Oppong, C. (1974). *Marriage among a matrilineal elite: A family study of Ghanaian senior civil servants.* New York: Cambridge University Press.

Ottenberg, S. (1971). *Leadership and authority in an African society.* Seattle: University of Washington Press.

Pagel, M. D., W. W. Erdly, and J. Becker (1987). Social networks: We get by with (and in spite of) a little help from our friends. *Journal of Personality and Social Psychology 53*:793–804.

Palmore, E. B., and D. Maeda (1985). *The honorable elders: A cross-cultural study of aging in Japan.* Durham, NC: Duke University Press.

Palmore, E. B., and K. M. Manton (1974). Modernization and status of the aged: International correlations. *Journal of Gerontology 29*(2): 205–210.

Park, J-H., Y. N. Park, and H. J. Ko (1991). Modification of the mini-mental state examination for use with the elderly in a non-Western society. Part 2: Cutoff points and their diagnostic validities. *International Journal of Geriatric Psychiatry 6*:875–882.

Parkin, D., and D. Nyamwaya (Eds.) (1989). *Transformation of African marriage.* Manchester: Manchester University Press.

Patterson, M. B., A. H. Schnell, R. J. Martin, et al. (1990). Assessment of behavioral and affective symptoms in Alzheimer's disease. *Journal of Geriatric Psychiatry and Neurology 3*:21–30.

Pearson, M. B., and D. E. Crews (1989). Evolutionary, biosocial, and cross-cultural perspectives on the variability in human biological aging. *American Journal of Human Biology 1*:303–306.

Peil, M. (1985). Old age in West Africa: Social support and quality of life. In J. H. Morgan (Ed.), *Aging in developing societies: A reader in Third World gerontology* (vol. 2, pp. 1–21). Bristol, IN: Wyndham Hall Press.

———— (1988). *Family support for the Nigerian elderly.* African Studies Association of the United Kingdom.

Peil, M., A. Bamisaiye, and S. Ekpenyong (1989). Health and physical support for the elderly in Nigeria. *Journal of Cross-Cultural Gerontology 4*:89–106.

Pillemer, K. A. (1985). The dangers of dependency: New findings on domestic violence against the elderly. *Social Problems 33*:146–158.

Plath, D. W. (1983). *Work and the lifecourse in Japan.* Albany: State University of New York Press.

Plato, C. C. (1987). The effects of aging on bioanthropological variables: Changes in bone mineral density with increasing age. *Colloquium in Anthropology 11*:59–72.

Poon, L. W. (Ed.) (1992a). The Georgia centenarian study. *International Journal of Aging and Human Development 34*(1):Special issue.

———— (1992b). Epilogue: Ode to three wise men. *International Journal of Aging and Human Development 34*:87–89.

Population Reference Bureau (1991). *1991 Population Data Sheet.* Washington, DC.: Population Reference Bureau.

Preston, S. H. (1984). Children and the elderly in the U.S. *Scientific American 251*(6):44–49.

Reaven, G. M., and E. P. Reaven (1985). Age, glucose intolerance, and non-insulin-dependent diabetes mellitus. *Journal of the American Geriatrics Society 33*:286–290.

Rhoads, E. C., and L. D. Holmes (1981). Mapuifagalele, Western Samoa's home for the aged—a cultural enigma. *International Journal of Aging and Human Development 13*:121–135.

Riley, M. W. (1979). Introduction: Life course perspectives. In M. W. Riley (Ed.), *Aging from birth to death: Interdisciplinary perspectives* (pp. 3–13). Boulder: Westview Press.

—— (1985). Women, men, and the lengthening life course. In A. S. Rossi (Ed.), *Gender and the life course* (pp. 333–347). New York: Aldine.

—— (Ed.) (1988). *Sociological lives: Social change and the life course, vol. 2.* Newbury Park, CA: Sage.

Riley, M. W., B. J. Huber, and B. B. Hess (Eds.) (1988). *Social structures and human lives: Social change and the life course, vol. 1.* Newbury Park, CA: Sage.

Riley, M. W., M. Johnson, and A. Foner (Eds.) (1972). *Aging and society, vol. 3: A sociology of age stratification.* New York: Russell Sage Foundation.

Roberts, R. E. L., and V. Bengston (1990). Is intergenerational solidarity a unidimensional construct? A second test of a formal model. *Journal of Gerontology, Social Sciences 45*(1):12–20.

Roberto, K. A., and J. P. Scott (1986a). Friendships of older men and women: Exchange patterns and satisfaction. *Psychology and Aging 1*:103–109.

—— (1986b). Equity considerations in the friendships of older adults. *Journal of Gerontology 41*:241–247.

Rook, K. S. (1987). Reciprocity of social exchange and social satisfaction among older women. *Journal of Personality and Social Psychology 52*:145–154.

Rook, K. S., and P. Pietromonaco (1987). Close relationships: Ties that heal or ties that bind? *Advances in Personal Relationships 1*:1–35.

Romney, A. K., S. C. Weller, and W. H. Batchelder (1986). Culture as consensus: A theory of culture and informant accuracy. *American Anthropologist 88*:313–338.

Romney, A. K., W. H. Batchelder, and S. C. Weller (1987). Recent applications of consensus theory. *American Behavioral Scientist 31*: 163–177.

Rose, M. R., and J. L. Graves (1989). What evolutionary biology can do for gerontology. *Journal of Gerontology, Biological Sciences 44*(2): 27–29.

Rosenberg, H. G. (1990). Complaint discourse, aging, and caregiving among the !Kung San of Botswana. In J. Sokolovsky (Ed.), *The cultural context of aging: Worldwide perspectives* (pp. 19–42). New York: Bergin and Garvey.

Rosenmayr, L. (1988). More than wisdom: A field study of the old in an African village. *Journal of Cross-Cultural Gerontology 3*:21–41.

Rosow, I. (1967). *Social integration of the aged.* New York: Free Press.

Rossi, A. S. (1985). Gender and parenthood. In A. S. Rossi (Ed.), *Gender and the life course* (pp. 161–191). New York: Aldine.

Rossi, A. F., and P. H. Rossi (1990). *Of Human bonding: Parent-child relations across the life course.* New York: Aldine.

Rowe, J. W., and K. L. Minaker (1985). Geriatric medicine. In E. L. Schneider and J. W. Rowe (Eds.), *Handbook of the biology of aging* (pp. 932–959). New York: Van Nostrand.

Rubinstein, R. L. (1990). Nature, culture, gender, and age: A critical review. In R. L. Rubinstein (Ed.), *Anthropology and gerontology: Comprehensive reviews* (pp. 109–128). Dordrecht: Kluwer Press.

——— (1992). Anthropological methods in gerontological research: entering the realm of meaning. *Journal of Aging Studies 6*:57–66.

Rubinstein, R. L., and P. T. Johnsen (1982). Toward a comparative perspective on filial response to aging populations. *Studies in Third World Societies 22*:115–171.

Sacher, G. A. (1959). Relationships of lifespan to brain weight and body weight in mammals. In G. Wolstenholme and M. O'Connor (Eds.), *The lifespan of animals, CIBA Foundation colloquia on aging* (vol. 5, pp. 115–133). Boston: Little, Brown.

——— (1978). Evolution of longevity and survival characteristics in mammals. In E. L. Schneider (Ed.), *The genetics of aging* (pp. 151–167). New York: Plenum.

Sackett, D. L., and G. W. Torrance (1978). The utility of different health states as pereceived by the general public. *Journal of Chronic Disease 31*:697–704.

Sahlins, M. (1972). *Stone age economics.* Chicago: University of Chicago Press.

Saluter, A. F. (1990). *Marital status and living arrangements: March 1989.* Current Population Reports. Series P–20, no. 445. Washington, DC: Bureau of the Census.

Sangree, W. H. (1966). *Age, prayer and politics in Tiriki, Kenya.* Oxford: Oxford University Press.

——— (1987). The childless elderly in Tiriki, Kenya, and Irigwe, Nigeria. *Journal of Cross-Cultural Gerontology 2*:201–224.

——— (1992). Grandparenthood and modernization: The changing

status of male and female elders in Tiriki, Kenya, and Irigwe, Nigeria. *Journal of Cross-Cultural Gerontology 7*:331–362.

Sankar, A. (1991). *Dying at home.* Baltimore: Johns Hopkins University Press.

Savishinsky, J. S. (1991). *The ends of time: Life and work in a nursing home.* New York: Bergin and Garvey.

Scheer, J., and N. Groce (1986). Impairment as a human constant: Cross-cultural and historical perspectives on variation. *Journal of Social Issues 44*:23–37.

Schorr, A. (1980). *Thy father and thy mother: A second look at filial obligation and family policy.* Washington, DC: U.S. Government Printing Office.

Shanas, E. (1979). The family as a social support system in old age. *The Gerontologist 19*:169–174.

Shanas, E., P. Townsend, D. Wedderburn, et al. (1968). *Old people in three industrial societies.* New York: Atherton.

Shelton, A. (1972). The aged and eldership among the Igbo. In D. Cowgill and L. Holmes (Eds.), *Aging and modernization.* New York: Appleton-Century-Crofts.

Shield, R. R. (1988). *Uneasy endings: Daily life in an American nursing home.* Ithaca, NY: Cornell University Press.

Shock, N. W., R. C. Greulich, and R. Andres (1984). *Normal human aging: The Baltimore study of aging.* N.I.H. Publication no. 84–2450. Washington DC: U.S. Government Printing Office.

Shryock, H. S., and J. S. Siegel (1971). *The methods and materials of demography, vol. 2.* Washington, DC: U.S. Government Printing Office.

Siegel, J. S., and M. Davidson (1984). *Demographic and socioeconomic aspects of aging in the United States.* Current Population Reports, Series P–23, No. 138. U.S. Bureau of the Census. Washington, DC: U.S. Government Printing Office.

Siegel, J. S., and S. L. Hoover (1984). *International trends and perspectives: Aging.* Washington, DC: U.S. Bureau of the Census. (International research Document, no. 12)

Silverman, P. (1987a). Family life. In P. Silverman (Ed.), *The elderly as modern pioneers* (pp. 205–233). Bloomington: Indiana University Press.

——— (1987b). Community settings. In P. Silverman (Ed.), *The elderly as modern pioneers* (pp. 234–262). Bloomington: Indiana University Press.

———— (1987c). Comparative studies. In P. Silverman (Ed.), *The elderly as modern pioneers* (pp. 312–344). Bloomington: Indiana University Press.

Silverman, P., and R. J. Maxwell (1978). How do I respect thee? Let me count the ways: Deference toward elderly men and women. *Behavior Science Research 13*(2):91–108.

———— (1983). The significance of information and power in the comparative study of the aged. In J. Sokolovsky (Ed.), *Growing old in different societies* (pp.43–55). Belmont, CA: Wadsworth.

Simic, A. (1990). Aging, world view, and intergenerational relations in America and Yugoslavia. In J. Sokolovsky (Ed.), *The cultural context of aging: Worldwide perspectives* (pp. 89–108). New York: Bergin and Garvey.

Simmons, L. (1945). *The role of the aged in primitive society.* New Haven, CT: Yale University Press.

Smith, D. S. (1981). Historical changes in the household structure of the elderly in economically developed societies. In R. W. Fogel, et al. (Eds.), *Aging: Stability and change in the family* (pp. 94–114). New York: Academic.

Sokolovsky, J. (Ed.) (1990). *The cultural context of aging: Worldwide perspectives.* New York: Bergin and Garvey.

Solomon, L. (1979). Bone density in aging Caucasian and African populations. *Lancet*:1,326–1,329.

Soper, R. (Ed.) (1986). *Kenya socio-cultural profiles: Busia district.* Nairobi: Ministry of Planning and National Development and Institute of African Studies, University of Nairobi.

Sorensen, A. B., F. E. Weinert, and L. R. Sherrod (Eds.) (1986). *Human development and the life course.* Hillsdale, NJ: Erlbaum.

Spector, W. (1991). Cognitive impairment and disruptive behaviors among community-based elderly persons: implications for targeting long-term care. *The Gerontologist 31*:51–59.

Spencer, P. H. (1965). *The Samburu: A study in gerontocracy in a nomadic tribe.* London: Routledge & Kegan Paul.

———— (1973). *Nomads in alliance: Symbiosis and growth among the Rendille and Samburu of Kenya.* Oxford: Oxford University Press.

———— (Ed.) (1990). *Anthropology and the riddle of the Sphinx:*

Paradoxes of change in the life course. London and New York: Routledge & Kegan Paul.

Stack, C. (1974). *All our kin.* New York: Harper & Row.

Stewart, F. H. (1977). *Fundamentals of age-group systems.* New York: Academic.

Stone, R., G. Cafferata, and L. Sangl (1987). Caregivers of the frail elderly: A national profile. *The Gerontologist 27*:616–626.

Stucki, B. (1992). The long voyage home: Return migration among aging cocoa farmers of Ghana. *Journal of Cross-Cultural Gerontology 7*:363–378.

Sudman, S. (1983). Applied sampling. In P. H. Rossi, J. D. Wright, and A. B. Anderson (Eds.), *Handbook of survey research* (pp. 145–193). New York: Academic.

Szathmary, E. J. E. (1990). Diabetes in Amerindian populations: The Dogrib studies. In A. C. Swedlund and G. J. Armelagos (Eds.), *Disease in populations in transition: Anthropological and epidemiological perspectives* (pp. 75–104). Westport, CT: Bergin and Garvey.

Tapper, N. (1978). The women's subsociety among the Shahsevan nomads of Iran. In L. Beck and N. Keddie (Eds.), *Women in the Muslim world.* Cambridge, MA: Harvard University Press.

Tatara, T. (1990). *Summaries of national elder abuse data: An exploratory study of state statistics based on a survey of state adult protective service and aging agencies.* Washington, DC: National Aging Resource Center on Elder Abuse.

Teitelbaum, M. (1988). Singing for their supper and other productive work of African elderly. In E. Gort (Ed.), *Aging in cross-cultural perspective: Africa and the Americas* (pp. 61–68). New York: The Phelps-Stokes Fund.

Thomas, K., and A. Wister (1984). Living arrangements of older women: The ethnic dimension. *Journal of Marriage and the Family 46*:301–311.

Thomas, S. P. (1992). *Old age in Meru, Kenya: Adaptive reciprocity in a changing rural community.* Ph.D. dissertation, University of Florida.

Thompson, S. (1990). Metaphors the Chinese age by. In P. Spencer (Ed.), *Anthropology and the riddle of the Sphinx* (pp. 102–120). London and New York: Routledge & Kegan Paul.

Togonu-Bickersteth, F. (1989). Conflicts over caregiving: A discussion of filial obligations among adult Nigerian children. *Journal of Cross-Cultural Gerontology* 4:35–48.

Torrey, B. R., K. Kinsella, and C. M. Taeuber (1987). *An aging world.* International population reports. Series P–95, no. 78. Bureau of the Census. Washington, DC: U.S. Government Printing Office.

Torrey, B. B. (1982). The lengthening of retirement. In M. W. Riley, R. P. Abeles, and M. S. Teitelbaum (Eds.), *Aging from birth to death. Vol. 2: Sociotemporal perspectives* (pp. 181–196). Boulder: Westview Press.

Townsend, P. (1957). *The family life of old people: An inquiry in East London.* London:Routledge & Kegan Paul.

Travis, S. S., and W. J. McAuley (1990). Simple counts of the number of basic ADL dependencies for long-term care research and practice. *Health Services Research* 25(2):349–360.

Tufte, V., and B. Myerhoff (1979). *Changing images of the family.* New Haven, CT: Yale University Press.

Turke, P. W. (1990). Evolution of the 100 year lifespan. Unpublished manuscript.

Uhlenberg, P. (1979). Demographic change and problems of the aged. In M. W. Riley (Ed.), *Aging from birth to death, vol. 1: Interdisciplinary perspectives* (pp. 153–166). Boulder: Westview Press.

United Nations (1989). *World population prospects.* U.N. Population Division. New York: United Nations.

United States Bureau of the Census (1988). *Who's helping out? Support networks among American families.* Current Population Reports. Series P–70, no. 13. Washington, DC: U.S. Government Printing Office.

Vatuk, S. (1980). Withdrawal and disengagement as a cultural response to aging in India. In C. L. Fry (Ed.), *Aging in culture and society: Comparative viewpoints and strategies* (pp. 126–148). New York: Praeger.

Vatuk, S. (1982). Old age in India. In P. N. Stearns (Ed.), *Old age in preindustrial society* (pp. 70–103). New York: Holmes and Meier.

Weihl, H. (1983). Three issues from the Israeli scene. *The Gerontologist* 23(6):576–578.

Weisner, T. S., C. Bradley, and P. L. Kilbride (Eds.) (n.d.). Troubled families: Intergenerational relationships and ecology in contemporary western Kenya. (in preparation)

Weiss, K. M. (1981). Evolutionary perspectives on human aging. In P. T. Amoss and S. Harrell (Eds.), *Other ways of growing old: Anthropological perspectives* (pp. 25–58). Stanford, CA: Stanford University Press.

————— (1984). On the number of members of *Genus homo* who have ever lived, and some evolutionary interpretations. *Human Biology 56*:637–649.

————— (1989a). Are known chronic diseases related to the human lifespan and its evolution? *American Journal of Human Biology 1*:307–319.

————— (1989b). A survey of human biodemography. *Journal of Quantitative Anthropology 1*(1–2):79–152.

————— (1990). Transitional diabetes and gallstones in Amerindian peoples: Genes or environment? In A. C. Swedlund and G. J. Armelagos (Eds.), *Disease in populations in transition: Anthropological and epidemiological perspectives* (pp. 105–124). Westport, CT: Bergin and Garvey.

Weissman, M. M., J. K. Myers, G. L. Tischler, et al. (1985). Psychiatric disorders (DSM-III) and cognitive impairment among the elderly in a U.S. urban community. *Acta Psychiatrica Scandinavica 71*:366–379.

Wentowski, G. (1981). Reciprocity and the coping strategies of older people. *The Gerontologist 21*:600–609.

White, N. (1985). Sex differences in Australian aboriginal subsistence: Possible implications for the biology of hunter-gatherers. In J. Ghesquiere, R. D. Martin, and F. Newcombe (Eds.), *Human sexual dimorphism*. London: Taylor & Francis.

Whiting, J. W. M. (1968). Methods and problems in cross-cultural research. In G. Lindzey and E. Aronson (Eds.), *The handbook of social psychology* (vol. 2, pp. 693–728). Reading, MA: Addison-Wesley.

Whiting, B. B. (1963). *Six cultures*. New York: Wiley.

World Health Organization (1991). *World Health Statistics Annual 1990*. Geneva: World Health Organization.

Wurtman, J. J., H. Liberman, R. Tsay, et al. (1988). Caloric and nutrient intakes of elderly and young subjects measured under identical conditions. *Journal of Gerontology, Biological Sciences 43*:174–180.

Yu, E. S. H., W. T. Liu, P. Levy, et al. (1989). Cognitive impairment among elderly adults in Shanghai, China. *Journal of Gerontology, Social Sciences 44*(3):97–106.

Zborowski, M., and E. Herzog (1952). *Life is with people: The Jewish little-town of Europe*. New York: International Universities Press.

Index

Abuse, elder, 234–37
  among Native Americans, 235–36
  in the United States, 235
Activity
  involuntary, 189, 193, 219–20, 247
  theory, 151–52
ADL measures, 128, 195–98, 207
Age, definitions of
  biologic, 11, 19–20, 35
  chronological, 13–14, 19–20, 26,
    35, 60, 72, 79
  social/cultural, 4–5, 35, 69, 75–76
Age sets (groups), 58, 68–70, 72
  in Kenya, 70
  in Tanzania, 70–71
  transitions in, 71–72
Age stratification, 58–50. *See also*
  Age sets
Aging, biology of, 17–34.
  of populations, 35–36
  and survivorship, 22–26, 32
  See also Age; Longevity; Senes-
    cence
Alzheimer's disease, 21, 199, 233
Ancestors, 66–68
Autonomy, personal, 193, 228. *See
  also* Independence

Birth order, 61, 122

Caregiver selection, 89, 114–15,
    128–38, 243
  and affection, 131–32
  demographic factors in, 130–31
  in Nigeria, 133–35
  in Somalia, 1269–179
  in Taiwan, 135–37
  in the United States, 132–33
Caregiving, 40, 96, 114, 129–38,
    242–43
  among Italian-Americans, 115
  in Kenya, 77, 93–94
  in the United States, 110
  in Yugoslavia, 114
  See also Caregiver selection; Ex-
    change; Filial obligation; Last
    year of life; Living arrange-
    ments
Centenarians, 29, 78, *See also* Lon-
    gevity
Comparison, of developing and de-
    veloped countries, 44, 49–50,
    52, 53, 86–87, 89–90, 95–96,
    103, 119–120, 139, 193, 209

283